Editorial project:
2019 © **booq** publishing, S.L.
c/ Domènech, 7-9, 2º 1ª
08012 Barcelona, Spain
T: +34 93 268 80 88
www.booqpublishing.com

ISBN 978-84-9936-897-9 [EN]
ISBN 978-84-9936-715-6 [ES]

Editorial coordinator:
Claudia Martínez Alonso

Art director:
Mireia Casanovas Soley

Editor:
Francesc Zamora Mola

Layout:
Cristina Simó Perales

Printing in China

The San Francisco Bay Area has an attractive architectural scene promoted by a great economic vitality and steady population growth. Architecturally speaking, the Bay Area is brimming with energy, featuring buildings and spaces reflecting a mix of geographical, cultural, technological, and ecological influences.

New buildings rise despite the challenges and concerns inherent to constructing in a historically and culturally significant region. At the same time, the same challenges promote the renovation of existing constructions, preserving the architectural heritage of the Bay Area. These projects are built, in part, thanks to generations of local architects, sensitive to its distinct environment. The works of early generations of architects such as Bernard Maybeck, Julia Morgan, William Wurster, Joseph Esherick, and William Turnbull have set a precedent for the contemporary architecture that continues to shape the built environment of the Bay Area. Their works are examples of deep reverence to the region's geographical qualities, climate, topography, and culture. The works of today's local architects show the same great respect, deference that contributes to the preservation of an inherently San Francisco and Bay Area expression.

Innovative approaches to dealing with the landscape, climate, and use of sustainable strategies and materials on the one hand, and a desire to make good design available to all people and communities, on the other hand, are a common thread in all their work.

The projects featured in this volume go beyond the creation of architectural atmospheres attuned to the needs and concerns of their occupants. The result is an architecture aimed at enhancing human experience and capable of eliciting emotions.

Die San Francisco Bay Area verfügt über eine attraktive Architekturszene, die durch eine große wirtschaftliche Vitalität und ein stetiges Bevölkerungswachstum gefördert wird. Architektonisch ist die Bay Area voll von Energie, mit Gebäuden und Räumen, die eine Mischung aus geografischen, kulturellen, technologischen und ökologischen Einflüssen widerspiegeln.

Neue Gebäude entstehen trotz der Herausforderungen und Bedenken, die mit dem Bauen in einer historisch und kulturell bedeutenden Region verbunden sind. Gleichzeitig fördern eben diese Herausforderungen die Renovierung bestehender Gebäude und bewahren das architektonische Erbe der Bay Area. Diese Projekte werden teilweise dank den Generationen lokaler Architekten realisiert, welche die besondere Umgebung berücksichtigen. Die Werke früher Generationen von Architekten wie Bernard Maybeck, Julia Morgan, William Wurster, Joseph Esherick und William Turnbull haben Präzedenzfälle für die zeitgenössische Architektur geschaffen, die die bauliche Umgebung der Bay Area bis heute prägen. Ihre Werke sind Beispiele für die tiefe Verehrung der geografischen Qualitäten, des Klimas, der Topographie und der Kultur der Region. Die Werke der heutigen lokalen Architekten zeigen den gleichen großen Respekt, der zur Erhaltung eines inhärenten Ausdrucks von San Francisco und der Bay Area beiträgt.

Innovative Ansätze im Umgang mit Landschaft, Klima und der Nutzung nachhaltiger Strategien und Materialien auf der einen und der Wunsch, gutes Design allen Menschen und Gemeinschaften zugänglich zu machen, auf der anderen Seite, sind ein roter Faden in all ihrer Arbeit.

Die in diesem Band vorgestellten Projekte gehen über die Schaffung von architektonischen Atmosphären, die auf die Bedürfnisse und Anliegen ihrer Bewohner abgestimmt sind, hinaus. Das Ergebnis ist eine Architektur, die darauf abzielt, das menschliche Erleben zu verbessern und Emotionen hervorzurufen.

La région de la baie de San Francisco possède une scène architecturale attrayante favorisée par une grande vitalité économique et une croissance démographique constante. D'un point de vue architectural, la région de la baie déborde d'énergie, avec des bâtiments et des espaces qui reflètent un mélange d'influences géographiques, culturelles, technologiques et écologiques.

De nouveaux bâtiments s'élèvent malgré les préoccupations et les défis inhérents à la construction dans une région d'importance historique et culturelle. En même temps, les mêmes défis favorisent la rénovation des constructions existantes, en préservant le patrimoine architectural de la région de la baie. Ces projets sont réalisés, en partie, grâce à des générations d'architectes locaux, sensibles à l'environnement distinctif de la baie. Les œuvres des premières générations d'architectes telles que Bernard Maybeck, Julia Morgan, William Wurster, Joseph Esherick et William Turnbull ont créé un précédent pour l'architecture contemporaine qui continue à façonner l'environnement bâti de la aie. Leurs œuvres témoignent d'un profond respect pour les qualités géographiques, le climat, la topographie et la culture de la région. Les œuvres des architectes locaux d'aujourd'hui font preuve du même respect, de la même déférence qui contribue à la préservation d'une expression inhérente à la région de San Francisco et de la baie.

D'une part, des approches innovantes en matière de paysage, de climat et d'utilisation de stratégies et de matériaux durables et, d'autre part, la volonté de rendre le design accessible à tous les individus et à toutes les communautés, sont le fil conducteur de tout leur travail.

Les projets présentés dans ce volume vont au-delà de la création d'ambiances architecturales adaptées aux besoins et aux préoccupations de leurs occupants. Le résultat est une architecture visant à valoriser l'expérience humaine et capable de susciter des émotions.

El Área de la Bahía de San Francisco tiene una atractiva escena arquitectónica promovida por una gran vitalidad económica y un crecimiento poblacional constante. Desde el punto de vista arquitectónico, esta zona está llena de energía, con edificios y espacios que reflejan una mezcla de influencias geográficas, culturales, tecnológicas y ecológicas.

Nuevos edificios se levantan a pesar de los retos y preocupaciones inherentes a la construcción en una región histórica y culturalmente significativa. Al mismo tiempo, los mismos desafíos promueven la renovación de las construcciones existentes, preservando el patrimonio arquitectónico. Estos proyectos se construyen, en parte, gracias a generaciones de arquitectos locales, sensibles a su entorno. Las obras de las primeras generaciones de arquitectos como Bernard Maybeck, Julia Morgan, William Wurster, Joseph Esherick y William Turnbull han sentado un precedente para la arquitectura contemporánea que continúa dando forma al entorno construido del "Bay Area". Sus obras son ejemplos de profunda reverencia a las cualidades geográficas, climáticas, topográficas y culturales de la región. Las obras de los arquitectos locales actuales muestran el mismo gran respeto que contribuye a la preservación de una expresión inherente a San Francisco y su bahía.

Los enfoques innovadores para abordar el paisaje, el clima y el uso de estrategias y materiales sostenibles, por un lado, y el deseo de poner el buen diseño a disposición de todas las personas y comunidades, por otro, son un hilo conductor de todos sus trabajos.

Los proyectos que se presentan en este volumen van más allá de la creación de atmósferas arquitectónicas en sintonía con las necesidades y preocupaciones de sus ocupantes. El resultado es una arquitectura orientada a mejorar la experiencia humana y capaz de provocar emociones.

ANDREW MANN
ARCHITECTURE

🌐 www.andrewmannarchitecture.com 📷 andrewmannarchitecture

The work of Andrew Mann Architecture expands the tradition of the Bay Area Style to contemporary needs, specifically inspired by the works of, and the precedent set by, earlier generations of architects such as Bernard Maybeck, Julia Morgan, William Wurster, Joseph Esherick, and William Turnbull. Andrew Mann Architecture continues this tradition by focusing on the particularities of each project's site and context, by establishing a strong connection between building and landscape and by using natural materials. Andrew has been designing residential architecture in the San Francisco Bay Area since 1989. His work encompasses a range of building types, from rural vacation retreats to sophisticated urban residences. He currently sits on the Design Committee of The Sea Ranch and board of the Northern California Chapter of the Institute for Classical Art and Architecture.

Das Werk von Andrew Mann Architecture erweitert die Tradition des Bay Area Style auf zeitgenössische Bedürfnisse, insbesondere inspiriert von den Werken früherer Architektengenerationen wie Bernard Maybeck, Julia Morgan, William Wurster, Joseph Esherick und William Turnbull. Andrew Mann Architecture setzt diese Tradition fort, indem man sich auf die Besonderheiten des Standorts und des Kontextes jedes Projekts konzentriert, eine starke Verbindung zwischen Gebäude und Landschaft herstellt und natürliche Materialien verwendet. Andrew entwirft seit 1989 Wohnarchitektur in der San Francisco Bay Area. Seine Arbeit umfasst eine Reihe von Gebäudetypen, von ländlichen Ferienresidenzen bis hin zu anspruchsvollen urbanen Wohnsitzen. Derzeit ist er Mitglied des Designkomitees der Sea Ranch und Mitglied des Vorstands des Northern California Chapter des Institute for Classical Art and Architecture.

L'œuvre d'Andrew Mann Architecture étend la tradition du Bay Area Style aux besoins contemporains, en s'inspirant spécifiquement des œuvres des générations précédentes d'architectes tels que Bernard Maybeck, Julia Morgan, William Wurster, Joseph Esherick et William Turnbull, et du précédent établi par ces derniers. Andrew Mann Architecture perpétue cette tradition en se concentrant sur les particularités du site et du contexte de chaque projet, en établissant un lien fort entre le bâtiment et le paysage et en utilisant des matériaux naturels. Andrew conçoit l'architecture résidentielle dans la région de la baie de San Francisco depuis 1989. Son travail englobe une gamme de types de bâtiments, allant des résidences de vacances à la campagne aux résidences urbaines sophistiquées. Il siège actuellement au comité de conception du Sea Ranch et au conseil d'administration du Northern California Chapter de l'Institute for Classical Art and Architecture.

El trabajo de Andrew Mann Architecture expande la tradición del Bay Area Style a las necesidades contemporáneas, inspirándose específicamente en las obras de generaciones precedentes de arquitectos tales como Bernard Maybeck, Julia Morgan, William Wurster, Joseph Esherick y William Turnbull. Andrew Mann Architecture continúa esta tradición centrándose en las particularidades del lugar y contexto de cada proyecto, estableciendo una fuerte conexión entre la construcción y el paisaje y haciendo uso de materiales naturales. Andrew ha estado diseñando arquitectura residencial en el área de la Bahía de San Francisco desde 1989. Su trabajo abarca una amplia gama de tipos de edificios, desde retiros de vacaciones rurales hasta sofisticadas residencias urbanas. Actualmente forma parte del Comité de Diseño de The Sea Ranch y es miembro de la junta directiva del Northern California Chapter del Institute for Classical Art and Architecture.

This weekend getaway for busy professionals looking to unwind and connect with nature creates a relaxing environment. While iconic and modern in form, the home—originally built in 1974—was in need of an interior refresh. A series of new interventions including a thoughtfully planned kitchen, new bathrooms and stairs, as well as new lighting and casework throughout create a new "heart of the home". The renovation also enhances the outdoor experience through the creation of a new vegetable garden and pavilion. The pavilion's shed roof evokes the rural architecture of Northern California, while the symmetrical curves of the garden beds, which respond to the existing typography, blend into the landscape to create a lush architectural framework.

Dieser Wochenendsitz für vielbeschäftigte Profis, die sich entspannen und mit der Natur verbinden möchten, schafft eine entspannende Umgebung. Obwohl ikonisch und modern in der Form, war für das 1974 erbaute Haus eine Erneuerung des Innenraums erforderlich. Eine Reihe neuer Maßnahmen, darunter eine durchdachte Küche, neue Bäder und Treppen sowie ein neues Beleuchtungskonzept schaffen ein neues Herzstück des Hauses. Die Renovierung wertet auch das Outdoor-Erlebnis durch die Schaffung eines neuen Gemüsegartens und Pavillons. Das Sheddach des Pavillons erinnert an die ländliche Architektur Nordkaliforniens, während sich die symmetrischen Kurven der Gartenbeete, die auf die vorhandene Typografie reagieren, in die Landschaft einfügen und einen üppigen architektonischen Rahmen schaffen.

Cette résidence de fin de semaine pour les professionnels occupésqui cherchent à se détendre et à se connecter à la nature crée un environnement relaxant. Bien qu'emblématique et moderne dans sa forme, la maison, construite à l'origine en 1974, avait besoin d'un rafraîchissement intérieur. Une série de nouvelles interventions, y compris une cuisine bien pensée, de nouvelles salles de bains et des escaliers, ainsi qu'un nouvel éclairage et un nouveau mobilier, crée un nouveau cœur de la maison. La rénovation rehausse également l'expérience en plein air grâce à la création d'un nouveau jardin potager et d'un pavillon. Le toit en cabanon du pavillon évoque l'architecture rurale du nord de la Californie, tandis que les courbes symétriques des plates-bandes, qui répondent à la typographie existante, se fondent dans le paysage pour créer un cadre architectural luxuriant.

Esta casa de fin de semana para profesionales ocupados que buscan relajarse y conectarse con la naturaleza crea un ambiente sosegado. A pesar de su forma icónica y moderna, la casa —construida originalmente en 1974— requería una renovación interior. Una serie de nuevas intervenciones que incluyen una cocina cuidadosamente planeada, nuevos baños y escaleras, así como nueva iluminación y el trabajo de carpintería, crean un nuevo corazón de la casa. La renovación también mejora la experiencia al aire libre mediante la creación de un nuevo huerto y pabellón. El tejado del pabellón evoca la arquitectura rural del norte de California, mientras que las curvas simétricas de los parterres, que responden a la tipografía existente, se mezclan con el paisaje para crear un marco arquitectónico exuberante.

Originally constructed in 1925 on an oak-studded property facing a meadow, this two-story residence was thoughtfully re-imagined to realize the owners' desire for a light-filled, airy, and spatially rich home that effortlessly connects with its magnificent surroundings. The contemporary update employs simplified traditional forms that enhance the existing home's character. The key design moves create a vocabulary of elements with modern detailing, clean lines, and a color palette of whites, grays and blues. The design also develops strong linear axes favoring visual connection between the different interior spaces and minimizing indoor-outdoor boundaries through large paned windows and French doors opening directly to wooden decks.

Ursprünglich 1925 auf einem mit Eichen bewachsenen Grundstück mit Blick auf eine Wiese erbaut, wurde diese zweistöckige Residenz sorgfältig neu gestaltet, um den Wunsch der Eigentümer nach einem lichtdurchfluteten, luftigen und geräumigen Haus zu verwirklichen, das sich mühelos mit seiner herrlichen Umgebung verbindet. Das zeitgenössische Update verwendet vereinfachte traditionelle Formen, die den Charakter des bestehenden Hauses unterstreichen. Die wichtigsten Designbewegungen erzeugen ein Vokabular aus Elementen mit modernen Details, klaren Linien und einer Farbpalette aus Weiß, Grau und Blau. Das Design entwickelt auch starke Linearachsen, die eine visuelle Verbindung zwischen den verschiedenen Innenräumen ermöglichen und die Grenzen zwischen Innen- und Außenbereich durch große verglaste Fenster und Fenstertüren, die sich direkt zu Holzterrassen öffnen, minimieren.

Construite à l'origine en 1925 sur une propriété à colombages de chênes face à une prairie, cette résidence de deux étages a été pensée pour répondre au désir des propriétaires pour une maison lumineuse, aérée et riche en espace qui s'intègre sans effort à son magnifique environnement. La mise à jour contemporaine utilise des formes traditionnelles simplifiées qui rehaussent le caractère de la maison existante. Les mouvements de conception clé créent un vocabulaire d'éléments avec des détails modernes, des lignes pures et une palette de couleurs de blancs, de gris et de bleus. Le design développe également des axes linéaires forts favorisant la connexion visuelle entre les différents espaces intérieurs et minimisant les frontières intérieures-extérieures à travers de grandes fenêtres à carreaux et des portes-fenêtres ouvrant directement sur des terrasses en bois.

Construida originalmente en 1925 en una propiedad repleta de robles frente a un prado, esta residencia de dos pisos fue cuidadosamente reinventada para hacer realidad el deseo de los propietarios de una casa llena de luz, espaciosa y rica en espacio que conecte sin esfuerzo con sus magníficos alrededores. La renovación contemporánea emplea formas tradicionales simplificadas que realzan el carácter de la casa original. Los movimientos clave del diseño crean un vocabulario de elementos con detalles modernos, líneas limpias y una paleta de colores de blancos, grises y azules. El diseño también desarrolla ejes lineales fuertes que favorecen la conexión visual entre los diferentes espacios interiores y minimizan los límites interior-exterior a través de grandes ventanales y puertas francesas que se abren directamente a las terrazas de madera.

Designed for an avid collector, this modern interpretation of Craftsman style architecture provides gallery space for the owner's Native American artifacts, baskets, craftsman furniture, landscape paintings, and other decorative objects. Clean lines, simple details, and a consistent vocabulary of materials contrast with the traditional character of the furniture, artwork, and artifacts. Given the confined configuration of the house, focus was given to pulling as much natural light into the interior spaces as possible. The entry hall, formal living room, and dining room at the front of the house maintain their authentic character. The new master bedroom takes advantage of a large expanse of windows and doors to visually connect to the garden and create a bright, airy space.

Diese moderne Interpretation der handwerklichen Architektur, die für einen begeisterten Sammler entworfen wurde, bietet Galerieraum für die indianischen Artefakte, Körbe, handgefertigten Möbel, Landschaftsgemälde und anderen dekorativen Objekte des Besitzers. Klare Linien, einfache Details und ein einheitliches Vokabular an Materialien stehen im Gegensatz zum traditionellen Charakter der Möbel, Kunstwerke und Artefakte. Angesichts der engen Konfiguration des Hauses wurde darauf geachtet, so viel natürliches Licht wie möglich in die Innenräume zu bringen. Die Eingangshalle, das formelle Wohnzimmer und das Esszimmer an der Vorderseite des Hauses behalten ihren authentischen Charakter. Das neue Hauptschlafzimmer nutzt die Vorteile einer großen Fenster- und Türfläche, um sich optisch mit dem Garten zu verbinden und einen hellen, luftigen Raum zu schaffen.

Conçue pour un collectionneur avide, cette interprétation moderne de l'architecture de style artisanal offre un espace d'exposition pour les artefacts, paniers, meubles d'artisanat, peintures de paysage et autres objets décoratifs amérindiens du propriétaire. Des lignes épurées, des détails simples et un vocabulaire cohérent des matériaux contrastent avec le caractère traditionnel des meubles, des œuvres d'art et des artefacts. Étant donné la configuration confinée de la maison, l'accent a été mis sur l'apport d'un maximum de lumière naturelle dans les espaces intérieurs. Le hall d'entrée, le salon formel et la salle à manger à l'avant de la maison conservent leur caractère authentique. La nouvelle chambre des maîtres profite d'une grande étendue de fenêtres et de portes pour se connecter visuellement au jardin et créer un espace lumineux et aéré.

Diseñado para un ávido coleccionista, esta interpretación moderna de la arquitectura de estilo artesanal proporciona espacio de galería para los utensilios, canastas, muebles artesanales, pinturas paisajísticas y otros objetos decorativos indios americanos del propietario. Líneas limpias, detalles simples y un vocabulario consistente de materiales contrastan con el carácter tradicional de los muebles, obras de arte y objetos. Dada la confinada configuración de la casa, se puso énfasis en atraer la mayor cantidad de luz natural posible hacia los espacios interiores. El vestíbulo de entrada, la sala de estar formal y el comedor en la parte delantera de la casa mantienen su carácter auténtico. El nuevo dormitorio principal aprovecha una gran extensión de ventanas y puertas para conectarse visualmente con el jardín y crear un espacio luminoso y aireado.

BEKOM
DESIGN

BeKom Design was founded in 2009 by designers Revital Kaufman-Meron and Susan Bowen. Specializing in single-family homes, the firm believes in a holistic approach, designing not only the structure but also the interior and outdoor spaces, and choosing the interior finishes. With modern aesthetics, the designs create intimate spaces with an emphasis on indoor-outdoor connections and natural light. By sharing strong work ethics and deep commitment to the homeowner's vision, BeKom Design provides its clients with a platform to envision, design and ultimately build the house of their dreams.

BeKom Design wurde 2009 von den Designern Revital Kaufman-Meron und Susan Bowen gegründet. Das auf Einfamilienhäuser spezialisierte Unternehmen setzt auf einen ganzheitlichen Ansatz, indem es nicht nur die Struktur, sondern auch die Innen- und Außenräume gestaltet und den Innenausbau wählt. Mit moderner Ästhetik schaffen die Entwürfe intime Räume mit Schwerpunkt auf Innen- und Außenverbindungen und natürlichem Licht. Mit seiner gemeinsamen Arbeitseinstellung und dem starken Engagement für die Vision des Hausbesitzers bietet BeKom Design seinen Kunden eine Plattform, sich das Haus ihrer Träume vorzustellen, zu gestalten und schließlich zu bauen.

BeKom Design a été fondé en 2009 par les designers Revital Kaufman-Meron et Susan Bowen. Spécialisée dans les maisons unifamiliales, l'entreprise croit en une approche holistique, concevant non seulement la structure mais aussi les espaces intérieurs et extérieurs et choisissant les finitions intérieures. Avec une esthétique moderne, les conceptions créent des espaces intimes en mettant l'accent sur les connexions intérieures-extérieures et la lumière naturelle. En partageant une solide éthique de travail et un engagement profond envers la vision du propriétaire, BeKom Design offre à ses clients une plateforme pour concevoir, concevoir et finalement construire la maison de leurs rêves.

BeKom Design fue fundada en 2009 por los diseñadores Revital Kaufman-Meron y Susan Bowen. Especializada en viviendas unifamiliares, la firma cree en un enfoque holístico, diseñando no solo la estructura sino también los espacios interiores y exteriores y eligiendo los acabados de los interiores. Con una estética moderna, los diseños crean espacios íntimos con énfasis en las conexiones interiores-exteriores y la luz natural. Al compartir una fuerte ética de trabajo y un profundo compromiso con la visión del propietario, BeKom Design proporciona a sus clientes una plataforma para visualizar, diseñar y, en última instancia, construir la casa de sus sueños.

Contemporary design meets modern elegance in this beautiful home. To bring the large proportions of the house down to a more human scale, the goal was to design individually intimate spaces. We wanted to create rooms flooded with natural light, but we also wanted to explore the limitless possibilities of artificial lighting. We focused on LED strips to frame different spaces. This lighting solution provided the spaces with a sophisticated touch and, from a technical point of view, allowed for the ceilings to be expressed as clean, continuous surfaces. A palette of warm, light colors combines with a variety of wood finishes and concrete elements to bring warmth and comfort while keeping the décor sleek and simple.

Zeitgemäßes Design trifft in diesem schönen Haus auf moderne Eleganz. Um die großen Teile des Hauses auf eine menschlichere Größe zu bringen, war es das Ziel, individuell intime Räume zu gestalten. Wir wollten Räume schaffen, die von natürlichem Licht durchflutet werden, aber wir wollten auch die grenzenlosen Möglichkeiten der künstlichen Beleuchtung erkunden. Wir haben uns auf LED-Streifen konzentriert, um verschiedene Räume zu umrahmen. Diese Lichtlösung verlieh den Räumen eine anspruchsvolle Note und ermöglichte es, technisch gesehen, die Decken als saubere, durchgehende Flächen auszudrücken. Eine Palette warmer, heller Farben wurde kombiniert mit einer Vielzahl von Holzoberflächen und Betonelementen, um Wärme und Komfort zu bringen und gleichzeitig das Dekor schlicht und einfach zu halten.

Le design contemporain rencontre l'élégance moderne dans cette belle maison. Afin de rendre les grandes proportions de la maison à une échelle plus humaine, l'objectif était de concevoir des espaces intimes et individuels. Nous voulions créer des pièces inondées de lumière naturelle, mais nous voulions aussi explorer les possibilités illimitées de l'éclairage artificiel. Nous nous sommes concentrés sur les bandes LED pour encadrer différents espaces. Cette solution d'éclairage a donné aux espaces une touche sophistiquée et, d'un point de vue technique, a permis aux plafonds de s'exprimer sous forme de surfaces propres et continues. Une palette de couleurs chaudes et lumineuses se marie à une variété de finis de bois et d'éléments de béton pour apporter chaleur et confort tout en gardant le décor épuré et simple.

El diseño contemporáneo se une a la elegancia moderna en esta hermosa residencia. Para reducir las grandes proporciones de la casa a una escala más humana, el objetivo era diseñar espacios íntimos individualmente. Queríamos crear estancias inundadas de luz natural, pero también queríamos explorar las posibilidades ilimitadas de la iluminación artificial. Nos centramos en las tiras de LEDs para enmarcar diferentes espacios. Esta solución de iluminación ha dotado a los espacios de un toque sofisticado y, desde un punto de vista técnico, permitió que los techos se expresaran como superficies limpias y continuas. Una paleta de colores cálidos y claros se combina con una variedad de acabados de madera y elementos de hormigón para aportar calidez y comodidad, manteniendo la decoración elegante y sencilla.

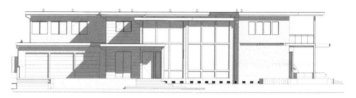

North elevation

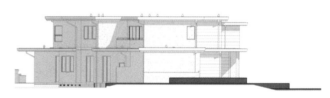

East elevation

South elevation

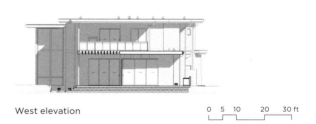

West elevation

0 5 10   20   30 ft

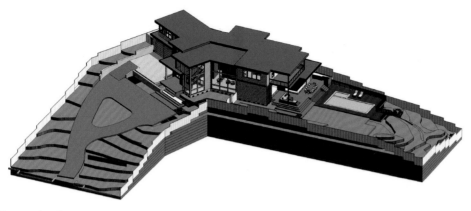

Perspective view

Second floor plan

First floor plan

0 5 10 20 30 ft

1. Entry
2. Office/suite
3. Powder room
4. Mud room
5. Elevator
6. Garage
7. Bedroom suite
8. Media room
9. Pantry
10. Living room
11. Wine room
12. Dining room
13. Great room
14. Outdoor covered patio
15. Outdoor dining area
16. Outdoor kitchen
17. Deck
18. Spa
19. Pool
20. Lawn
21. Natural boulder area
22. Hallway/gallery
23. Laundry room
24. Bedroom suite
25. Bedroom suite
26. Family room
27. Elevator
28. Balcony
29. Bedroom suite
30. Master bedroom
31. Walk-in-closet
32. Master bathroom
33. Master bedroom balcony

This unique lot presented many challenges common to hilltop properties: limited flat areas, slopes equal to or greater than 50%, a variety of mature trees subject to preservation laws, and the proximity to a road. These features guided—and limited—the location and scale of the construction. We designed a linear floor plan with the entertainment areas along the house perimeter to capitalize on the views. Natural lighting and indoor-outdoor connection are key components of the design. On the first floor, a courtyard can be accessed from the entry hall and the front-facing office, while providing the kitchen with views. To offset the lack of usable outdoor space on the lot, we turned part of the first-floor roof into an accessible roof deck, offering an alternative outdoor space and celebrating the most dramatic views from the house.

Das hügelige Gelände dieser einzigartigen Parzelle stellte die Architekten vor viele Herausforderungen: begrenzte ebene Flächen, Hänge mit mindestens 50% Steigung, eine Vielzahl von alten, denkmalgeschützten Bäumen und die Nähe zu einer Straße. Diese Merkmale bedingen – und begrenzen – die Ausrichtung und den Umfang der Konstruktion. Wir haben einen linearen Grundriss mit den Unterhaltungsbereichen entlang des Hausrandes entworfen, um die Aussicht zu nutzen. Natürliches Licht und der Anschluss an den Außenbereich sind wichtige Bestandteile des Designs. Im ersten Stock ist ein Innenhof von der Eingangshalle und dem vorderen Büro aus zugänglich, während die Küche einen Ausblick hat. Um den Mangel an nutzbarem Außenbereich auf dem Grundstück auszugleichen, haben wir einen Teil des Daches im ersten Stock in ein begehbares Dachgeschoss verwandelt, das einen alternativen Außenbereich bietet und die dramatischsten Ausblicke vom Haus aus zelebriert.

Ce terrain unique présentait de nombreux défis communs aux propriétés situées au sommet d'une colline : des surfaces planes limitées, des pentes égales ou supérieures à 50 %, une variété d'arbres matures assujettis aux lois de préservation et la proximité d'une route. Ces caractéristiques ont guidé et limité l'emplacement et l'échelle de la construction. Nous avons conçu un plan d'étage linéaire avec les zones de divertissement le long du périmètre de la maison pour capitaliser sur les vues. L'éclairage naturel et le raccordement intérieur-extérieur sont des éléments clés de la conception. Au premier étage, on accède à la cour par le hall d'entrée et le bureau en façade, tout en offrant une vue sur la cuisine. Pour compenser le manque d'espace extérieur utilisable sur le terrain, nous avons transformé une partie du toit du premier étage en une terrasse accessible, offrant un espace extérieur alternatif et célébrant les vues les plus spectaculaires de la maison.

Este terreno único presentó muchos desafíos comunes a las propiedades situadas en la cima de una colina: áreas planas limitadas, pendientes iguales o mayores al 50%, una variedad de árboles maduros sujetos a las leyes de preservación y la proximidad a una carretera. Estas características guiaron —y limitaron— la ubicación y la escala de la construcción. Diseñamos un plano lineal con las áreas de entretenimiento a lo largo del perímetro de la casa para aprovechar las vistas. La iluminación natural y la conexión interior-exterior son componentes clave del diseño. En la primera planta, se puede acceder a un patio desde el vestíbulo de entrada y el despacho de la parte delantera, al tiempo que se proporciona vistas a la cocina. Para compensar la falta de espacio exterior utilizable en el terreno, convertimos parte del tejado del primer piso en una cubierta accesible, ofreciendo un espacio exterior alternativo donde disfrutar de las vistas más espectaculares de la casa.

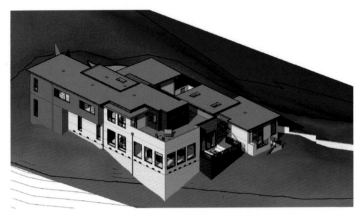

Perspective view

Northwest elevation

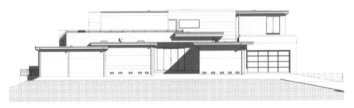

Northeast elevation

Southwest elevation

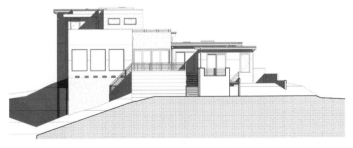

Southeast elevation

0 5 10   20   30 ft

Ground floor plan

Second floor plan

0 5 10 20 30 ft

1. Entry
2. Garage
3. Laundry room
4. Media room
5. Dining room
6. Wine room
7. Living room
8. Office
9. Courtyard
10. Kitchen
11. Family room/
    guest suite
12. Outdoor kitchen
13. Deck
14. Bedroom suite
15. Bedroom
16. Bedroom
17. Bathroom
18. Master bedroom
19. Walk-in-closet
20. Master bathroom
21. Roof deck

This unique steep lot offered three defined plateaux. This allowed us to explore various unique layout configurations of an existing two-story house. The result is a home that is modern and feels open, while at the same time offering spaces that are warm and intimate. Forging a strong indoor-outdoor connection was paramount in the design of the house, whether it was visual through dramatic bay views or physical through the creation of access points to generous outdoor spaces. Large-span folding doors minimized the boundaries between the interior and the exterior, while also optimizing natural lighting and openness. The hardscape design was conceived to provide specific areas for dining and cooking as well as lounging and gathering areas around a cascading water feature and fire pit.

Dieses einzigartige steile Grundstück bot drei definierte Plateaus. Dies ermöglichte uns, verschiedene, einzigartige Layout-Konfigura-tionen für ein zweistöckiges Haus zu erforschen. Das Ergebnis ist ein Haus, das modern ist und sich offen anfühlt, aber gleichzeitig Räume bietet, die warm und intim sind. Die Herstellung einer starken Verbin-dung zwischen innen und außen war für die Gestaltung des Hauses von größter Bedeutung, sei es visuell durch einen dramatischen Blick auf die Bucht oder physisch durch die Schaffung von Zugangspunk-ten zu großzügigen Außenräumen. Falttüren mit großer Spannweite minimieren die Grenzen zwischen innen und außen und optimieren gleichzeitig die natürliche Beleuchtung und Offenheit. Das Hards-cape-Design wurde konzipiert, um spezifische Bereiche für das Essen und Kochen sowie Lounge- und Sammelbereiche um ein kaskadieren-des Wasserspiel und eine Feuerstelle zu schaffen.

Ce terrain unique et escarpé offrait trois plateaux bien définis. Cela nous a permis d'explorer diverses configurations d'aménagement uniques d'une maison existante à deux étages. Le résultat est une maison moderne et ouverte, qui offre des espaces chaleureux et intimes. L'établissement d'un lien solide entre l'intérieur et l'exté-rieur était primordial dans la conception de la maison, qu'il s'agisse de l'aspect visuel grâce à des vues spectaculaires sur la baie ou de l'aspect physique grâce à la création de points d'accès aux généreux espaces extérieurs. Les portes pliantes à grande portée réduisaient au minimum les limites entre l'intérieur et l'extérieur, tout en optimi-sant l'éclairage naturel et l'ouverture. L'aménagement paysager a été conçu pour offrir des espaces spécifiques pour les repas et la cuisine, ainsi que des aires de détente et de rassemblement autour d'un point d'eau en cascade et d'un foyer.

Este terreno de características únicas y forma empinada ofrecía tres niveles definidos en forma de mesetas, lo que permitió explorar varias configuraciones de distribución en una casa de dos pisos ya existen-te. El resultado es un hogar moderno y abierto, a la vez que ofrece es-pacios cálidos e íntimos. Forjar una fuerte conexión interior-exterior fue fundamental en el diseño de la casa, ya fuera de forma visual, a través de vistas espectaculares de la bahía o física a través de la crea-ción de puntos de acceso a amplios espacios exteriores. Las puertas plegables de gran envergadura minimizan los límites entre el interior y el exterior, a la vez que optimizan la iluminación natural. Un diseño de paisaje "duro" fue concebido para proporcionar áreas específicas para comer y cocinar, así como para descansar y reunir zonas alrede-dor de una fuente de agua en cascada y una chimenea.

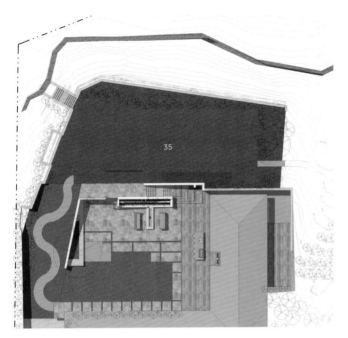

Upper terrace plan

Second floor plan

Ground floor plan

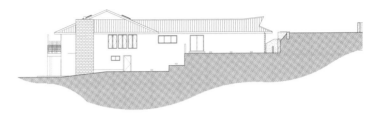

Northwest elevation

Southeast elevation

Northeast elevation

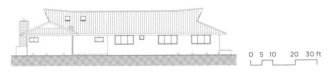

Southwest elevation

0 5 10   20 30 ft

1. Entry
2. Mud room
3. Garage
4. Media room
5. Wine room/wet bar
6. Guest suite
7. Bathroom/
   steam room
8. Storage
9. Bedroom
10. Jack and Jill
    Bathroom
11. Bedroom
12. Bedroom suite
13. Laundry room
14. Master bedroom
15. Walk-in-closet
16. Master bathroom
17. Balcony
18. Living room
19. Balcony
20. Dining room
21. Lounge
22. Powder room
23. Pantry
24. Butler sink/wet bar
25. Kitchen
26. Family room
27. Guest suite
28. Deck
29. Outdoor kitchen
30. Patio
31. Water fountain
    and fire pit
32. Bathroom
33. Storage
34. Stair access to
    upper terrace
35. Grass area

CARY BERNSTEIN ARCHITECT

⊕ **www.cbstudio.com**

CARY BERNSTEIN ARCHITECT is a San Francisco-based architecture and design studio led by principal Cary Bernstein, AIA. Since its establishment in 1991, the firm's projects have won numerous awards and have been published locally, nationally, and internationally. Projects for residential, commercial, and arts-related clients have been completed in California, New York, and Moscow. The firm is known for site-specific, reductive, and well-crafted work, fostering meaningful connections to place and time. Ms. Bernstein graduated from Dartmouth College with a Bachelor of Arts degree in Philosophy and Russian Language and Literature, where she also managed the jewelry fabrication studio. She received her Master of Architecture degree from Yale University, where she also taught aesthetics and ethics in the Philosophy Department. The intersection of philosophy, craft, and culture forms the basis of her architectural practice.

CARY BERNSTEIN ARCHITECT ist ein in San Francisco ansässiges Architektur- und Designstudio unter der Leitung von Direktor Cary Bernstein, AIA. Seit seiner Gründung im Jahr 1991 wurden die Projekte des Studios mehrfach ausgezeichnet und lokal, national und international veröffentlicht. In Kalifornien, New York und Moskau wurden Projekte für Privat-, Geschäfts- und Kunstkunden abgeschlossen. Das Unternehmen ist bekannt für standortspezifische, reduzierende und gut gemachte Arbeit, die sinnvolle Verbindungen zu Ort und Zeit fördert. Frau Bernstein schloss das Dartmouth College mit einem Bachelor of Arts in Philosophie und Russischer Sprache und Literatur ab, wo sie auch das Studio für Schmuckherstellung leitete. Sie erwarb ihren Master of Architecture an der Yale University, wo sie auch Ästhetik und Ethik am Philosophischen Institut lehrte. Die Verbindung von Philosophie, Handwerk und Kultur bildet die Grundlage ihres architektonischen Arbeitens.

CARY BERNSTEIN ARCHITECT est un studio d'architecture et de design basé à San Francisco et dirigé par le principal Cary Bernstein, AIA. Depuis sa création en 1991, les projets du cabinet ont remporté de nombreux prix et ont été publiés à l'échelle locale, nationale et internationale. Des projets pour des clients résidentiels, commerciaux et artistiques ont été réalisés en Californie, à New York et à Moscou. L'entreprise est reconnue pour son travail réducteur et bien fait, qui favorise des liens significatifs avec le lieu et l'époque, et qui est propre à chaque site. Mme Bernstein a obtenu un baccalauréat ès arts en philosophie et en langue et littérature russes au Dartmouth College, où elle a également dirigé l'atelier de fabrication de bijoux. Elle est titulaire d'une maîtrise en architecture de l'université de Yale, où elle a également enseigné l'esthétique et l'éthique au sein du département de philosophie. L'intersection de la philosophie, de l'artisanat et de la culture est à la base de sa pratique architecturale.

CARY BERNSTEIN ARCHITECT es un estudio de arquitectura y diseño con sede en San Francisco dirigido por la Directora Cary Bernstein, AIA. Desde su fundación en 1991, los proyectos de la firma han ganado numerosos premios y han sido publicados a nivel local, nacional e internacional. Proyectos para clientes residenciales, comerciales y relacionados con las artes han sido completados en California, Nueva York y Moscú. La empresa es conocida por su buen trabajo, fomentando conexiones significativas con el lugar y el tiempo. Cary Bernstein se graduó en Dartmouth College con una licenciatura en Filosofía y Lengua y Literatura Rusa, donde también dirigió el estudio de fabricación de joyas. Obtuvo su Máster en Arquitectura en la Universidad de Yale, donde también enseñó estética y ética en el Departamento de Filosofía. La intersección de filosofía, artesanía y cultura forma la base de su práctica arquitectónica.

Hill House is the full transformation of a well-worn 1930s bungalow into a modern, urban home. The owners wanted a house that would be "just big enough," favoring quality over quantity. The project required an artful balance among concept, utility, value, and execution. To capitalize on its wide lot, the existing house was expanded laterally to the side property lines and a few feet to the rear. Sectional shifts in the architecture and landscape merge exterior and interior topographies. Warm, textured materials and natural forms from the surrounding gardens enrich the rigorously detailed construction. The interplay between architecture and landscape, intimacy and distance, solid and void, and light and dark inextricably joins Hill House with its site.

Hill House ist die vollständige Umwandlung eines gut erhaltenen Bungalows aus den 1930er Jahren in ein modernes, urbanes Zuhause. Die Besitzer wollten ein Haus, das „gerade groß genug" ist und Qualität vor Quantität stellt. Das Projekt erforderte ein ausgeklügeltes Gleichgewicht zwischen Konzept, Nutzen, Wert und Ausführung. Um das große Grundstück zu nutzen, wurde das bestehende Haus seitlich in Richtung der Grundstücksgrenzen und einige Meter nach hinten erweitert. Sektionale Verschiebungen in Architektur und Landschaft verschmelzen Außen- und Innentopographien. Warme, strukturierte Materialien und natürliche Formen aus den umliegenden Gärten bereichern die streng detaillierte Konstruktion. Das Zusammenspiel von Architektur und Landschaft, Intimität und Distanz, Solidität und Leere sowie Hell und Dunkel verbindet Hill House und seinen Standort untrennbar.

Hill House est la transformation complète d'un bungalow des années 1930 en une maison moderne et urbaine. Les propriétaires voulaient une maison « juste assez grande », privilégiant la qualité à la quantité. Le projet exigeait un équilibre ingénieux entre le concept, l'utilité, la valeur et l'exécution. Pour tirer profit de son vaste terrain, la maison existante a été agrandie latéralement jusqu'aux limites latérales de la propriété et à quelques mètres à l'arrière. Les changements de section dans l'architecture et le paysage fusionnent les topographies extérieure et intérieure. Les matériaux chauds et texturés et les formes naturelles des jardins environnants enrichissent la construction rigoureusement détaillée. L'interaction entre l'architecture et le paysage, l'intimité et la distance, le solide et le vide, la lumière et l'obscurité rejoignent inextricablement Hill House et son site.

Hill House es la transformación completa de un bungaló de los años 30 en una casa moderna y urbana. Los propietarios querían una casa que tuviera "el tamaño justo", favoreciendo la calidad por encima de la cantidad. El proyecto requería un equilibrio ingenioso entre concepto, utilidad, valor y ejecución. Para sacar provecho de su amplio terreno, la casa original se extendió lateralmente hasta los límites laterales de la propiedad y unos pocos metros hacia atrás. Los cambios seccionales en la arquitectura y el paisaje fusionan topografías exteriores e interiores. Los materiales cálidos y texturizados y las formas naturales de los jardines circundantes enriquecen la construcción rigurosamente detallada. La interacción entre la arquitectura y el paisaje, la intimidad y la distancia, la solidez y el vacío, y la luz y la oscuridad unen inextricablemente a Hill House con su emplazamiento.

East elevation

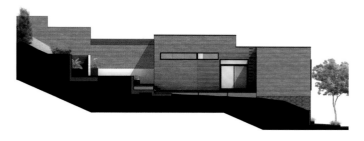

West elevation

Building section

North elevation

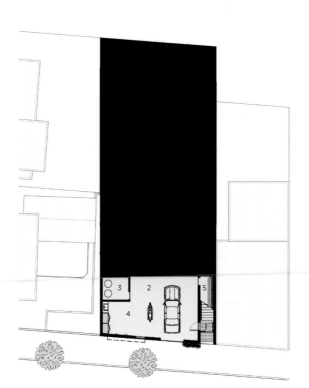

Ground floor plan

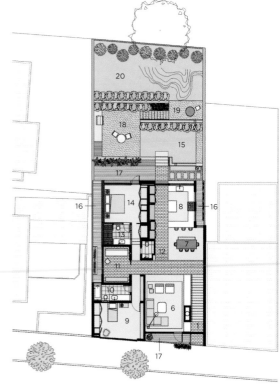

Second floor plan

1. Entry
2. Garage
3. Mechanical room
4. Workshop
5. Storage
6. Living area
7. Dining area
8. Kitchen
9. Bedroom
10. Bathroom
11. Study
12. Powder room
13. Master bathroom
14. Master bedroom
15. Garden
16. Side garden
17. Deck
18. Patio
19. Kitchen garden
20. Hill

0   5   10   20 ft

N

One & Co is part of a new generation of industrial design firms in San Francisco. Since its founding, the firm had made its home in a turn-of-the-century brick warehouse in the Mission District. When the need came to expand into an adjacent space, the three principals saw the opportunity to create a workspace that represents the culture of their collaborative studio, design values, and the firm's increasing prominence. The new studio nearly doubled the size of One & Co's original space, yet the design maintains enough intimacy to support fluid working relationships among the staff. A rigorous design language was established within the variable conditions of the old industrial building. Both the idealized new construction and eccentric older shell retain their individual identities while engaged in a vibrant dialogue.

One & Co ist Teil einer neuen Generation von Industriedesignunternehmen in San Francisco. Nach seiner Gründung hatte sich das Unternehmen in einem Backsteinlager aus der Jahrhundertwende im Mission District niedergelassen. Als die Notwendigkeit der Expansion in einen angrenzenden Raum entstand, sahen die drei Principals die Möglichkeit, einen Arbeitsplatz zu schaffen, der die Kultur ihres kollaborativen Studios, die Designwerte und die zunehmende Bedeutung des Unternehmens repräsentiert. Das neue Studio hat die Größe des ursprünglichen Raumes von One & Co fast verdoppelt, dennoch bleibt das Design so intim, dass es reibungslose Arbeitsabläufe zwischen den Mitarbeitern ermöglicht. Unter den variablen Bedingungen des alten Industriegebäudes wurde eine strenge Designsprache festgelegt. Sowohl der idealisierte Neubau als auch der alte exzentrische Rohbau behalten ihre individuelle Identität und pflegen einen lebendigen Dialog.

One & Co fait partie d'une nouvelle génération d'entreprises de design industriel à San Francisco. Depuis sa fondation, l'entreprise s'était installée dans un entrepôt en briques du début du siècle dans le quartier de la Mission. Lorsque le besoin s'est fait sentir d'ajouter un espace adjacent, les trois directeurs ont vu l'occasion de créer un espace de travail qui représente la culture de leur studio collaboratif, les valeurs du design et l'importance croissante de l'entreprise. Le nouveau studio a presque doublé la taille de l'espace d'origine de One & Co, tout en conservant une intimité suffisante pour permettre des relations de travail fluides entre les membres du personnel. Un langage de conception rigoureux a été établi dans les conditions variables de l'ancien bâtiment industriel. La nouvelle construction idéalisée et l'ancienne carcasse excentrique conservent leurs identités individuelles tout en s'engageant dans un dialogue animé.

One & Co es parte de una nueva generación de firmas de diseño industrial en San Francisco. Desde su fundación, la empresa había establecido su sede en un almacén de ladrillos de principios de siglo en el distrito de la Misión. Cuando surgió la necesidad de expandirse a un espacio adyacente, los tres directores vieron la oportunidad de crear un espacio de trabajo que representara la cultura de su estudio colaborativo, los valores del diseño y la creciente prominencia de la firma. El nuevo estudio casi duplicó el tamaño del espacio original de One & Co, sin embargo, el diseño mantiene suficiente intimidad como para mantener relaciones de trabajo fluidas entre el personal. Se estableció un riguroso lenguaje de diseño dentro de las condiciones variables del antiguo edificio industrial. Tanto la nueva construcción idealizada como el excéntrico armazón antiguo conservan sus identidades individuales a la vez que mantienen un vibrante diálogo.

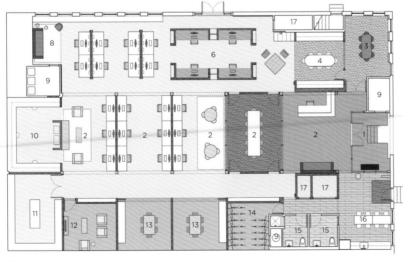

Floor plan

0 1   5   10 ft   N ⊕

1. Entry
2. Reception
3. Small conference
4. Material library
5. Large conference
6. Partners/Admin.
7. Open studio
8. Lounge
9. I.T./Mechanical

10. Clean shop
11. Dirty shop
12. Game room
13. War room
14. Bike storage
15. Bathroom
16. Kitchen
17. Closet

Teaberry is a master suite addition to a simple, single-story mid-century house on a wooded lot overlooking the northern San Francisco Bay. The owners dreamed of a serene, modern retreat immersed in nature. Architecture, landscape, and interior design form a unified dwelling narrative on this spectacular hillside site. The addition includes a bridge, porch, bedroom, and bath. The site and landscape design include a retaining wall, concrete, and heavy timber landscape stairs, and intimate planting areas adjacent to the building. The addition has a straight horizontal emphasis, but the sections differ along the shifting slope. Minimizing excavation and foundation areas provided both cost-saving benefits as well as expressive opportunities.

Teaberry ist eine Mastersuite als Ergänzung zu einem einfachen, einstöckigen Haus aus der Mitte des Jahrhunderts auf einem bewaldeten Grundstück mit Blick auf die nördliche San Francisco Bay. Die Besitzer träumten von einem ruhigen, modernen Rückzugsort inmitten der Natur. Architektur, Landschaft und Innenarchitektur bilden auf dieser spektakulären Hanglage ein kohärentes Wohnerlebnis. Die Ergänzung beinhaltet eine Brücke, eine Veranda, ein Schlafzimmer und ein Bad. Die Standort- und Landschaftsgestaltung umfasst eine Stützmauer, Beton- und schwere Holzlandschaftstreppen sowie intime Pflanzflächen neben dem Gebäude. Die Addition hat eine gerade horizontale Betonung, aber die Abschnitte unterscheiden sich entlang der Verschiebebahn. Die Minimierung von Aushub- und Fundamentflächen brachte sowohl Kostenvorteile als auch expressive Möglichkeiten.

Teaberry est une suite parentale qui s'ajoute à une maison simple de plain-pied du milieu du siècle sur un terrain boisé donnant sur le nord de la baie de San Francisco. Les propriétaires rêvaient d'un refuge serein et moderne en pleine nature. L'architecture, le paysage et l'aménagement intérieur forment un récit d'habitation unifié sur ce site spectaculaire à flanc de colline. L'ajout comprend un pont, un porche, une chambre à coucher et une salle de bain. Le site et l'aménagement paysager comprennent un mur de soutènement, du béton et des escaliers paysagers en bois massif, ainsi que des zones de plantation intimes adjacentes à l'édifice. L'ajout a une emphase horizontale droite, mais les sections diffèrent le long de la pente de déplacement. La réduction au minimum des zones d'excavation et de fondation a permis de réaliser des économies et de profiter d'occasions expressives.

Teaberry es una *suite* principal que se añade a una sencilla casa de un solo piso de mediados de siglo, en un terreno arbolado con vistas al norte de la Bahía de San Francisco. Los propietarios soñaban con un lugar de retiro sereno y moderno inmerso en la naturaleza. La arquitectura, el paisaje y el diseño de interiores forman una narración unificada de la vivienda en esta espectacular ladera. La adición incluye un puente, un porche, un dormitorio y un baño. El diseño del solar y del paisaje incluye un muro de contención, hormigón y escaleras de madera maciza, así como áreas de plantación íntimas adyacentes al edificio. La adición tiene un énfasis horizontal recto, pero las secciones difieren a lo largo de la pendiente de desplazamiento. La minimización de las áreas de excavación y cimentación proporcionó tanto beneficios de ahorro de costes como oportunidades expresivas.

North elevation

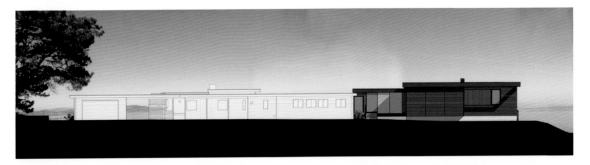

South elevation

Section through bedroom

Section through bridge

Section through bathroom

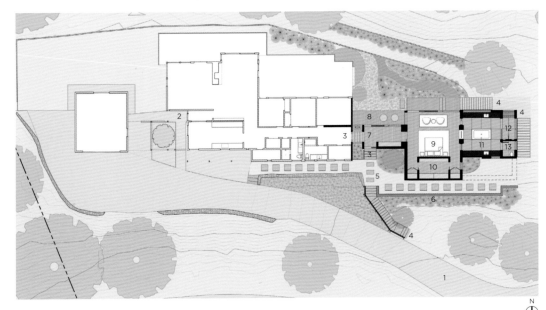

Floor plan

1. Driveway
2. Main house entry
3. Addition entry
4. Landscape stair
5. Gravel walkway
6. Retaining wall
7. Bridge
8. Porch
9. Bedroom
10. Dressing
11. Bathroom
12. Shower
13. Water closet

DESIGNPAD/
PATRICK PEREZ ARCHITECT

Understanding the client, their needs and dreams, and partnering with them to shape their living space has been the goal for the team at designpad architecture. This is accomplished by working with the narrative of how the client would like to experience their space on a day-to-day basis and proposing options and solutions that meet those goals, while also making the most of the natural light, views, comfort, and connection to the outside. Drawing from their experience with the design and fabrication of furniture, the team enjoys investigating design options at a fine detail level while tying that into the larger experiential level. Amelia Driscoll brings wide-ranging experience working in commercial and residential interior design while Patrick Perez draws on his many years of custom residential design. Together they provide thoughtful design solutions that seek to enhance and celebrate the common everyday experiences of their clients.

Den Kunden, seine Bedürfnisse und Träume zu verstehen und gemeinsam mit ihm seinen Lebensraum zu gestalten, war das Ziel des Teams von designpad architecture. Dies wird erreicht, indem man mit der Erzählung arbeitet, wie der Kunde seinen Raum im Alltag erleben möchte, und Optionen und Lösungen vorschlägt, die diese Ziele erfüllen, während man gleichzeitig das natürliche Licht, die Aussicht, den Komfort und die Verbindung nach außen optimal nutzt. Basierend auf ihren Erfahrungen mit dem Design und der Herstellung von Möbeln untersucht das Team gerne Designoptionen auf einer feinen Detaillierungsstufe und bindet diese an die größere Erfahrungsebene an. Amelia Driscoll bringt umfangreiche Erfahrung aus der Arbeit im Bereich der kommerziellen und privaten Innenarchitektur mit, während Patrick Perez auf sein langjähriges individuelles Wohndesign zurückgreift. Gemeinsam bieten sie durchdachte Designlösungen, die die gemeinsamen Alltagserfahrungen ihrer Kunden bereichern und feiern sollen.

Comprendre le client, ses besoins et ses rêves, et travailler en partenariat avec celui-ci pour façonner son espace de vie a été l'objectif de l'équipe de designpad architecture. Pour ce faire, il faut travailler avec le récit de la façon dont le client aimerait vivre son espace au quotidien et proposer des options et des solutions qui répondent à ces objectifs, tout en tirant le meilleur parti de la lumière naturelle, des vues, du confort et de la connexion avec l'extérieur. Forte de son expérience dans la conception et la fabrication de meubles, l'équipe aime étudier les options de conception dans les moindres détails tout en les rattachant au niveau expérientiel plus large. Amelia Driscoll apporte une vaste expérience dans la conception d'intérieurs commerciaux et résidentiels, tandis que Patrick Perez s'appuie sur ses nombreuses années de conception résidentielle sur mesure. Ensemble, ils fournissent des solutions de conception réfléchies qui cherchent à améliorer et à célébrer les expériences quotidiennes communes de leurs clients.

Entender al cliente, sus necesidades y sueños, y asociarse con ellos para dar forma a su espacio vital ha sido el objetivo del equipo de designpad architecture. Esto se logra trabajando con la narración de cómo el cliente desea experimentar su espacio en el día a día y proponiendo opciones y soluciones que cumplan con esos objetivos, a la vez que se aprovecha al máximo la luz natural, las vistas, el confort y la conexión con el exterior. Basándose en su experiencia en el diseño y fabricación de muebles, el equipo disfruta investigando las opciones de diseño a un nivel de detalle refinado, a la vez que las relaciona con el nivel de experiencia más amplio. Amelia Driscoll aporta una amplia experiencia de trabajo en el diseño de interiores comerciales y residenciales, mientras que Patrick Pérez se basa en sus muchos años de diseño residencial a medida. Juntos proporcionan soluciones de diseño cuidadosas que buscan mejorar y celebrar las experiencias cotidianas comunes de sus clientes.

The original structure was a very modest home built in the 1920s. The site enjoyed downtown San Francisco views at the front and access to a large rear yard and shared community green space at the rear. Initially comprised of one small main level with two bedrooms, the client sought to increase the amount of living space to accommodate their young and growing family. This was achieved by excavating the ground level to create more living space and a home office while also providing direct access to the rear yard garden. At the main level, the entire floor was opened up and expanded to the rear to provide for an open floor plan. Finally, a full third story was added to accommodate three bedrooms and two baths.

Das ursprüngliche Gebäude war ein sehr bescheidenes Haus aus den 1920er Jahren. Der Standort ermöglichte den Blick auf die Innenstadt von San Francisco an der Vorderseite und den Zugang zu einem großen Hinterhof und gemeinschaftlichen Grünflächen an der Rückseite. Ursprünglich bestand sie aus einer kleinen Hauptetage mit zwei Schlafzimmern, doch der Kunde wollte die Wohnfläche vergrößern, um seine junge und wachsende Familie unterzubringen. Dies wurde durch den Aushub des Erdgeschosses erreicht, um mehr Wohnraum und ein Heimbüro zu schaffen und gleichzeitig einen direkten Zugang zum Hinterhofgarten zu ermöglichen. Im Hauptgeschoss wurde der gesamte Boden geöffnet und nach hinten erweitert, um einen offenen Grundriss zu schaffen. Schließlich wurde ein vollständiges drittes Stockwerk hinzugefügt, um drei Schlafzimmer und zwei Bäder unterzubringen.

La structure originale était une maison très modeste construite dans les années 1920. Le site jouissait d'une vue sur le centre-ville de San Francisco à l'avant et d'un accès à une grande cour arrière et à un espace vert communautaire à l'arrière. Initialement composé d'un petit rez-de-chaussée principal avec deux chambres à coucher, le client cherchait à augmenter l'espace habitable pour accueillir sa jeune famille grandissante. Ceci a été réalisé en creusant le rez-de-chaussée pour créer plus d'espace de vie et un bureau à domicile tout en offrant un accès direct au jardin de la cour arrière. Au rez-de-chaussée, tout l'étage a été ouvert et agrandi vers l'arrière pour permettre un plan d'étage ouvert. Enfin, un troisième étage a été ajouté pour accueillir trois chambres à coucher et deux salles de bains.

La estructura original era una casa muy modesta construida en la década de 1920. El sitio disfrutaba de las vistas del centro de San Francisco en la parte delantera y del acceso a un gran patio trasero y a un espacio verde comunitario compartido en la parte trasera. Inicialmente compuesto de un pequeño nivel principal con dos dormitorios, el cliente buscó aumentar la cantidad de espacio habitable para acomodar a su joven y creciente familia. Esto se logró excavando el nivel del suelo para crear más espacio habitable y una oficina en casa, al tiempo que se proporcionaba acceso directo al jardín del patio trasero. En el nivel principal, todo el piso se abrió y se expandió hacia atrás para proporcionar una planta abierta. Finalmente, se añadió un tercer piso completo para acomodar tres dormitorios y dos baños.

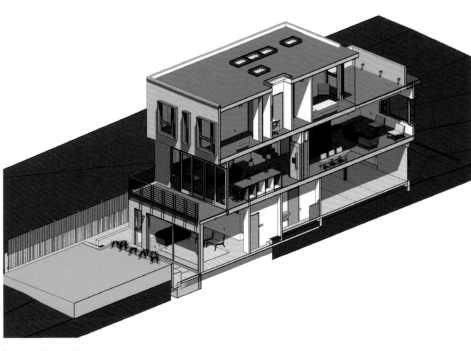

Perspective section

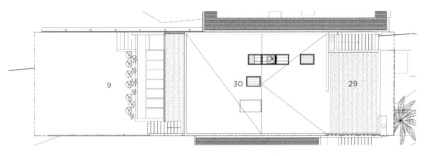

Roof plan

Third floor plan

Second floor plan

New ——|—— Existing

New ——|—— Existing

Ground floor plan

Longitudinal section

1. Garage
2. New study
3. New laundry
4. New bathroom
5. New den
6. Rotating wood slat screen
7. Lower patio
8. Concrete bench
9. Rear yard
10. New deck
11. Family room
12. Kitchen
13. Open below
14. Open above
15. Wood slat screen
16. Dining room
17. Hall
18. Powder room
19. Entry
20. Living room
21. Fireplace
22. Built-in storage
23. New bedroom
24. New landing
25. New skylight
26. New master bathroom
27. New closet
28. New master bathroom
29. New roof deck
30. New roof

This ranch style home was built in the 1950s. Its interior had been modified and renovated once before, but the spaces remained small and dark. The client purchased the home with the intention of modernizing the layout and spaces while also significantly adding to the home to accommodate his growing family. Taking into account the spacious backyard and wanting to utilize it as an additional room, the floor plan was redesigned so that there was a constant and seamless connection to this central backyard. To capitalize on natural light and the volume of the main space, the roof was reconfigured to create a split-level clerestory. This served to flood the living spaces with morning light and to create a sense of spaciousness while also keeping the building footprint relatively small.

Dieses Haus im Ranchstil wurde in den 1950er Jahren gebaut. Sein Inneres war bereits einmal umgebaut und renoviert worden, aber die Räume blieben klein und dunkel. Der Kunde kaufte das Haus in der Absicht, den Grundriss und die Räume zu modernisieren und gleichzeitig das Haus deutlich zu erweitern, um seine wachsende Familie unterzubringen. Unter Berücksichtigung des großzügigen Hinterhofes und des Planes, ihn als zusätzlichen Raum zu nutzen, wurde der Grundriss neu gestaltet, sodass eine ständige und nahtlose Verbindung zu diesem zentralen Hinterhof besteht. Um das natürliche Licht und das Volumen des Hauptraumes zu nutzen, wurde das Dach zu einem geteilten Obergeschoss umgebaut. Dies diente dazu, die Wohnräume mit Morgenlicht zu überfluten und ein Gefühl von Weite zu schaffen, während gleichzeitig die Grundfläche relativ klein gehalten wurde.

Cette maison de style ranch a été construite dans les années 1950. Son intérieur avait été modifié et rénové une fois auparavant, mais les espaces restaient petits et sombres. Le client a acheté la maison dans l'intention d'en moderniser l'aménagement et les espaces, tout en y ajoutant des agrandissements importants pour accommoder sa famille grandissante. Compte tenu de l'arrière-cour spacieuse et de la volonté de l'utiliser comme pièce supplémentaire, le plan de l'étage a été redessiné afin qu'il y ait une connexion constante et continue avec cette cour arrière centrale. Pour tirer parti de la lumière naturelle et du volume de l'espace principal, le toit a été reconfiguré pour créer un étage à claire-voie à deux niveaux. Cela a permis d'inonder les espaces de vie de lumière matinale et de créer un effet d'espace tout en gardant l'empreinte du bâtiment relativement petite.

Esta casa estilo rancho fue construida en la década de 1950. Su interior había sido modificado y renovado una vez anteriormente, pero los espacios seguían siendo pequeños y oscuros. El cliente compró la casa con la intención de modernizar la distribución y los espacios, al mismo tiempo que aumentaba significativamente la capacidad de la casa para acomodar a su creciente familia. Contando con el amplio patio trasero para utilizarlo como una habitación adicional, se rediseñó el plano del piso para que hubiera una conexión constante y sin fisuras con este patio trasero central. Para aprovechar la luz natural y el volumen del espacio principal, se reconfiguró el tejado para crear un claristorio de dos niveles. Esto sirvió para inundar los espacios con la luz de la mañana y para crear una sensación de amplitud, al mismo tiempo que se mantenía la huella del edificio relativamente pequeña.

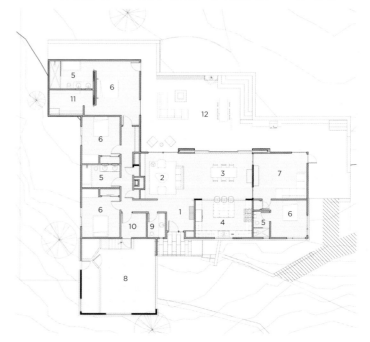

Floor plan

1. Entry
2. Living room
3. Dining room
4. Kitchen
5. Bathroom
6. Bedroom
7. Den
8. Garage
9. Powder room
10. Laundry room
11. Closet
12. Patio

The original building was comprised of two separate structures that were a mirror image of each other. Built in the early 1900s, the structures were renovated, partitioned, and added to overtime. Their floor plans were not very efficient and their original detailing was lost with the alterations. Our client purchased the properties with the idea of salvaging their exterior charm while modernizing and reconfiguring the interiors and also adding living space for her and her family. The floor plans were redesigned to add living space on both the ground and top floors while attempting to conceal the top floor addition from street view. Furthermore, it was important to provide access to the rear yard. Flow, connection, and natural light were integral to the design.

Die ursprüngliche Anlage bestand aus zwei getrennten, spiegelsymmetrischen Strukturen. Die in den frühen 1900er Jahren errichteten Gebäude wurden renoviert und neu aufgeteilt. Ihre Grundrisse waren nicht sehr effizient und ihre ursprüngliche Detaillierung ging mit den Änderungen verloren. Unser Kunde kaufte die Immobilien mit der Idee, ihren äußeren Charme zu erhalten, indem er die Innenräume modernisierte und umgestaltete und gleichzeitig den Lebensraum für sich und seine Familie vergrößerte. Die Grundrisse wurden neu gestaltet, um sowohl im Erd- als auch im Obergeschoss Wohnraum zu schaffen und gleichzeitig zu versuchen, den Anbau des Obergeschosses vor der Straßenansicht zu verbergen. Darüber hinaus war es wichtig, den Zugang zum Hinterhof zu ermöglichen. Fluss, Verbindung und natürliches Licht waren integraler Bestandteil des Designs.

Le bâtiment d'origine se composait de deux structures distinctes qui étaient un miroir l'une de l'autre. Construites au début des années 1900, les structures ont été rénovées, cloisonnées et ajoutées avec le temps. Leurs plans d'étage n'étaient pas très efficaces et les détails d'origine ont été perdus avec les modifications. Notre cliente a acheté les propriétés avec l'idée de récupérer leur charme extérieur tout en modernisant et reconfigurant les intérieurs et en ajoutant un espace de vie pour elle et sa famille. Les plans des étages ont été redessinés pour ajouter de l'espace habitable au rez-de-chaussée et au dernier étage tout en essayant de dissimuler l'ajout du dernier étage à la vue de la rue. De plus, il était important de donner accès à la cour arrière. L'écoulement, la connexion et la lumière naturelle faisaient partie intégrante de la conception.

El edificio original estaba compuesto por dos estructuras separadas que eran un espejo el uno del otro. Construidas a principios del siglo XX, las estructuras fueron renovadas, divididas y añadidas con el paso del tiempo. Sus planos no eran muy eficientes y sus detalles originales se perdieron con las modificaciones. Nuestra clienta compró las propiedades con la idea de recuperar su encanto exterior mientras modernizaba y reconfiguraba los interiores y también añadía espacio habitable para ella y su familia. Los planos fueron rediseñados para agregar espacio habitable tanto en la planta baja como en la superior, intentando además y ocultar la adición de la planta superior de la vista de la calle. Además, era importante proporcionar acceso al patio trasero. El flujo, la conexión y la luz natural fueron parte integral del diseño.

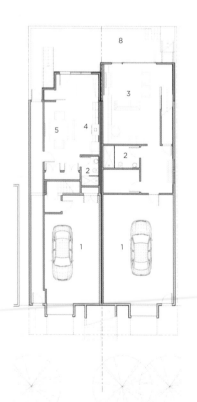

Garage level floor plan

New second level floor plan

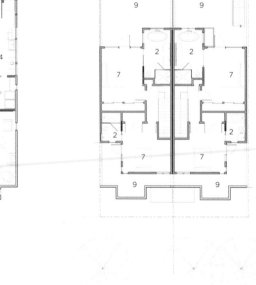

New third level floor plan

1. Garage
2. Bathroom
3. Den
4. Kitchen
5. Living room
6. Dining room
7. Bedroom
8. Rear yard
9. Roof deck

DIEBEL AND COMPANY
ARCHITECTS

⊕ **www.diebelstudio.com** ⓘ **diebelstudio**

Diebel and Company | Architects is an architecture firm based in the San Francisco Bay Area. We work closely with our clients to thoroughly understand their needs and to develop solutions that are unique, appropriate, and strategic responses to the constraints and opportunities of the project. Rigorous and thoughtful consideration is given to all projects to produce the best results for our clients. Publications and awards have recognized the consistent quality of the firm's work. The firm is interested in a search of design solutions that are refined, cost-effective, and environmentally sensitive. We have developed close working relationships with consultants and contractors who are available to assist our clients.

Diebel and Company | Architects ist ein Architekturbüro mit Sitz in der San Francisco Bay Area. Wir arbeiten eng mit unseren Kunden zusammen, um ihre Bedürfnisse gründlich zu verstehen und Lösungen zu entwickeln, die einzigartige, angemessene und strategische Antworten auf die Möglichkeiten und Beschränkungen des Projekts sind. Alle Projekte werden sorgfältig geprüft, um die besten Ergebnisse für unsere Kunden zu erzielen. Veröffentlichungen und Auszeichnungen würdigen die gleichbleibende Qualität der Arbeit unseres Unternehmens. Wir sind stets auf der Suche nach Designlösungen, die raffiniert, kostengünstig und umweltfreundlich sind. Zu diesem Zweick haben wir enge Arbeitsbeziehungen zu Beratern und Auftragnehmern aufgebaut, die unseren Kunden zur Seite stehen.

Diebel and Company | Architects est un cabinet d'architectes basé dans la région de la baie de San Francisco. Nous travaillons en étroite collaboration avec nos clients afin de bien comprendre leurs besoins et de développer des solutions uniques, appropriées et stratégiques pour répondre aux contraintes et aux opportunités du projet. Une attention rigoureuse et réfléchie est accordée à tous les projets afin de produire les meilleurs résultats pour nos clients. Des publications et des prix ont reconnu la qualité constante du travail du cabinet. L'entreprise s'intéresse à la recherche de solutions de conception raffinées, rentables et respectueuses de l'environnement. Nous avons développé des relations de travail étroites avec des consultants et des entrepreneurs qui sont disponibles pour aider nos clients.

Diebel and Company | Architects es un estudio de arquitectura con sede en el área de la Bahía de San Francisco. Trabajamos en estrecha colaboración con nuestros clientes para comprender a fondo sus necesidades y desarrollar soluciones que sean únicas, apropiadas y respuestas estratégicas a las limitaciones y oportunidades del proyecto. Todos los proyectos son considerados rigurosa y cuidadosamente para producir los mejores resultados para nuestros clientes. Las publicaciones y los premios han reconocido la calidad constante del trabajo de la firma. El estudio está interesada en una búsqueda de soluciones de diseño que sean refinadas, rentables y respetuosas con el medio ambiente. Hemos desarrollado estrechas relaciones de trabajo con consultores y contratistas que están disponibles para ayudar a nuestros clientes.

The project started as a remodel to an existing house that was built decades ago by the owner's father. Because the house no longer satisfied the requirements of a contemporary living style, a new house was planned. Now the original owner's son has built a new house just where his father did many years ago. Tall flowing spaces are full of natural light and maximize the interaction between indoor and outdoor areas. The home flows among three domains for public and private uses and is planned to take advantage of daylighting and views of the surrounding landscape. Spatial interest is developed with varying ceiling heights in the one-story house. Calming blue accents highlight the architecture. The architecture is inspired by mid-century architecture with the house opening to exterior spaces.

Das Projekt begann als Umbau eines bestehenden Hauses, das vor Jahrzehnten vom Vater des Eigentümers gebaut worden war. Da das Haus nicht mehr den Anforderungen an einen zeitgemäßen Wohnstil entsprach, wurde neu geplant. Jetzt hat der Sohn des ursprünglichen Besitzers ein neues Haus errichtet, genau dort, wo sein Vater es vor vielen Jahren getan hatte. Hohe, fließende Räume sind voll von natürlichem Licht und maximieren die Interaktion zwischen Innen- und Außenbereich. Das Haus erstreckt sich über drei Bereiche für die gemeinschaftliche und private Nutzung und soll offen sein für Tageslicht und die Aussicht auf die umliegende Landschaft. Im eingeschossigen Haus werden räumliche Interessen mit unterschiedlichen Deckenhöhen entwickelt. Beruhigende blaue Akzente unterstreichen die Architektur. Das moderne Design ist von der Architektur des Mittelalters inspiriert, wobei sich das Haus nach außen öffnet.

Le projet a commencé comme le remodelage d'une maison existante construite il y a des décennies par le père du propriétaire. Comme la maison ne répondait plus aux exigences d'un style de vie contemporain, une nouvelle maison a été planifiée. Aujourd'hui, le fils du propriétaire initial a construit une nouvelle maison exactement comme son père l'avait fait il y a de nombreuses années. Les grands espaces fluides sont pleins de lumière naturelle et maximisent l'interaction entre l'intérieur et l'extérieur. La maison s'écoule entre trois domaines pour des usages publics et privés et est conçue pour permettre de profiter de l'éclairage naturel et de la vue sur le paysage environnant. L'intérêt spatial est développé avec des hauteurs de plafond variables dans la maison de plain-pied. Des accents bleus apaisants mettent en valeur l'architecture. Le design moderne s'inspire de l'architecture du milieu du siècle dernier, la maison s'ouvrant sur l'extérieur.

El proyecto comenzó como una remodelación de una casa existente que fue construida hace décadas por el padre del dueño. Debido a que la casa ya no satisfacía los requisitos de un estilo de vida contemporáneo, se planificó una nueva casa. Ahora el hijo del dueño original ha construido una nueva casa justo donde su padre lo hizo hace muchos años. Los espacios altos y fluidos están llenos de luz natural y maximizan la interacción entre las áreas interiores y exteriores. La casa fluye entre tres dominios para uso público y privado y está planeada para aprovechar la luz natural y las vistas del paisaje circundante. El interés espacial se desarrolla con diferentes alturas de techo en la casa de una planta. Las relajantes notas de color azul resaltan la arquitectura. El diseño moderno se inspira en la arquitectura de mediados del siglo XX con la casa abriéndose a los espacios exteriores.

North elevation

South elevation

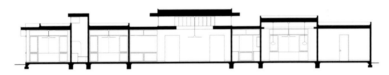

Building section

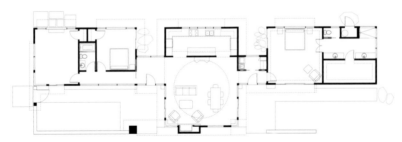

Floor plan

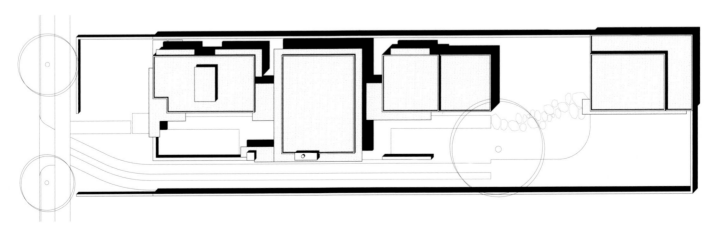

Site plan

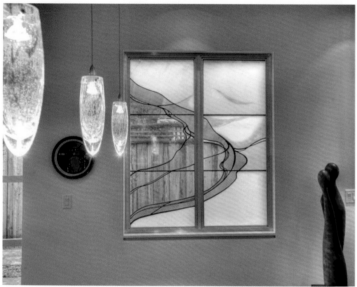

Easton Residence is a modern departure from the 1920s California Spanish architectural grandeur. Its original romantic charm is transformed with contemporary design, highlighting a modern take on characteristic stucco walls, low-pitched clay tile roofs, sweeping arches, and wrought-iron railings. The design blends previous expansions with a sleek reconfiguration of the house for contemporary living. A combination of conspicuous silhouettes, restrained color choices, and rich textures provide a soothing retreat. A generally muted palette of pleasing neutrals is enhanced with unexpected appealing color in the home's overall comfortable décor. In the kitchen and baths, streamlined surfaces give the home a sophisticated, modern style. The landscaping and exterior living spaces capitalize on the temperate climate providing for interior spaces seamlessly flowing to exterior areas.

Easton Residence ist eine moderne Entwicklung der architektonischen Größe, die den spanischen neokolonialen Stil der 1920er Jahre in Kalifornien prägt. Sein ursprünglicher romantischer Charme wird mit einem zeitgenössischen Design erneuert, das die Modernität der Stuckmauern, die sanft abfallenden Keramikziegeldächer, Rundbögen und schmiedeeisernen Geländer unterstreicht. Das Design verschmilzt frühere Erweiterungen mit einer eleganten Reorganisation des Hauses für einen zeitgemäßen Lebensstil. Eine Kombination aus auffälligen Silhouetten, nüchternen Farben und satten Texturen sorgt für eine gemütliche Atmosphäre. Die komfortable Einrichtung des Hauses konzentriert sich auf eine Reihe neutraler Farbtöne, die durch kräftige Farbakzente ergänzt werden. In Küche und Bad verleihen die gereinigten Oberflächen dem Haus einen anspruchsvollen Stil. Landschaftsgestaltung und Außenwohnflächen nutzen das gemäßigte Klima und ermöglichen einen reibungslosen Übergang der Innenräume in die Außenbereiche.

Easton Residence est une évolution moderne de la grandeur architecturale qui caractérise le style néocolonial espagnol des années 1920 en Californie. Son charme romantique original est renouvelé par un design contemporain qui met en valeur la modernité des murs en stuc, des toits en tuiles de céramique en pente douce, des arcs en plein cintre et des rampes de fer forgé. Le design fusionne les extensions précédentes avec une élégante réorganisation de la maison pour un style de vie contemporain. Une combinaison de silhouettes remarquables, de couleurs sobres et de textures riches procure une atmosphère chaleureuse. Le décor confortable de la maison met l'accent sur une gamme de tons neutres qui est complétée par des touches de couleurs vives. Dans la cuisine et les salles de bains, les surfaces épurées donnent à la maison un style sophistiqué. L'aménagement paysager et les espaces de vie extérieurs profitent du climat tempéré et permettent aux espaces intérieurs de s'intégrer harmonieusement aux espaces extérieurs.

Easton Residence es una evolución moderna de la grandeza arquitectónica que caracteriza el estilo neocolonial español de la década de 1920 en California. Su encanto romántico original se renueva con un diseño contemporáneo, resaltando la modernidad de las paredes de estuco, los tejados de suave inclinación con teja de cerámica, los arcos de medio punto y las barandillas de hierro forjado. El diseño fusiona ampliaciones anteriores con una elegante reorganización de la casa para una estilo de vida contemporáneo. Una combinación de siluetas conspicuas, colores sobrios y texturas ricas proporcionan un ambiente acogedor. La decoración cómoda de la casa se centra en una gama de tonos neutros que se completa con toques de color llamativos. En la cocina y en los baños, las superficies depuradas dan a la casa un estilo sofisticado. El paisajismo y los espacios de vida exteriores aprovechan el clima templado y permiten que los espacios interiores fluyan sin problemas hacia las áreas exteriores.

TellApart is a fast-growing advertising technology startup company. Their headquarters is in an adaptive reuse building that was converted from an industrial facility into 26,000 square feet of tech office space. A unique office environment was created around the company's culture. The facility encourages flexible working arrangements, promotes collaboration, and fosters productivity. Open spaces and enclosed rooms are used for suitability to the task at hand and to satisfy personal working preferences. The building was retrofitted with glazed overhead doors and folding doors opening to exterior spaces. TellApart was named one of the best places to work in the Bay Area by San Francisco Business Times.

TellApart ist ein schnell wachsendes Startup-Unternehmen für Werbetechnologie. Der Hauptsitz befindet sich in einem adaptiven Mehrzweckgebäude, das von einer Industrieanlage in eine technische Bürofläche von 2.400 Quadratmetern umgewandelt wurde. Gemäß der Unternehmenskultur wurde eine einzigartige Büroumgebung geschaffen. Die Einrichtung fördert flexible Arbeitsregelungen, Zusammenarbeit und Produktivität. Freiflächen und geschlossene Räume werden für nachhaltiges Arbeiten und zur Befriedigung der persönlichen Arbeitspräferenzen genutzt. Das Gebäude wurde mit verglasten Überkopftüren und nach außen offenen Falttüren nachgerüstet. TellApart wurde von der San Francisco Business Times als einer der besten Arbeitgeber in der Bay Area ausgezeichnet.

TellApart est une jeune entreprise de technologie publicitaire en pleine croissance. Leur siège social est situé dans un immeuble de réutilisation adapté qui a été reconverti en bureaux techniques d'une superficie de 2.400 mètres carrés à partir d'une installation industrielle. Un environnement de bureau unique a été créé autour de la culture de l'entreprise. L'installation encourage la souplesse des modalités de travail, favorise la collaboration et favorise la productivité. Des espaces ouverts et des pièces fermées sont utilisés pour s'adapter à la tâche à accomplir et pour satisfaire les préférences de travail personnelles. Le bâtiment a été réaménagé avec des portes basculantes vitrées au plafond et des portes pliantes ouvrant sur l'extérieur. TellApart a été nommé l'un des meilleurs endroits pour travailler dans la région de la Baie par le San Francisco Business Times.

TellApart es una empresa del sector de la tecnología publicitaria en pleno crecimiento. Su sede se encuentra en un edificio de reutilización adaptable que fue convertido a partir de una instalación industrial en un espacio de oficinas tecnológicas de 2.400 metros cuadrados. En torno a la cultura de la empresa se creó un entorno de oficina único. La instalación fomenta procesos de trabajo flexibles, promueve la colaboración y fomenta la productividad. Los espacios abiertos y los espacios cerrados se utilizan para adaptarse a la tarea que se está llevando a cabo y para satisfacer las preferencias personales de trabajo. El edificio fue reequipado con puertas batientes acristaladas y puertas plegables que se abren a los espacios exteriores. TellApart fue nombrado uno de los mejores lugares para trabajar en el Área de la Bahía por el San Francisco Business Times.

DIEGO PACHECO
DESIGN PRACTICE

🌐 www.diegopacheco.com ⓘ diego.pacheco.design

Diego Pacheco is the owner and founder of Diego Pacheco Design Practice, a San Francisco-based architectural planning and design firm specializing in high-end residential work. Diego was born in Colombia and studied architecture in Berkeley, Barcelona, and London before receiving his Masters of Architecture from the University of Pennsylvania. Over the course of his career, Diego has worked on architectural projects across the US, several of which have been featured in Elle Décor, California Home+Design, Dwell Magazine, and Spaces Magazine. He began his career at Karl G. Smith Associates, followed by tenure at Gemmill Design, Aidlin Darling Design, and MAK Studio, prior to starting his own firm in 2012. The firm's design work is informed by a close collaboration with the client and strives to achieve simplicity, tranquility, and balance.

Diego Pacheco ist Eigentümer and Gründer von Diego Pacheco Design Practice, einem in San Francisco ansässigen Architekturbüro für Planung und Design, das sich auf hochwertige Wohnarbeiten spezialisiert hat. Diego wurde in Kolumbien geboren und studierte Architektur in Berkeley, Barcelona und London, bevor er seinen Master of Architecture an der University of Pennsylvania erhielt. Im Laufe seiner Karriere hat Diego an Architekturprojekten in den Vereinigten Staaten gearbeitet, von denen mehrere in Elle Décor, California Home+Design, Dwell Magazineund Spaces Magazine vorgestellt wurden. Er begann seine Karriere bei Karl G. Smith Associates, gefolgt von Anstellungen bei Gemmill Design, Aidlin Darling Design und MAK Studio, bevor er 2012 seine eigene Firma gründete. Die Designarbeit des Unternehmens wird durch eine enge Zusammenarbeit mit dem Kunden bestimmt und strebt nach Einfachheit, Ruhe und Ausgeglichenheit.

Diego Pacheco est le propiétaire et fondateur de Diego Pacheco Design Practice, un cabinet d'architecture et de design basé à San Francisco spécialisé dans les travaux résidentiels haut de gamme. Diego est né en Colombie et a étudié l'architecture à Berkeley, Barcelone et Londres avant de recevoir sa maîtrise en architecture de l'Université de Pennsylvanie. Au cours de sa carrière, Diego a travaillé sur des projets architecturaux aux États-Unis, dont plusieurs ont été présentés dans Elle Décor, California Home+Design, Dwell Magazine et Spaces magazine. Il a commencé sa carrière chez Karl G. Smith Associates, puis a travaillé chez Gemmill Design, Aidlin Darling Design et MAK Studio, avant de créer son propre cabinet en 2012. Le travail de conception de l'entreprise s'appuie sur une étroite collaboration avec le client et s'efforce d'atteindre la simplicité, la tranquilité et l'équilibre.

Diego Pacheco es el propietario y fundador de Diego Pacheco Design Practice, un estudio de planificación y diseño arquitectónico con sede en San Francisco, especializado en trabajos residenciales de alto nivel. Diego nació en Colombia y estudió arquitectura en Berkeley, Barcelona y Londres antes de recibir su Master en Arquitectura de la Universidad de Pennsylvania. A lo largo de su carrera, Diego ha trabajado en proyectos arquitectónicos en todo Estados Unidos, varios de los cuales han sido presentados en Elle Décor, California Home+Design, Dwell Magazine y Spaces Magazine. Comenzó su carrera en Karl G. Smith Associates, seguido de un periodo en Gemmill Design, Aidlin Darling Design y MAK Studio, antes de comenzar su propia firma en 2012. El trabajo de diseño de la empresa se basa en una estrecha colaboración con el cliente y se esfuerza por lograr la simplicidad, la tranquilidad y el equilibrio.

The original residence was designed in 1952 by John Bolles, a prominent San Francisco architect. The structure is a fine example of Bay Region Modernism, with exposed wood beam ceilings and a mural in the dining area that features a spectacular cityscape painted by artist Jose Moya del Pino. The current owners hired Diego Pacheco to update the home in 2014. While the original spirit of the house was preserved and the mural was restored, the historic house was reorganized around a new open central stair below an operable skylight. The redesigned backyard is now a roof garden above an underground addition that includes a gym, wine cellar, and great room for entertaining. Landscape elements include mature olive trees and succulents in the private garden and colorful maples along the street.

Die ursprüngliche Residenz wurde 1952 von John Bolles, einem bedeutenden Architekten aus San Francisco, entworfen. Die Struktur ist ein schönes Beispiel für den Modernismus der Bay Region, mit freiliegenden Holzbalkendecken und einem Wandbild im Essbereich, das ein spektakuläres Stadtbild des Künstlers Jose Moya del Pino zeigt. Die derzeitigen Eigentümer beauftragten Diego Pacheco 2014 mit der Modernisierung des Hauses. Während der ursprüngliche Geist des Hauses bewahrt und das Wandbild restauriert wurde, wurde das historische Haus um eine neue offene zentrale Treppe unter einem bedienbaren Oberlicht herum neu organisiert. Der neu gestaltete Hinterhof ist heute ein Dachgarten über einem unterirdischen Anbau, der eine Turnhalle, einen Weinkeller und einen großen Raum für Unterhaltung beinhaltet. Zu den Landschaftselementen gehören reife Olivenbäume und Sukkulenten im privaten Garten und bunte Ahorne entlang der Straße.

La résidence originale a été conçue en 1952 par John Bolles, un éminent architecte de San Francisco. La structure est un bon exemple de modernisme dans la région de la Baie, avec des plafonds à poutres en bois et une peinture murale dans la salle à manger qui présente un paysage urbain spectaculaire peint par l'artiste José Moya del Pino. Les propriétaires actuels ont engagé Diego Pacheco pour rénover la maison en 2014. Tout en préservant l'esprit original de la maison et en restaurant la peinture murale, la demeure historique a été réorganisée autour d'un nouvel escalier central ouvert sous un puits de lumière utilisables. L'arrière-cour réaménagée est maintenant un jardin sur le toit au-dessus d'une extension souterraine qui comprend un gymnase, une cave à vin et une grande salle de récréation. Les éléments du paysage comprennent des oliviers mûrs et succulents dans le jardin privé et des érables colorés le long de la rue.

La residencia original fue diseñada en 1952 por John Bolles, un destacado arquitecto de San Francisco. La estructura es un buen ejemplo del Modernismo de la Región de la Bahía, con techos de vigas de madera y un mural en el comedor que presenta un espectacular paisaje urbano pintado por el artista José Moya del Pino. Los actuales propietarios contrataron a Diego Pacheco para actualizar la casa en 2014. Mientras que el espíritu original de la casa fue preservado y el mural restaurado, la casa histórica fue reorganizada alrededor de una nueva escalera central abierta debajo de un tragaluz practicable. El patio trasero rediseñado es ahora un jardín en la azotea sobre una ampliación subterránea que incluye un gimnasio, una bodega de vinos y un gran salón para el esparcimiento. Los elementos del paisaje incluyen olivos maduros y suculentas en el jardín privado y coloridos arces a lo largo de la calle.

Upper level floor plan

Main level floor plan

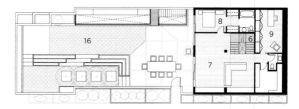

Garden level floor plan

Garage level floor plan

1. Garage
2. Home gym
3. Great room
4. Light well
5. Wine cellar
6. Central stair
7. Playroom
8. Guest suite
9. Office
10. Living room
11. Dining room
12. Kitchen
13. Master suite
14. Office
15. Bedroom
16. Garden

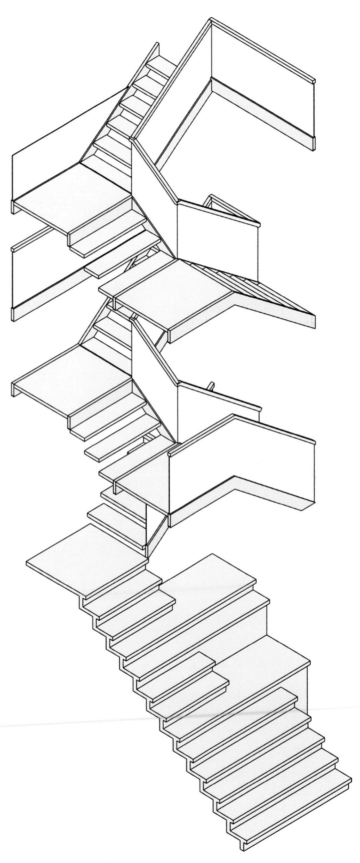

Axonometric of central four-level open staircase

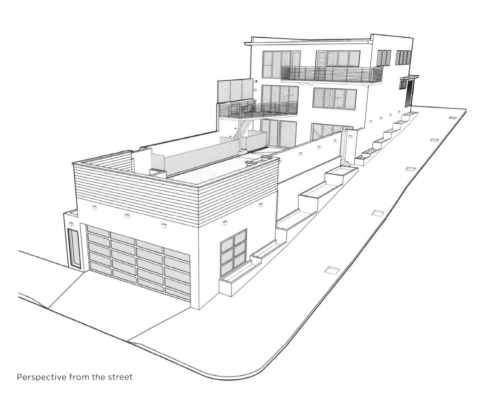

Perspective from the street

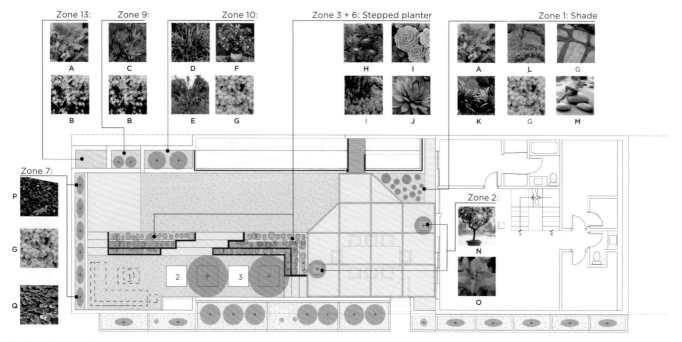

Planting design. Private garden

1. Fire pit
2. Herb Garden
3. Water feature

A. Giant chain fern
B. Clematis cart avalanche vine
C. Icee blue
D. Apple tree
E. Mondo grass
F. Eureka lemon tree
G. Baby tears

H. Hens and chicks succulents
I. Low succulents
J. Medium succulents
K. Nano mondo grass
L. Star creeper
M. Seating
N. Meyer lemon tree

O. Mint
P. Espalier limes
Q. Wild ginger
R. Blue fescue grass
S. Golden variegated sweet flag
T. Juncus elk blue
U. Provence lavender

V. Columnar hornbeam trees
W. Variegated string of buttons
X. Agave attenuata
Y. Japanese maple

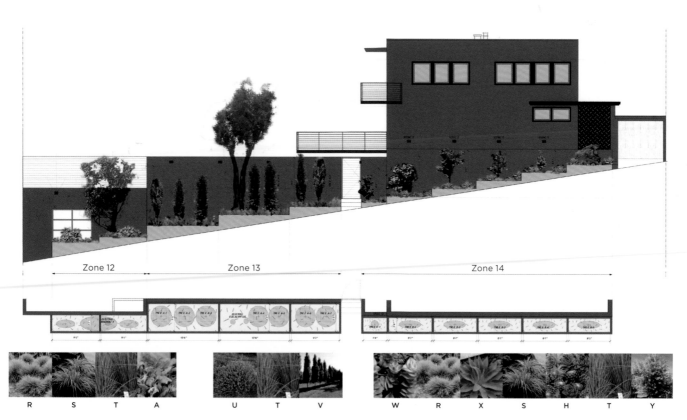

Planting design. Street elevation

A 1940 Mediterranean bungalow was opened up and reconfigured for indoor/outdoor open-plan living. The existing house was dark and cramped and had no connection to the outdoors. The walls between the separate rooms were removed to create a continuous open space that flows from the front entry through the living room, kitchen, and dining area into the backyard. The kitchen, featuring a 20-foot-long marble island, vaulted ceiling, and 20-foot-long skylight is the focal point of the public space. The private side of the house is separated from the public side by pocket doors. The sloping rear yard was terraced to create a flat patio for outdoor living with a strong connection to the main public space, blurring the lines between interior and exterior.

Ein mediterraner Bungalow aus dem Jahr 1940 wurde geöffnet und für das offene Wohnen im Innen- und Außenbereich umgestaltet. Das bestehende Haus war dunkel und eng und hatte keine Verbindung zur Außenwelt. Die Wände zwischen den einzelnen Räumen wurden entfernt, um einen durchgehenden offenen Raum zu schaffen, der vom vorderen Eingang durch das Wohnzimmer, die Küche und den Essbereich in den Hinterhof fließt. Die Küche mit einer sechs Meter langen Marmorinsel, gewölbter Decke und 20 Fuß langem Oberlicht ist der Mittelpunkt des öffentlichen Raumes. Die private Seite des Hauses ist durch eine Taschentür von der öffentlicheren Seite getrennt. Der schräge Hinterhof wurde terrassenförmig angelegt, um eine flache Terrasse für das Wohnen im Freien zu schaffen, die eine starke Verbindung zum öffentlichen Hauptraum aufweist und die Grenzen zwischen innen und außen verwischt.

Un bungalow méditerranéen de 1940 a été ouvert et reconfiguré pour l'habitat intérieur/extérieur à aire ouverte. La maison existante était sombre et exiguë et n'avait aucun lien avec l'extérieur. Les murs entre les pièces séparées ont été enlevés pour créer un espace ouvert continu qui s'écoule de l'entrée avant vers le salon, la cuisine et la salle à manger dans la cour arrière. La cuisine, avec son îlot de marbre de six mètres de long, son plafond voûté et sa lucarne de six mètres de long, est le point central de l'espace public. Le côté privé de la maison est séparé du côté public par des portes à poche. La cour arrière en pente a été aménagée en terrasse pour créer un patio plat pour la vie en plein air avec une forte connexion à l'espace public principal, estompant les lignes entre l'intérieur et l'extérieur.

Un bungaló mediterráneo de 1940 fue abierto y reconfigurado para vivir en interiores y exteriores. La casa original era oscura y estrecha y no tenía conexión con el exterior. Las paredes que separaban las estancias fueron eliminadas para crear un espacio abierto continuo que fluye desde la entrada principal a través de la sala de estar, la cocina y el comedor hacia el patio trasero. La cocina, con una isla de mármol de seis metros de largo, techo abovedado y tragaluz de seis metros de largo, es el punto focal del espacio público. El lado privado de la casa está separado del lado público por puertas corredizas. El jardín trasero inclinado fue adosado para crear un patio plano para vivir al aire libre con una fuerte conexión con el espacio público principal, desdibujando las líneas entre el interior y el exterior.

Original main floor plan

Renovated main floor plan

Original ground floor plan

Renovated ground floor plan

1. Garage
2. Mud room/laundry
3. Playroom
4. Guest suite
5. Living room
6. Kitchen
7. Dining room
8. Master suite
9. Bedroom

A renovation to a 1905 Victorian house was conceived as a progression from traditional design elements to modern as one circulates from public to private spaces. The Victorian façade remains intact, and the rooms at the front of the house maintain all their original details. The back of the main level—containing three separate rooms for kitchen, living, and dining—was opened up into one singular space that blends some of the Victorian elements with a modern kitchen and sleek steel and glass balcony and staircase that connects to the backyard below, a new lush garden oasis. The living space was expanded into the garden level that was previously basement space behind the garage. The expansion allows for a spacious modern master suite with generous closets and a zen-like spa bathroom.

Eine Renovierung eines viktorianischen Hauses aus dem Jahr 1905 wurde als Witerentwicklung von traditionellen Designelementen zur Moderne konzipiert, eine Zirkulation von öffentlichen zu privaten Räumen. Die viktorianische Fassade bleibt intakt, und die Räume an der Vorderseite des Hauses behalten alle ihre ursprünglichen Details. Die Rückseite der Hauptebene mit drei separaten Räumen für Küche, Wohnen und Essen wurde zu einem einzigen Raum geöffnet, der einige der viktorianischen Elemente mit einer modernen Küche und einem schlanken Stahl-Glas-Balkon und einer Treppe verbindet, die mit dem darunter liegenden Hinterhof, einer neuen üppigen Gartenoase, verbunden ist. Die Wohnfläche wurde in die Gartenebene erweitert, die früher Kellerraum hinter der Garage war. Die Erweiterung ermöglichte eine geräumige, moderne Mastersuite mit großzügigen Schränken und einem zenähnlichen Wellnessbad.

La rénovation d'une maison victorienne de 1905 a été conçue comme une progression des éléments de design traditionnels vers un style moderne au fur et à mesure que l'on passe des espaces publics aux espaces privés. La façade victorienne reste intacte et les pièces situées devant la maison conservent tous leurs détails d'origine. L'arrière du rez-de-chaussée, qui contient trois pièces séparées pour la cuisine, le salon et la salle à manger, a été ouvert dans un espace singulier qui mélange certains des éléments victoriens avec une cuisine moderne, un balcon et un escalier en acier et en verre élégant qui relie la cour arrière, un nouvel oasis de jardin luxuriant. L'espace habitable a été agrandi au niveau du jardin qui était auparavant un sous-sol derrière le garage. L'agrandissement permet d'avoir une suite des maîtres spacieuse et moderne avec des placards généreux et une salle de bain spa zen.

La renovación de una casa victoriana de 1905 se concibió como una progresión de los elementos de diseño tradicionales a los modernos, a medida que uno circula de los espacios públicos a los privados. La fachada victoriana permanece intacta, y las estancias que dan a la fachada de la casa conservan todos sus detalles originales. La parte trasera del nivel principal —que contenía tres estancias separadas, cocina, sala de estar y comedor— se abrió en un espacio singular que combina algunos de los elementos victorianos con una cocina moderna y un elegante balcón y escalera de acero y cristal que conecta con el patio trasero de abajo, un nuevo y exuberante oasis de jardín. El espacio habitable se amplió hasta el nivel del jardín, que antes era un sótano detrás del garaje. La ampliación permite una espaciosa y moderna habitación principal con generosos armarios y un cuarto de baño *spa* estilo zen.

Renovated main floor plan

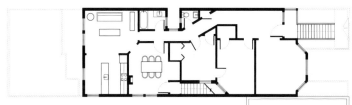

Original main floor plan

Renovated lower floor plan

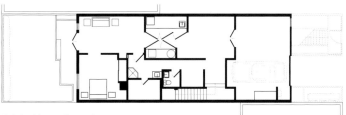

Original lower floor plan

1. Garage
2. Mud room
3. Washer/dryer
4. Wine cellar
5. Closet
6. Mechanical
7. Master bathroom
8. Master bedroom
9. Foyer
10. Parlor
11. Guest room
12. Office
13. Great room

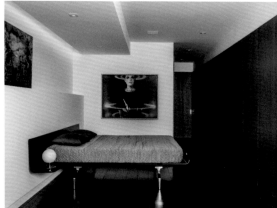

DUMICAN MOSEY
ARCHITECTS

SOMA RESIDENCE, ARTIST GALLERY & STUDIO

Photography: **Cesar Rubio Photography and Kirsten Hepburn Photography**
Location: **San Francisco, California**
Area: **8,200 Sq. Ft.**
General Contractor: **Interspace Builders Inc.**
Structural Engineering: **Provest Structural Engineering**
Acoustical Consultant: **Charles M Salter Associates Inc.**
Geotechnical Engineering: **Herzog Geotechnical Consulting Services**
Waterproofing Consultant: **Blanco Architecture Inc.**

ATHERTON RESIDENCE

Photography: **Cesar Rubio Photography**
Location: **Atherton, California**
Area: **10,280 Sq. Ft.**
General Contractor: **Plath & Company**
Structural Engineering: **GFDS Engineers**
Geotechnical Engineering: **Romig Engineers**
Civil Engineering: **Lea & Braze Engineering**
MEP Engineering: **CB Engineers**
Acoustical Consultants: **Charles M Salter Associates Inc.**
Lighting Designer: **Jeffrey Nathan Lighting Design**
Owner's Representative: **Kemnitzer**

MENLO PARK COURTYARD RESIDENCE

Photography: **John Edward Linden and Mariko Reed**
Location: **Menlo Park, California**
Area: **4,990 Sq. Ft.**
General Contractor: **Matarozzi Pelsinger Builders**
Structural Engineering: **Provest Structural Engineering**
Civil Engineering: **Lea & Braze Engineering**

⊕ **www.dumicanmosey.com** ⦾ dumicanmoseyarchitects

DUMICAN MOSEY Architects is a San Francisco-based firm established by Eric Dumican and Matthew Mosey in 2006, specializing in design-oriented architecture and interior design projects. The firm is guided by the principle that great projects are made in the marriage of pragmatism and poetry. Through a vocabulary of warm materials, an artful flow of space, and dynamic connections between indoors and out—imbued with a Modern sensibility—we strive for work that stands the test of time. Each project is developed in a structured sequence of interactive decision-making that tests alternative solutions against stated objectives and seeks consensus based on clearly defined priorities. The results are cohesive living environments that consistently exceed expectations.

DUMICAN MOSEY Architects ist ein in San Francisco ansässiges Büro, das 2006 von Eric Dumican und Matthew Mosey gegründet wurde und sich auf designorientierte Architektur- und Innenarchitekturprojekte spezialisiert hat. Die Firma orientiert sich am Grundsatz, dass große Projekte in der Verbindung von Pragmatismus und Poesie entstehen. Durch ein Vokabular aus warmen Materialien, einen raffinierten Raumfluss und dynamische Verbindungen zwischen innen und außen – erfüllt von einer modernen Sensibilität – streben wir nach zeitgemäßer Arbeit. Jedes Projekt wird in einer strukturierten Abfolge interaktiver Entscheidungen entwickelt, die alternative Lösungen anhand vorgegebener Ziele testen und einen Konsens auf der Grundlage klar definierter Prioritäten suchen. Das Ergebnis sind kohärente Lebensumgebungen, die die Erwartungen immer wieder übertreffen.

DUMICAN MOSEY Architects est un cabinet d'architectes basé à San Francisco, fondé par Eric Dumican et Matthew Mosey en 2006, spécialisé dans les projets d'architecture et de design d'intérieur. Le cabinet est guidé par le principe que les grands projets se réalisent par l'union du pragmatisme et de la poésie. Grâce à un vocabulaire de matériaux chauds, un flux d'espace artistique et des connexions dynamiques entre l'intérieur et l'extérieur avec une sensibilité moderne, nous recherchons un travail qui résiste à l'épreuve du temps. Chaque projet est élaboré selon une séquence structurée de prises de décisions interactives qui met à l'essai des solutions de rechange par rapport aux objectifs énoncés et qui recherche un consensus fondé sur des priorités clairement définies. Il en résulte des milieux de vie cohésifs qui dépassent constamment les attentes.

DUMICAN MOSEY Architects es una firma con sede en San Francisco fundada por Eric Dumican y Matthew Mosey en 2006, especializada en proyectos de arquitectura orientada al diseño y al diseño de interiores. La firma se guía por el principio de que los grandes proyectos se realizan a través del matrimonio entre pragmatismo y poesía. Utilizan un vocabulario de materiales cálidos, un flujo ingenioso de espacio y conexiones dinámicas entre el interior y el exterior —imbuido de una moderna sensibilidad— el estudio se esfuerza por lograr un trabajo que resista la prueba del paso del tiempo. Cada proyecto se desarrolla en una secuencia estructurada de toma de decisiones interactiva que prueba soluciones alternativas frente a objetivos establecidos, buscando el consenso basado en prioridades claramente definidas. Los resultados son ambientes cohesivos que consistentemente exceden las expectativas.

An existing historic industrial building provided a unique canvas for a carefully considered owner-occupied adaptive re-use project in the evolving SOMA neighborhood of San Francisco. The project features a strong interplay between art and the newly conceived architecture, which focuses on the qualities of light, space, and materiality. Historic elements of the front facade were restored and refurbished, while new modernist elements were introduced, creating a dynamic relationship. A two-car garage, a residential guest unit, and a studio/gallery space for the internationally exhibited artist Klari Reis occupy the ground floor. The second level was transformed into a 4,500-square-foot residential loft for the owners. The new home is organized around a 20′ x 20′ courtyard with an operable glass roof and has access to an expansive roof deck.

Ein bestehendes historisches Industriegebäude bot eine einzigartige Kulisse für ein sorgfältig durchdachtes, eigengenutztes, adaptives Wiederverwendungsprojekt im sich entwickelnden SOMA-Viertel von San Francisco. Das Projekt zeichnet sich durch ein starkes Zusammenspiel zwischen Kunst und der neu konzipierten Architektur aus, die sich auf die Eigenschaften von Licht, Raum und Materialität konzentriert. Historische Elemente der Vorderfassade wurden restauriert und renoviert, während neue modernistische Elemente eingeführt wurden, die eine dynamische Beziehung herstellen. Im Erdgeschoss befinden sich eine Doppelgarage, eine Gästewohnung und ein Studio/Galerie für den international ausstellenden Künstler Klari Reis. Die zweite Etage wurde für die Eigentümer in ein 420 Quadratmeter großes Wohnloft umgewandelt. Das neue Haus ist um einen 6 x 6 Meter großen Innenhof mit einem intakten Glasdach herum organisiert und hat Zugang zu einer großzügigen Dachterrasse.

Un bâtiment industriel historique existant a fourni une toile unique pour un projet de réutilisation adaptative soigneusement étudié par le propriétaire-occupant dans le quartier SOMA de San Francisco, en pleine évolution. Le projet se caractérise par une forte interaction entre l'art et l'architecture nouvellement conçue, qui met l'accent sur les qualités de la lumière, de l'espace et de la matérialité. Les éléments historiques de la façade avant ont été restaurés et rénovés, tandis que de nouveaux éléments modernistes ont été introduits, créant une relation dynamique. Le rez-de-chaussée est occupé par un garage pour deux voitures, une unité résidentielle pour les invités et un atelier/galerie pour l'artiste Klari Reis, exposé à l'échelle internationale. Le deuxième niveau a été transformé en loft résidentiel de 420 mètres carrés pour les propriétaires. La nouvelle maison est organisée autour d'une cour de 6 x 6 mètres avec un toit en verre opérable et a accès à un vaste toit-terrasse.

Un edificio industrial histórico proporcionó un lienzo único para un proyecto de reutilización adaptable, cuidadosamente estudiado por el propietario, en el barrio SOMA de San Francisco. El proyecto presenta una fuerte interacción entre el arte y la arquitectura recién concebida, que se centra en las cualidades de la luz, el espacio y la materialidad. Los elementos históricos de la fachada frontal fueron restaurados y renovados, a la vez que se introdujeron nuevos elementos modernistas, creando una relación dinámica. En la planta baja hay un garaje para dos coches, una zona residencial para invitados y un estudio/galería para el artista Klari Reis, que ha expuesto internacionalmente. El segundo nivel fue transformado en un *loft* residencial de 420 metros cuadrados para los propietarios. La nueva casa está organizada alrededor de un patio de 6 x 6 metros con un techo de vidrio operable y tiene acceso a una amplia azotea.

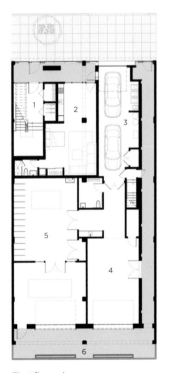

First floor plan

Second floor plan

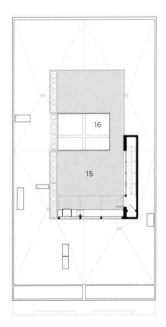

Roof plan

1. Mian entry unit #1
2. Residential studio unit #2
3. Garage
4. Art gallery
5. Artist studio
6. Lower terrace
7. Living/Dining/Kitchen
8. Courtyard
9. Library/Media room
10. Study
11. Master bedroom
12. Children bedroom
13. Guest bedroom
14. Main entry stair/Fiat at ceiling
15. Roof deck
16. Courtyard below

Designed for Bay Area luminaries in Atherton, this residence reflects a well-orchestrated response to a host of requirements, technologies, and amenities. Built for living, working, entertaining, and playing, the diverse building program created the opportunity to weave a rich tapestry of form, materials, and details that reveal themselves at every corner. Anchored by the primary palette of Sapele wood and Jerusalem limestone, the structure radiates warmth and elegance. By "folding" the front yard down to the basement level, the building sensitively reduces its height and impact on the site, while expansive glass and openings create an engaging interior-exterior dialogue.

Entworfen für die Leuchten der Bay Area in Atherton, spiegelt diese Residenz eine gut abgestimmte Antwort auf eine Vielzahl von Anforderungen, Technologien und Annehmlichkeiten wider. Gebaut zum Leben, Arbeiten, Unterhalten und Spielen, schuf das vielfältige Bauprogramm die Möglichkeit, einen reichen Teppich aus Formen, Materialien und Details zu weben, der sich an jeder Ecke offenbart. Verankert in einer Primärpalette aus Sapellholz und Jerusalemer Kalkstein, strahlt die Struktur Wärme und Eleganz aus. Durch das „Falten" des Vorhofs bis zum Untergeschoss reduziert das Gebäude sensibel seine Höhe und seinen Einfluss auf den Platz, während großzügige Glasflächen und Öffnungen einen ansprechenden Dialog zwischen innen und außen schaffen.

Conçue pour les sommités de la Bay Area à Atherton, cette résidence reflète une réponse bien orchestrée à une foule d'exigences, de technologies et de commodités. Construit pour vivre, travailler, se divertir et jouer, le programme de construction diversifié a été l'occasion de tisser une riche tapisserie de formes, de matériaux et de détails qui se révèlent à chaque coin. Ancrée dans la palette primaire du bois de Sapele et de la pierre de Jérusalem, la structure rayonne de chaleur et d'élégance. En « rabattant » la cour avant jusqu'au sous-sol, le bâtiment réduit sensiblement sa hauteur et son impact sur le site, tandis que les grandes baies vitrées et les ouvertures créent un dialogue intérieur-extérieur engageant.

Diseñada para las celebridades de la Bay Area en Atherton, esta residencia refleja una respuesta bien orquestada a una gran cantidad de requisitos, tecnologías y servicios. Construido para vivir, trabajar, recibir visitas y jugar, el variado programa de construcción creó la oportunidad de tejer un rico tapiz de formas, materiales y detalles que se revelan en cada esquina. Anclada en la paleta primaria de madera de Sapeli y piedra caliza de Jerusalén, la estructura irradia calidez y elegancia. Al "plegar" el patio delantero hasta el nivel del sótano, el edificio reduce sensiblemente su altura y su impacto en el lugar, mientras que el vidrio expansivo y las aberturas crean un diálogo atractivo entre el interior y el exterior.

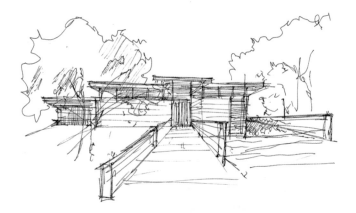

Designed for a young family from New Zealand, the 5,000-square-foot residence located on the edge of downtown Menlo Park is a new leaf on the branch of classic Californian Modernism. Beyond the aesthetic indebtedness of form and materials, the seamless connection to the outdoors was established as a refrain for the house's organization and articulation. A forty-foot-wide pocketing glass door opening creates a dramatic dissolution of the separation between a great room living space and the pool deck beyond. In the master bedroom, similar pocketing doors retract at the corner to link the space with an intimate outdoor sitting area.

Die 465 Quadratmeter große Residenz am Rande der Innenstadt von Menlo Park wurde für eine junge Familie aus Neuseeland entworfen und ist ein neues Kapitel in der klassischen kalifornischen Moderne. Über die ästhetische Verschuldung von Form und Materialien hinaus wurde die nahtlose Verbindung zur Außenwelt als Refrain für die Organisation und Artikulation des Hauses etabliert. Eine zwölf Meter breite Glasschiebetüröffnung schafft eine dramatische Auflösung der Trennung zwischen einem großen Wohnraum und dem Pooldeck dahinter. Im Hauptschlafzimmer ziehen sich ähnliche Schiebetüren an der Ecke zurück, um den Raum mit einer intimen Sitzecke im Freien zu verbinden.

Conçue pour une jeune famille néo-zélandaise, cette résidence de 465 mètres carrés située en bordure du centre-ville de Menlo Park est une nouvelle feuille de route sur la branche du modernisme californien classique. Au-delà de l'endettement esthétique de la forme et des matériaux, la connexion sans couture avec l'extérieur a été établie comme un refrain pour l'organisation et l'articulation de la maison. Une porte vitrée coulissante de douze mètres de large crée une dissolution dramatique de la séparation entre une grande pièce à vivre et le bord de la piscine au-delà. Dans la chambre principale, des portes coulissantes similaires se rétractent à l'angle pour relier l'espace à un coin salon extérieur intime.

Diseñada para una familia joven de Nueva Zelanda, la residencia de 465 metros cuadrados ubicada en el límite del centro de Menlo Park es una nueva hoja de la rama del clásico modernismo californiano. Más allá del endeudamiento estético de la forma y los materiales, la conexión sin fisuras con el exterior se estableció como un estribillo para la organización y articulación de la casa. Una puerta de vidrio corredera de doce metros de ancho crea una disolución absoluta de la separación entre una gran sala de estar y la cubierta de la piscina más allá. En el dormitorio principal, puertas correderas similares se retraen en la esquina para unir el espacio con una íntima zona de estar al aire libre.

EAG STUDIO

Crafting inspirational, sustainable spaces drive the architectural and design teams of EAG Studio. From concept to completion, they are consummate client advocates throughout their integrated design approach to ensure success in the many aspects of each project. Utilizing the latest visual rendering technologies, EAG's client can share, experience, and collaborate with the place and space before breaking ground.

Die Gestaltung inspirierender, nachhaltiger Räume bestimmt die Arbeit des Architektur- und Designteams von EAG Studio. Von der Konzeption bis zur Fertigstellung sind sie voll-wertige Kundenvertreter in ihrem integrierten Designansatz, um den Erfolg in den vielen Aspekten jedes Projekts sicherzustellen. Durch die Verwendung der neuesten visuellen Rendering-Technologien kann der Kunde mit der EAG Ort und Raum teilen, Erfahrungen sammeln und zusammenarbeiten, bevor er den ersten Schritt macht.

La création d'espaces inspirants et durables anime les équipes d'architectes et de desi-gners du studio EAG. De la conception à la réalisation, ils sont des défenseurs acharnés des clients tout au long de leur approche de conception intégrée afin d'assurer le succès dans les nombreux aspects de chaque projet. Utilisant les dernières technologies de ren-du visuel, le client d'EAG peut partager, expérimenter et collaborer avec le lieu et l'espace avant d'innover.

La creación de espacios inspiradores y sostenibles es el motor de los equipos de arquitec-tura y diseño de EAG Studio. Desde el concepto hasta la finalización, son defensores con-sumados del cliente a través de su enfoque de diseño integrado para asegurar el éxito en los muchos aspectos de cada proyecto. Utilizando las últimas tecnologías de renderizado visual, el cliente de EAG puede compartir, experimentar y colaborar con el lugar y el espa-cio antes de llevar a cabo la obra.

Located in the hills of Eureka Valley this LEED Platinum residence has sweeping views of downtown San Francisco and Twin Peaks. The custom-built family home provides a unique blend of the latest in green engineering, technology, and design with timeless modern finishes and an open plan, which optimizes natural light and indoor-outdoor lifestyle. The central stairway spans all levels to five bedrooms and four and one-half baths. The wood of a fallen down ancient Laurel tree from Marin County accents the kitchen counter with a "live" edge lasered around the stone. The rainwater harvesting system circulates as a fountain feature before it is filtered and sent to water tank fencing for future irrigation.

Diese LEED Platinum View Residenz liegt in den Hügeln des Eureka Valley und bietet einen weiten Blick auf die Innenstadt von San Francisco und die Twin Peaks. Das maßgeschneiderte Einfamilienhaus bietet eine einzigartige Mischung aus modernster grüner Technik, Technologie und Design mit zeitlos modernen Oberflächen und einem offenen Grundriss, der das natürliche Licht und den Lebensstil im Innen- und Außenbereich optimiert. Die zentrale Treppe erstreckt sich über alle Ebenen zu fünf Schlafzimmern und viereinhalb Bädern. Ein heruntergefallener alter Lorbeerbaum aus Marin Country akzentuiert die Küchenzeile mit einer „lebenden" Kante, die um den Stein gelasert ist. Im Regengewinnungssystem fungiert als Quelle, bevor es das Wasser filtert und zur späteren Bewässerung an den Stauraumzaun leitet.

Située dans les collines de Eureka Valley, cette résidence avec certificat LEED Platinum offre une vue imprenable sur le centre-ville de San Francisco et Twin Peaks. La maison familiale construite sur mesure offre un mélange unique des plus récents progrès en matière d'ingénierie, de technologie et de design écologiques, avec des finitions modernes intemporelles et un plan ouvert qui optimise la lumière naturelle et le style de vie intérieur-extérieur. L'escalier central enjambe tous les niveaux jusqu'à cinq chambres à coucher et quatre salles de bains et une toilette. Le bois d'un laurier ancien de Marin County, tombé au sol, accentue le comptoir de la cuisine d'un bord « vivant » au laser autour de la pierre. Le système de collecte des eaux de pluie circule comme une fontaine avant d'être filtré et envoyé à la clôture de réservoirs d'eau pour l'irrigation future.

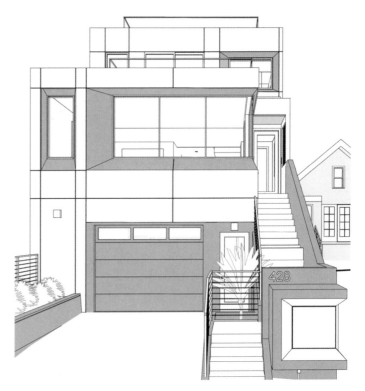

Perspective view from the street

Ubicada en las colinas de Eureka Valley, esta residencia con certificado LEED Platinum tiene vistas impresionantes del centro de San Francisco y Twin Peaks. La casa familiar construida a medida proporciona una mezcla única de lo último en ingeniería, tecnología y diseño ecológicos con acabados modernos y atemporales y un plano abierto, que optimiza la luz natural y el estilo de vida interior-exterior. La escalera central se extiende por todos los niveles hasta cinco dormitorios y cuatro baños y un aseo. La madera de un viejo laurel caído de Marin County acentúa el mostrador de la cocina con un borde "vivo" cortado con láser alrededor de la piedra. El sistema de recolección de agua de lluvia funciona como una fuente antes de filtrar el agua y enviarla al vallado de depósitos para el riego futuro.

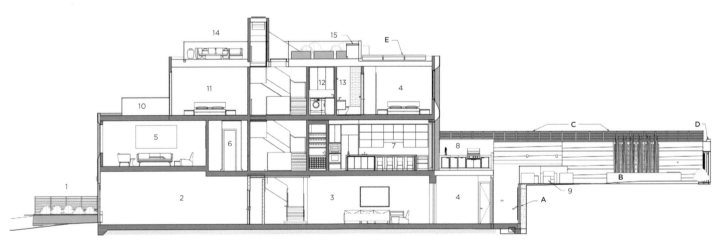

Building section

1. Front yard and driveway
2. Garage
3. Media room
4. Bedroom
5. Living room
6. Powder room
7. Kitchen
8. Outdoor kitchen

9. Outdoor lounge and firepit
10. Front deck
11. Master bedroom
12. Laundry room
13. Bathroom
14. Roof deck
15. Roof kitchen

A. Living wall
B. Planters and lawn
C. Reclaimed wood fence
D. Rainwater fence tanks
E. Solar panels

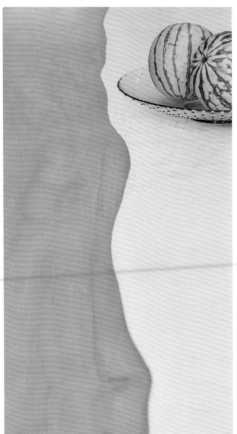

From the elegant foyer crowned by a stunning glass chandelier, a wrapped floating oak stairway leads to the top floor of this reverse floor plan home featuring expansive northeast views of downtown San Francisco, the Bay Bridge, and Coit Tower. Two peaked skylights and numerous windows on all four elevations provide an abundance of natural light throughout the four bedrooms and six-bath home. The living wall staircase to the panoramic roof deck brings nature to the main floor via a glass wall. A backlit onyx wall highlights the dining room and horizontal straight-grained oak built-ins and wine storage. State-of-the-art security video access, lighting, environmental, entertainment A/V controls finish this truly smart home.

Von dem eleganten Foyer, das von einem atemberaubenden Glasleuchter gekrönt wird, führt eine umhüllte, schwimmende Eichentreppe in das oberste Stockwerk dieses Hauses mit großzügigem Nordostblick auf die Innenstadt von San Francisco, die Bay Bridge und den Coit Tower. Zwei spitze Oberlichter und zahlreiche Fenster auf allen vier Fassaden sorgen für eine Fülle an natürlichem Licht in den vier Schlafzimmern und den sechs Bädern. Die Wohnwandtreppe zur Panoramadachterrasse bringt die Natur über eine Glaswand ins Erdgeschoss. Eine hinterleuchtete Onyxwand betont das Esszimmer und die horizontalen, geradfaserigen Eicheneinbauten und die Weinlagerung. Modernste Sicherheitsvideozugangs-, Beleuchtungs-, Umwelt- und Unterhaltungs-A/V-Steuerungen runden dieses wirklich intelligente Zuhause ab.

De l'élégant foyer couronné par un magnifique lustre de verre, un escalier flottant en chêne enveloppé mène à l'étage supérieur de cette maison en plan inversé avec vue sur le centre-ville de San Francisco, le Bay Bridge et la Coit Tower, au nord-est. Deux puits de lumière et de nombreuses fenêtres sur les quatre façades offrent une abondance de lumière naturelle dans les quatre chambres à coucher et les six salles de bains de la maison. Le mur végétal de l'escalier menant à la terrasse panoramique du toit apporte la nature au rez-de-chaussée par l'intermédiaire d'un mur vitré. Un mur d'onyx rétro-éclairé met en valeur la salle à manger et les encadrements horizontaux en chêne à grain droit et le rangement à vin. L'accès vidéo de sécurité, l'éclairage, l'environnement et les commandes audiovisuelles de divertissement à la fine pointe de la technologie complètent cette maison intelligente.

Desde el elegante vestíbulo coronado por una impresionante lámpara de araña de cristal, una escalera de roble flotante envuelta conduce al último piso de esta casa de planta inversa con amplias vistas del noreste del centro de San Francisco, el Bay Bridge y la Coit Tower. Dos claraboyas y numerosas ventanas en las cuatro fachadas proporcionan abundante luz natural a esta casa de cuatro dormitorios y seis baños. El jardín vertical de la escalera que conduce a la azotea panorámica lleva la naturaleza a la planta principal a través de una pared de cristal. Una pared de ónix retroiluminada hace resaltar el comedor y los armarios empotrados horizontales de roble y el armario para vinos. Los controles de video de seguridad de última generación para el acceso, la iluminación, el medio ambiente, y los mandos A/V de entretenimiento completan esta casa verdaderamente inteligente.

Library perspectives

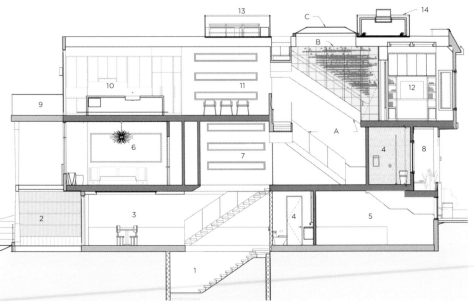

Longitudinal section

Cross section

1. Staircase to wine cellar and gym
2. Courtyard
3. Media room
4. Bathroom
5. Bedroom
6. Master bedroom
7. Hall
8. Foyer
9. Rear deck
10. Kitchen
11. Dining room
12. Library
13. Roof lounge
14. Outdoor kitchen
15. Wine cellar
16. Gym
17. Garage
18. Laundry room
19. Hall
20. Family room
A. Floating staircase with glass guardrail
B. Green wall
C. Peaked Skylight

Views of the Golden Gate Bridge and Fort Mason Park complement the warm palette of finishes for this Marina home. A glass-paneled, wood wrapped staircase tie together the four levels with four bedrooms and four and two half-baths. The ground level offers a family/media room with full-length sliding doors to the backyard with living wall fencing. On the main floor, the 16-foot-long kitchen island is a gathering spot.

Der Blick auf die Golden Gate Bridge und den Fort Mason Park ergänzt die warme Palette der Oberflächen für dieses Marina-Haus. Eine verglaste, holzverkleidete Treppe verbindet die vier Ebenen mit vier Schlafzimmern und viereinhalb Bädern. Im Erdgeschoss befindet sich ein Familien-/Medienraum mit durchgehenden Schiebetüren zum Hinterhof mit Wohnwandabtrennung. Im Erdgeschoss ist die 5 Meter lange Kücheninsel ein Treffpunkt.

Les vues du Golden Gate Bridge et du parc Fort Mason complètent la chaleureuse palette de finitions de cette maison Marina. Un escalier vitré en bois enveloppé de panneaux de verre relie les quatre niveaux avec quatre chambres à coucher et quatre salles de bains et deux toilettes. Le rez-de-chaussée offre une salle familiale/médiatique avec des portes coulissantes sur toute la longueur menant à la cour arrière et une clôture murale vivante. Au rez-de-chaussée, l'îlot de cuisine de 5 mètres de long est un lieu de rassemblement.

Las vistas del Golden Gate Bridge y del Fort Mason Park complementan la cálida paleta de acabados de esta casa de la Marina. Una escalera de cristal, revestida de madera, une los cuatro niveles con cuatro dormitorios y cuatro baños y dos aseos. La planta baja ofrece una sala para la familia y para audiovisuales con puertas correderas de longitud completa hacia el patio trasero con cerramiento de plantas. En el piso principal, la isla de cocina de 5 metros de largo es un punto de reunión.

FELDMAN ARCHITECTURE

BUTTERFLY HOUSE

Photography: Joe Fletcher Photography and Jason Liske
Location: Carmel, California
Area: 2,900 Sq. Ft.
General Contractor: Groza Construction
Landscape Architect: Ground Studio Landscape Architecture
Structural Engineering: Sheerline Structural Engineering
Lighting Consultant: Kim Cladas Lighting Design
Audio Visual Consultant: MetroEighteen

THE SANCTUARY

Photography: Joe Fletcher Photography
Location: Palo Alto, California
Area: 4,289 Sq. Ft.
Interior Design: Feldman Architecture
Landscape Architect: Ground Studio Landscape Architecture
Builder: Baywest Builders
Arborist: Urban Tree Management
Structural Engineering: Stranberg Engineering
Civil Engineering: BKF Engineers
Geotechnical Engineering: Romig Engineers
Lighting Consultant: Kim Cladas Lighting Design

DOSA BY DOSA

Photography: Kassie Borreson
Location: Oakland, California
Area: 3,530 Sq. Ft.
General Contractor: Terra Nova Industries
Furnishings and Interior Consultants: Anna Molina A2M Design
Kitchen Consultant: Next Step Design and Nahum Goldberg Associates
Mechanical Engineering: MHC Engineers
Lighting Design: Melinda Morrison Lighting
Structural Engineering: Coffman Engineers
Restaurant and Brand Innovation Partner: IDEO

🌐 **www.feldmanarchitecture.com** ⃞ feldmanarchitecture

Feldman Architecture is dedicated to creating buildings that sit gracefully and lightly on the earth: beautiful, healthful, and soulful spaces that enhance our clients' lives, our communities, and the environment. We work in conversation with clients and colleagues, listening without preconception, sharing visions and values, generating ideas and sifting possibilities together, finding a clear and compelling focus. This collaborative process helps us devise solutions that are responsive to program and context, sustainable, and elegant. We believe in the importance of great design because we understand that the quality of architecture shapes the quality of life and that what we create can be meaningful for many generations.

Feldman Architecture widmet sich der Schaffung von Gebäuden, die anmutig und leicht auf der Erde sitzen: schöne, gesunde und beseelte Räume, die das Leben unserer Kunden, unserer Gemeinden und die Umwelt verbessern. Wir arbeiten im Gespräch mit Kunden und Kollegen, hören ohne Vorurteile zu, teilen Visionen und Werte, generieren Ideen, prüfen gemeinsam Möglichkeiten und finden einen klaren und überzeugenden Fokus. Dieser kollaborative Prozess hilft uns, Lösungen zu entwickeln, die auf Programm und Kontext reagieren und nachhaltig und elegant sind. Wir glauben an die Bedeutung großartigen Designs, weil wir verstehen, dass die Qualität der Architektur die Lebensqualität prägt und dass das, was wir schaffen, für viele Generationen sinnvoll sein kann.

Feldman Architecture se consacre à la création de bâtiments qui s'installent gracieusement et légèrement sur la terre : des espaces beaux, sains et empreints d'âme qui améliorent la vie de nos clients, de nos communautés et de l'environnement. Nous travaillons en conversation avec nos clients et collègues, en écoutant sans préconception, en partageant nos visions et nos valeurs, en générant des idées et en passant au crible les possibilités ensemble, en trouvant une orientation claire et convaincante. Ce processus de collaboration nous aide à concevoir des solutions adaptées au programme et au contexte, durables et élégantes. Nous croyons en l'importance d'un grand design parce que nous comprenons que la qualité de l'architecture façonne la qualité de la vie et que ce que nous créons peut avoir un sens pour plusieurs générations.

Feldman Architecture se dedica a crear edificios que se asientan con elegancia y ligereza en la tierra: espacios hermosos, saludables y conmovedores que mejoran las vidas de nuestros clientes, nuestras comunidades y el medio ambiente. Trabajamos conjuntamente con clientes y colegas, escuchando sin prejuicios, compartiendo visiones y valores, generando ideas y tamizando posibilidades juntos, encontrando un enfoque claro y convincente. Este proceso de colaboración nos ayuda a idear soluciones que son sensibles al programa y al contexto, sostenibles y elegantes. Creemos en la importancia de un gran diseño porque entendemos que la calidad de la arquitectura da forma a la calidad de vida y que lo que creamos puede ser significativo para muchas generaciones.

Butterfly House is a retreat befitting the natural beauty of a hilly site covered with native grasses and studded with oak, redwood and pine trees. The clients were meticulous in the selection of the site, searching for two years for a spectacular piece of land that was flat enough to accommodate living on one level. Sitting lightly on the land, the house is divided into three pavilions that are topped by expressive butterfly roofs. The distinct roof shapes are a take on the clients' vision of butterflies alighting on the meadow site. The pavilions are modest in size, yet each expands into an outdoor room opening up to dramatic views of the canyon below and hills above. The house uses little energy as a result of extensive day lighting and passive thermal strategies.

Butterfly House ist ein Rückzugsort, der der natürlichen Schönheit einer hügeligen Gegend entspricht, die mit einheimischen Gräsern bewachsen ist und mit Eichen, Rotholz und Kiefern übersät ist. Die Kunden wählten den Standort sorgfältig aus und suchten zwei Jahre lang nach einem spektakulären Grundstück, das flach genug war, um das Leben auf einer Ebene zu ermöglichen. Das leicht auf dem Land gelegene Haus ist in drei Pavillons unterteilt, die von ausdrucksstarken Schmetterlingsdächern überdacht werden. Die markanten Dachformen nehmen die Vision der Kunden auf, dass Schmetterlinge auf der Wiese landen. Die Pavillons sind bescheiden in der Größe, aber jedes erstreckt sich in einen Außenraum, der sich für einen dramatischen Blick auf den Canyon unten und die Hügel oben öffnet. Durch umfangreiche Tageslichttechnik und passive Wärmeverfahren verbraucht das Haus wenig Energie.

Butterfly House est une retraite digne de la beauté naturelle d'un site vallonné couvert d'herbes indigènes et parsemé de chênes, de séquoias et de pins. Les clients ont été méticuleux dans le choix du site, à la recherche pendant deux ans d'un terrain spectaculaire, suffisamment plat pour accueillir une habitation de plain-pied. Légèrement assise sur le terrain, la maison est divisée en trois pavillons coiffés de toits papillon expressifs. Les formes distinctes des toits sont une représentation de la vision que les clients eurent des papillons se posant sur le site de la prairie. Les pavillons sont de taille modeste, mais chacune s'étend vers une pièce extérieure offrant une vue spectaculaire sur le canyon en contrebas et les collines en haut. La maison consomme peu d'énergie en raison de l'éclairage naturel intensif et des stratégies thermiques passives.

Butterfly House es un refugio digno de la belleza natural de un paraje ondulado cubierto de pastos nativos y salpicado de robles, secuoyas y pinos. Los clientes fueron meticulosos en la elección del emplazamiento, buscando durante dos años un terreno espectacular, lo suficientemente plano como para albergar una vivienda de una sola planta. Apoyada ligeramente en el suelo, la casa está dividida en tres pabellones coronados por expresivos tejados en mariposa. Las distintas formas de los tejados son una representación de la visión que los clientes tuvieron de las mariposas posándose en la pradera. Los pabellones son modestos en tamaño, pero cada uno se extiende a un espacio al aire libre con una vista espectacular del cañón y de las colinas. La casa consume poca energía gracias a la intensa iluminación natural y a las estrategias térmicas pasivas.

North elevation

East elevation

South elevation

West elevation

0 4 8 16 ft

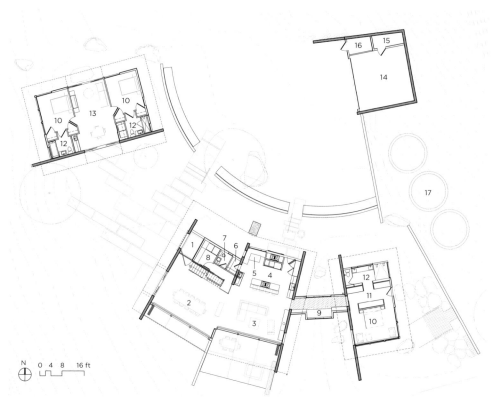

Floor plan

1. Entry
2. Dining room
3. Living room
4. Kitchen
5. Nook
6. Pantry
7. Powder room
8. Laundry room
9. Office
10. Bedroom
11. Dressing room
12. Bathroom
13. Family room
14. Garage
15. Wine cellar
16. Garbage
17. Water tanks
18. Stairs to media loft

N   0 4 8   16 ft

SOLAR ELECTRICITY HARVESTING
The south facing garage roof harvests solar energy on a 7kw solar array.

WATER HARVESTING
Butterfly roofs carefully channel rainwater in two directions, spilling over in a dramatic waterfall onto splash pads below. The water is the piped up to 3 concrete water tanks. 30,000 gallons of collected rainwater help irrigate the restored meadow of native grasses & wildflowers.

THERMAL MASS
Board formed concrete walls and concrete floors serve as heat sink to keep temperatures well regulated. Radiant floor heating in concrete floors keep the building warm in the winter with less energy. Walls help absorb excess solar heat to keep interiors cool.

PASSIVE SOLAR (WINTER)
South facing window wall allows light and heat to penetrate on winter days. Deep awnings and roof overhangs block out the hotter steeper summer solar energy.

PASSIVE COOLING (SUMMER)
Deep awnings and roof overhangs block out the hotter steeper summer solar energy. Strategically placed windows provide cross ventilation in all pavilions. Thermal mass in concrete walls also helps absorb excess daytime heat in the summer.

Sustainability diagram

The Sanctuary responds to the clients' desire to downsize and simplify in the design of their new Palo Alto home. When they purchased the property, an old wooden fence across the front yard closed off the site from the street. Behind this rough presentation, however, was an urban refuge of lush vegetation. This sense of discovery served as the original inspiration for the design of the house. The proximity of the downtown Palo Alto area was fundamental to the clients' decision to purchase this lot, and their belief in building to a higher density in an urban setting, lead to the inclusion of a second-story apartment. The Sanctuary is a modern house that allows the landscape to speak first. The design features many hidden courtyards, inviting guests to experience the same sense of wonder that first drew our clients to this urban oasis.

The Sanctuary entspricht dem Wunsch der Kunden, das Design ihres neuen Palo Alto Hauses zu verkleinern und zu vereinfachen. Als sie das Grundstück kauften, schloss ein alter Holzzaun über dem Vorplatz das Gelände von der Straße ab. Hinter dieser groben Darstellung verbirgt sich jedoch ein urbanes Refugium mit üppiger Vegetation. Dieses Entdeckungserlebnis war die ursprüngliche Inspiration für die Gestaltung des Hauses. Die Nähe zur Innenstadt von Palo Alto war für die Entscheidung der Kunden, dieses Grundstück zu erwerben, von grundlegender Bedeutung, und ihr Glaube an eine höhere Dichte in einem städtischen Umfeld führte zur Aufnahme einer Wohnung im zweiten Stock. The Sanctuary ist ein modernes Haus, das es der Landschaft ermöglicht, zuerst zu sprechen. Das Design bietet viele versteckte Innenhöfe und lädt die Gäste ein, das gleiche Gefühl des Staunens zu erleben, das unsere Kunden zum ersten Mal in diese urbane Oase zog.

The Sanctuary répond au désir des clients de réduire et de simplifier la conception de leur nouvelle maison Palo Alto. Lorsqu'ils ont acheté la propriété, une vieille clôture en bois de l'autre côté de la cour avant a fermé le site de la rue. Derrière cette présentation sommaire se cachait cependant un refuge urbain à la végétation luxuriante. Ce sens de la découverte a servi d'inspiration originale pour la conception de la maison. La proximité du centre-ville de Palo Alto a joué un rôle fondamental dans la décision des clients d'acheter ce terrain, et leur croyance dans la construction d'un immeuble à plus forte densité en milieu urbain a mené à l'inclusion d'un appartement au deuxième étage. The Sanctuary est une maison moderne qui permet au paysage de parler en premier. Les nombreuses cours intérieures cachées invitent les visiteurs à vivre l'émerveillement qui a d'abord attiré nos clients dans cette oasis urbaine.

The Sanctuary responde al deseo de los clientes de reducir y simplificar el diseño de su nueva casa en Palo Alto. Cuando compraron la propiedad, una vieja cerca de madera a través del patio delantero separaba el solar de la calle. Detrás de esta presentación áspera, sin embargo, había un refugio urbano de exuberante vegetación. Este sentido de descubrimiento sirvió de inspiración original para el diseño de la casa. La proximidad del centro de Palo Alto que fue fundamental para que los clientes finalmente compraran este solar, y su firme convicción de construir en mayor densidad en un entorno urbano, llevó a la inclusión de un apartamento en un segundo piso. the Sanctuary es una casa moderna que permite que el paisaje hable primero. El diseño presenta muchos patios ocultos, invitando a los huéspedes a experimentar la misma sensación de asombro que atrajo a nuestros clientes a este oasis urbano.

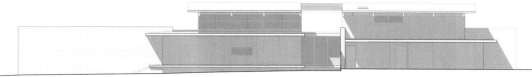

North elevation

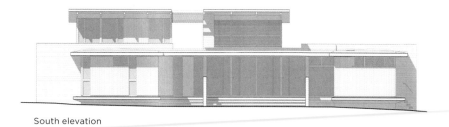

South elevation

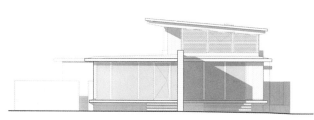

East elevation

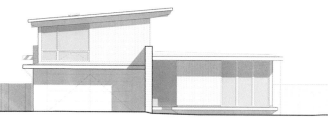

West elevation

Site plan

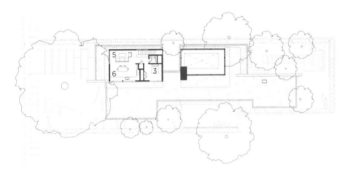

Upper floor plan

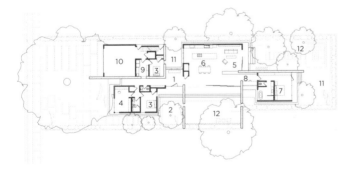

Lower floor plan

N

0 8 16   32 ft

1. Entry
2. Entry courtyard
3. Bedroom
4. Office
5. Living room
6. Kitchen
7. Master bedroom
8. Study
9. Laundry room
10. Garage
11. Courtyard
12. Firepit

dosa by DOSA brings the energetic warmth and spirit of Mumbai street food to the easy-going Uptown Oakland neighborhood. The design takes full advantage of high ceilings and abundant natural light in the century-old, brick-and-timber building. Hand-crafted interpretations of traditional Indian elements play with new and old, developing an enduring design idiom for future dosa by DOSA locations. The experience at dosa by DOSA is guided by its architectural simplicity, true to Feldman Architecture's objectives to create beautiful, healthful, soulful spaces that inspire people and enhance communities while aligning with the client's vision. This Uptown Oakland project's resourceful design, fine materials, and thoughtful detailing make dosa by DOSA both journey and destination.

dosa von DOSA bringt die energetische Wärme und den Geist des Mumbai Street Food in das unkomplizierte Uptown Oakland Viertel. Das Design nutzt die hohen Decken und das reichlich vorhandene natürliche Licht im jahrhundertealten Ziegel- und Holzgebäude voll aus. Handgefertigte Interpretationen traditioneller indischer Elemente spielen mit Neuem und Altem und entwickeln eine nachhaltige Designsprache für zukünftige Dosa von DOSA-Standorten. Die Erfahrung bei der Dosa von DOSA wird von der architektonischen Einfachheit geleitet, getreu den Zielen von Feldman Architecture, schöne, gesunde, seelenvolle Räume zu schaffen, die Menschen inspirieren und Gemeinschaften verbessern, während sie mit der Vision des Kunden übereinstimmen. Das einfallsreiche Design, die feinen Materialien und die durchdachten Details dieses Uptown Oakland-Projekts machen Dosa von DOSA zu einer Reise und einem Ziel.

dosa by DOSA apporte la chaleur énergique et l'esprit de la cuisine de rue de Mumbai dans le quartier paisible d'Uptown Oakland. La conception tire pleinement parti des hauts plafonds et de l'abondante lumière naturelle de ce bâtiment centenaire en briques et en bois. Des interprétations artisanales d'éléments traditionnels indiens jouent avec le nouveau et l'ancien, en développant un langage de conception durable pour les futures implantations de dosa by DOSA. L'expérience à dosa by DOSA est guidée par sa simplicité architecturale, fidèle aux objectifs de Feldman Architecture de créer des espaces beaux, sains et pleins d'âme qui inspirent les gens et améliorent les communautés tout en s'alignant avec la vision du client. La conception ingénieuse du projet à Uptown Oakland, les matériaux fins et les détails soignés de ce projet font de dosa by DOSA à la fois un voyage et une destination.

dosa by DOSA trae el calor energético y el espíritu de la comida callejera de Mumbai al tranquilo barrio de Uptown Oakland. El diseño aprovecha al máximo los techos altos y la abundante luz natural en el edificio de ladrillo y madera de un siglo de antigüedad. Interpretaciones artesanales de los elementos tradicionales de la India juegan con lo nuevo y lo viejo, desarrollando un lenguaje de diseño duradero para los futuros emplazamientos de dosa by DOSA. La experiencia en dosa by DOSA está guiada por su simplicidad arquitectónica, fiel a los objetivos de Feldman Architecture de crear espacios hermosos, saludables y emotivos que inspiren a las personas y mejoren las comunidades a la vez que se alinean con la visión del cliente. El diseño ingenioso de este proyecto de Uptown Oakland, los materiales finos y los detalles cuidados hacen de dosa by DOSA a la vez un viaje y un destino.

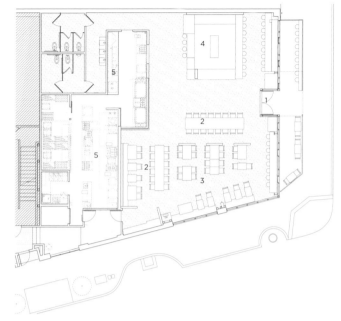

Floor plan

1. Entry/outdoor seating
2. Communal dining table
3. Dining
4. Bar
5. Kitchen

FOUGERON
ARCHITECTURE

CUT OUT HOUSE

Photography: **Joe Fletcher Photography**
Location: **SanFrancisco, California**
Area: **2,500 Sq. Ft.**
Interior Design: **Fougeron Architecture**
Landscape Architect: **Shades of Green
Landscape Architecture**
General Contractor: **Dermot Barry Construction**
Structural Engineering: **Endres Studio**

FALL HOUSE

Photography: **Joe Fletcher Photography**
Location: **Big Sur, California**
Area: **3,800 Sq. Ft.**
Interior Design: **Fougeron Architecture**
Landscape Architect: **Blasen Landscape
Architects**
General Contractor: **Tom George Construction**
Structural Engineering: **Endres Studio**
Civil Engineering: **Grice Engineering
and Geology**

SUSPENSION HOUSE

Photography: **Joe Fletcher Photography**
Location: **Napa, California**
Area: **4,875 Sq. Ft.**
Interior Design: **Feldman Architecture**
General Contractor: **Dermot Barry Construction**
Structural Engineering: **Endres Studio**
Civil Engineering: **Adobe Associates**
Geotechnical Engineering: **Rockridge
Geothechnical**

🌐 **www.fougeron.com**

Fougeron Architecture is a nationally recognized design firm whose work exhibits a strong commitment to clarity of thought, design integrity, and quality of architectural detail. The firm's decidedly modernist attitude is the result of founder Anne Fougeron's vision to create a practice dedicated to finding the perfect alignment between architectural idea and built form. Her work can be defined by three basic tenets: Architectural space is modulated by the quality and character of the natural light; innovative use of structure becomes the architectural ornament, and exploration into the visual and tactile nature of materials enhances how people engage a building. Ms. Fougeron's keen interest in crossing disciplinary boundaries has led the firm to develop a collaborative creative process that capitalizes on her relationships with craftsmen and artists who are experts in their fields.

Fougeron Architecture ist ein national anerkanntes Designbüro, dessen Arbeit ein starkes Engagement für Klarheit des Denkens, Designintegrität und Qualität der architektonischen Details zeigt. Die entschieden modernistische Haltung des Architekturbüros ist das Ergebnis der Vision der Gründerin Anne Fougeron: eine Praxis zu schaffen, die sich der perfekten Abstimmung zwischen architektonischer Idee und gebauter Form widmet. Ihre Arbeit lässt sich durch drei Grundprinzipien definieren: Der architektonische Raum wird durch die Qualität und den Charakter des natürlichen Lichts moduliert; die innovative Nutzung der Struktur wird zum architektonischen Ornament, und die Erforschung der visuellen und taktilen Natur von Materialien verstärkt die Art und Weise, wie Menschen ein Gebäude nutzen. Frau Fougerons großes Interesse an der Überschreitung von Disziplingrenzen hat die Firma veranlasst, einen kollaborativen kreativen Prozess zu entwickeln, der von ihren Beziehungen zu Handwerkern und Künstlern profitiert, die Experten auf ihrem Gebiet sind.

Fougeron Architecture est une firme de conception reconnue à l'échelle nationale dont le travail témoigne d'un engagement ferme envers la clarté de pensée, l'intégrité de la conception et la qualité du détail architectural. L'attitude résolument moderniste de l'entreprise est le résultat de la vision de la fondatrice Anne Fougeron de créer un cabinet dédié à trouver l'alignement parfait entre l'idée architecturale et la forme construite. Son travail peut être défini par trois principes de base : l'espace architectural est modulé par la qualité et le caractère de la lumière naturelle ; l'utilisation novatrice de la structure devient l'ornement architectural, et l'exploration de la nature visuelle et tactile des matériaux rehausse l'engagement des gens envers un bâtiment. Le vif intérêt de Mme Fougeron pour le franchissement des frontières disciplinaires a amené le cabinet à développer un processus créatif collaboratif qui s'appuie sur ses relations avec des artisans et des artistes experts dans leur domaine.

Fougeron Architecture es una empresa de diseño reconocida a nivel nacional cuyo trabajo exhibe un fuerte compromiso con la claridad de pensamiento, la integridad del diseño y la calidad de los detalles arquitectónicos. La actitud decididamente modernista de la firma es el resultado de la visión de su fundadora, Anne Fougeron, de crear un estudio dedicado a encontrar la alineación perfecta entre la idea arquitectónica y la forma construida. Su trabajo se puede definir por tres principios básicos: el espacio arquitectónico está modulado por la calidad y el carácter de la luz natural, el uso innovador de la estructura se convierte en el ornamento arquitectónico y la exploración de la naturaleza visual y táctil de los materiales aumenta la forma en que la gente se involucra en un edificio. El gran interés de la Sra. Fougeron en cruzar las fronteras disciplinarias ha llevado a la firma a desarrollar un proceso creativo colaborativo que capitaliza sus relaciones con artesanos y artistas que son expertos en sus campos.

The Cut Out House is a full remodel of a Victorian built over a century ago and previously untouched. The existing interior had to be completely reorganized to create a modern home. Solar orientation and natural light diffusion were paramount for making sure the home felt warm and open. We turned the back of the site into the main living area. Three slots puncture each floor so that the home is connected vertically rather than horizontally. Traditional Victorian homes are often poorly lit and are disconnected from floor to floor. By suspending floors, we achieved brightness and fluidity throughout the Cut Out House. The ground floor was excavated at the rear extension to maximize the small footprint of the house. The angle of the slanted façade over two stories maximizes space and square footage in the house.

The Cut Out House ist ein komplettes viktorianisches Haus, das vor über einem Jahrhundert erbaut und vor dem Umbau unberührt geblieben war. Das bestehende Interieur musste komplett saniert werden, um ein modernes Zuhause zu schaffen. Sonnenorientierung und natürliche Lichtstreuung waren entscheidend, um sicherzustellen, dass sich das Haus warm und offen anfühlt. Wir haben die Rückseite des Geländes zum Hauptwohnbereich umgebaut. Drei Schächte durchdringen jedes Stockwerk, so dass das Haus vertikal und nicht horizontal verbunden ist. Traditionelle viktorianische Häuser sind oft schlecht beleuchtet und von Stockwerk zu Stockwerk getrennt. Durch die Abhängung von Böden erreichten wir Helligkeit und Fließeigenschaften im gesamten Cut Out House. Das Erdgeschoss wurde am hinteren Anbau ausgehoben, um die geringe Grundfläche des Hauses zu maximieren. Der Winkel der schrägen Fassade über zwei Stockwerke maximiert die Fläche und die Quadratmeterzahl im Haus.

The Cut Out House est une rénovation complète d'une maison victorienne construite il y a plus d'un siècle et qui n'avait jamais été touchée auparavant. L'intérieur existant a dû être complètement réorganisé pour créer une maison moderne. L'orientation solaire et la diffusion de la lumière naturelle étaient primordiales pour que la maison soit chaude et ouverte. Nous avons transformé l'arrière du site en espace de vie principal. Trois fentes percent chaque étage de façon à ce que la maison soit reliée verticalement plutôt qu'horizontalement. Les maisons victoriennes traditionnelles sont souvent mal éclairées et déconnectées d'un étage à l'autre. En suspendant les planchers, nous avons obtenu de la luminosité et de la fluidité dans toute la Cut Out House. Le rez-de-chaussée a été excavé à l'extension arrière pour maximiser la petite surface au sol de la maison. L'angle de la façade inclinée sur deux étages maximise l'espace et la superficie de la maison.

La Cut Out House es una remodelación completa de una casa victoriana construida hace más de un siglo y que permanecía intacta. El interior existente tuvo que ser completamente reorganizado para crear un hogar moderno. La orientación solar y la difusión de la luz natural eran fundamentales para asegurar que la casa fuera cálida y abierta. Convertimos la parte trasera en la zona de estar principal. Tres aberturas perforan cada piso para que la casa esté conectada verticalmente en lugar de horizontalmente. Las casas victorianas tradicionales a menudo están mal iluminadas y están desconectadas de piso en piso. Al suspender los pisos, logramos claridad y fluidez en todo la Cut Out House. La planta baja fue excavada en la extensión trasera para maximizar la pequeña huella de la casa. El ángulo de la fachada inclinada sobre dos pisos maximiza el espacio y los metros cuadrados de la casa.

Third floor plan

Second floor plan

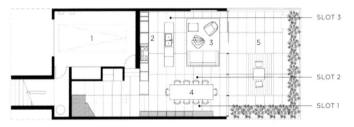

Ground floor plan

1. Garage
2. Kitchen
3. Living room
4. Dining room
5. Rear yard
6. Staircase
7. Entry
8. Kid's room
9. Office
10. Deck
11. Bedroom 3
12. Master bathroom
13. Master bedroom
14. Deck

3D section

This three-bedroom house is located on a spectacular site in the south coast of Big Sur, paying homage to the natural beauty and power of this California landscape. The site offers plunging views, a 250-foot drop to the Pacific Ocean both along the bluff and the western exposure. The house—a long thin volume—conforms and deforms to the natural contours of the land and the geometries of the bluff. It is cantilevered over the land 12 feet back from the bluff's edge, both to protect the delicate ecosystem of the cliff and to ensure the integrity and safety of the structure. The design strategy is one of embedding the building in the land, creating a structure that is inseparable from its context. It reinterprets the organic architectural vocabulary of Big Sur houses built in the 50s and 60s.

Dieses Haus mit drei Schlafzimmern befindet sich an einem spektakulären Ort an der Südküste von Big Sur und würdigt die natürliche Schönheit und Kraft dieser kalifornischen Landschaft. Der Standort bietet einen atemberaubenden Blick; ein 75 Meter tiefer Abstieg zum Pazifischen Ozean ist sowohl entlang der Klippe als auch in westlicher Richtung vorhanden. Das Haus – ein langes, schlankes Volumen – schmiegt sich an die natürlichen Konturen des Landes und die Geometrie der Klippe an. Es liegt knapp 4 Meter oberhalb des Randes der Klippe, sowohl um das empfindliche Ökosystem der Klippe zu schützen als auch um die Integrität und die Sicherheit der Struktur zu gewährleisten. Die Entwurfsstrategie besteht darin, das Gebäude in das Land einzubetten und eine Struktur zu schaffen, die untrennbar mit seinem Kontext verbunden ist. Es interpretiert das organische Architekturvokabular der Big Sur-Häuser aus den 50er und 60er Jahren neu.

Cette maison de trois chambres à coucher est située sur un site spectaculaire sur la côte sud de Big Sur, rendant hommage à la beauté naturelle et à la puissance de ce paysage californien. Le site offre des vues plongeantes, une chute de 75 mètres jusqu'à l'océan Pacifique le long de la falaise et de l'exposition ouest. La maison - un long et mince volume - se conforme et se déforme aux contours naturels du terrain et aux géométries de la falaise. Il est en porte-à-faux sur le terrain à 4 mètres du bord de la falaise, à la fois pour protéger l'écosystème fragile de la falaise et pour assurer l'intégrité et la sécurité de la structure. La stratégie de conception consiste à encastrer le bâtiment dans le terrain, créant ainsi une structure inséparable de son contexte. Il réinterprète le vocabulaire architectural organique des maisons Big Sur construites dans les années 50 et 60.

Esta casa de tres habitaciones está ubicada en un sitio espectacular en la costa sur de Big Sur, rindiendo homenaje a la belleza natural y el poder de este paisaje californiano. El sitio ofrece vistas profundas, una caída de 75 metros hacia el océano Pacífico, tanto a lo largo del acantilado como en la exposición occidental. La casa —un volumen largo y delgado— se adapta a los contornos naturales del terreno y a las geometrías del acantilado. Está en voladizo sobre la tierra a 4 metros de distancia del borde del acantilado, tanto para proteger el delicado ecosistema del acantilado como para garantizar la integridad y seguridad de la estructura. La estrategia de diseño consiste en encastrar el edificio en el terreno, creando una estructura inseparable de su contexto. Esta vivienda reinterpreta el vocabulario de la arquitectura orgánica de las casas de Big Sur construidas en los años 50 y 60.

1. Open plan for stack ventilation/passive cooling
2. Green roof
3. Limited glazing on South facade to avoid heat gain
4. Operable windows in all rooms (including bathrooms)
5. Flow through opening for natural ventilation

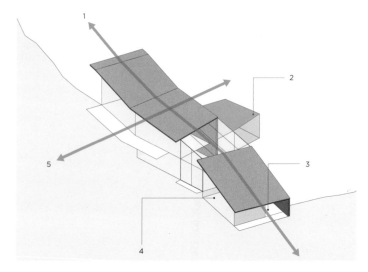

Sustainable strategies

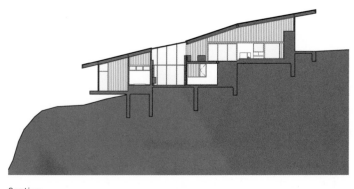

Section

0   32 ft

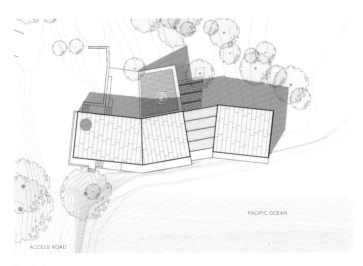

Roof plan

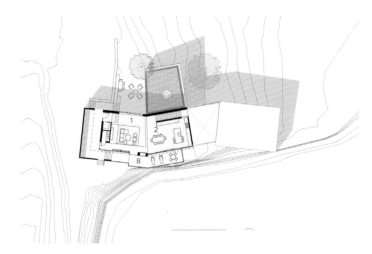

Upper floor plan

Lower floor plan

1. Living room
2. Kitchen/dining
3. Library
4. Master bedroom
5. Bedroom
6. Storage
7. Patio
8. Deck

Suspended between two hills, this house remodel spans a creek and has a waterfall in the backyard. In the state of California, it is no longer legal for homes to be suspended over creeks. Therefore, there were strict guidelines on how to use the existing structure as the basis for design. The goal with this unique site was to enhance the connection between the structure and the exceptional natural environment while best utilizing the site for the clients. Most importantly, the new home had to follow the exact outline of the existing house and decks. The new structural system was anchored to the bedrock of flanking hillsides, suspending the home completely over the creek. The use of transparent materials and the creation of outdoor spaces and sightlines opened the house on its front and back to the water features.

Zwischen zwei Hügeln aufgehängt, überspannt dieses Haus einen Bach und hat einen Wasserfall im Hinterhof. Aufgrund neuer, strenger Gesetzesvorgaben im Bundesstaat Kalifornien, welche die bauliche Integration von natürlichen Fließgewässern auf Privatgrundstücken regelt, musste die bestehende Struktur als Grundlage für die Gestaltung verwendet werden. Das Ziel für diesen einzigartigen Standort war die Stärkung der Verbindung zwischen dem Bauwerk und der außergewöhnlichen natürlichen Umgebung und gleichzeitig die bestmögliche Nutzung des Standorts für die Kunden. Am wichtigsten war, dass das neue Haus dem genauen Grundriss des bestehenden Hauses und der Terrassen folgte. Das neue Tragwerk wurde im Felsen der flankierenden Hänge verankert und hängte das Haus komplett über den Bach. Die Verwendung transparenter Materialien und die Schaffung von Außenräumen und Sichtlinien öffneten das Haus an seiner Vorder- und Rückseite zu den Wasserspielen.

Suspendue entre deux collines, cette maison rénovée enjambe un ruisseau et possède une chute d'eau dans la cour arrière. Dans l'État de Californie, il n'est plus légal que les maisons soient suspendues au-dessus des ruisseaux. Par conséquent, il y avait des directives strictes sur la façon d'utiliser la structure existante comme base pour la conception. L'objectif de ce site unique était d'améliorer le lien entre la structure et l'environnement naturel exceptionnel tout en utilisant au mieux le site pour les clients. Plus important encore, la nouvelle maison devait suivre les plans exacts de la maison et des terrasses existantes. Le nouveau système structural a été ancré au substrat rocheux des flancs des collines, ce qui a permis de suspendre complètement la maison au-dessus du ruisseau. L'utilisation de matériaux transparents et la création d'espaces extérieurs et de lignes de vue ont ouvert la maison à l'avant et à l'arrière sur les plans d'eau.

Suspendida entre dos colinas, esta casa remodelada se extiende sobre un arroyo y tiene una cascada en el patio trasero. En el estado de California, ya no es legal que las casas de nueva construcción queden suspendidas de esta forma así que había directrices estrictas sobre cómo utilizar la estructura existente como base para el diseño. El objetivo fue mejorar la conexión entre la estructura y un entorno natural excepcional. La nueva casa tenía que seguir el contorno exacto de la casa original y las cubiertas existentes. El nuevo sistema estructural se ancló en el lecho rocoso de las laderas, suspendiendo la casa por completo sobre el arroyo. El uso de materiales transparentes y la creación de espacios exteriores y el gusto por las vistas al paisaje abrieron la casa por ambos extremos.

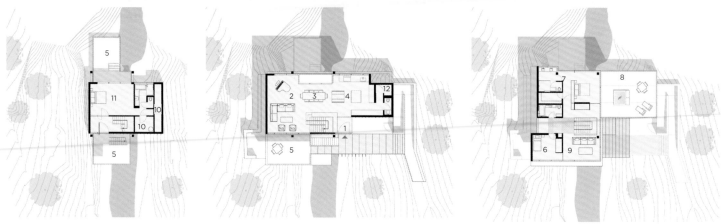

First floor plan

Second floor plan

Third floor plan

1. Entry
2. Living room
3. Dining area
4. Kitchen
5. Balcony
6. Bedroom
7. Master suite
8. Roof deck
9. Flex space
10. Utilities
11. Guest suite
12. Pantry

N

GEDDES ULINSKAS
ARCHITECTS

Geddes Ulinskas Architects has been orchestrating the interplay of light, material, and form with distinct creative vision in the San Francisco Bay Area for nearly fifteen years. In its refined work, including residential and commercial projects, this versatile firm marries a love of conceptual modeling with a deep reverence for site context and human experience, yielding timeless works. A unique series of commissions has demonstrated the firm's ability to utilize local craftsmen and artists in unique ways that redefine the San Francisco regional vernacular. "Beyond their structural role, materials define a home's emotional quality," says Mr. Ulinskas. "There's an art to highlighting and framing materials properly. We take a deliberate, typically minimalist approach and treat every building material with respect."

Geddes Ulinskas Architects inszeniert seit fast fünfzehn Jahren das Zusammenspiel von Licht, Material und Form mit ausgeprägt kreativer Vision in der San Francisco Bay Area. In ihrer raffinierten Arbeit – sowohl Wohn- als auch Gewerbeobjekte – verbindet die vielseitige Firma die Liebe zur konzeptionellen Modellierung mit einer tiefen Ehrfurcht vor dem Kontext des Ortes und der menschlichen Erfahrung und schafft zeitlose Werke. Eine einzigartige Reihe von Aufträgen hat gezeigt, dass das Unternehmen in der Lage ist, lokale Handwerker und Künstler auf einmalige Weise einzusetzen und den regionalen Dialekt von San Francisco neu zu definieren. „Über ihre strukturelle Rolle hinaus definieren Materialien die emotionale Qualität eines Hauses", sagt Herr Ulinskas. „Es ist die Kunst, Materialien richtig hervorzuheben und zu rahmen. Wir gehen bewusst minimalistisch vor und behandeln jedes Baumaterial mit Respekt."

Depuis près de quinze ans, Geddes Ulinskas Architects orchestre les jeux de lumière, de matière et de forme avec une vision créative distincte dans la région de la baie de San Francisco. Dans son travail raffiné, incluant des projets résidentiels et commerciaux, cette firme polyvalente marie l'amour de la modélisation conceptuelle avec un profond respect pour le contexte du site et l'expérience humaine, donnant lieu à des œuvres intemporelles. Une série unique de commandes a démontré la capacité de l'entreprise à utiliser les artisans et les artistes locaux d'une manière unique qui redéfinit la langue vernaculaire régionale de San Francisco. « Au-delà de leur rôle structurel, les matériaux définissent la qualité émotionnelle d'une maison », explique M. Ulinskas. « Il y a un art à mettre en valeur et à encadrer correctement les matériaux. Nous adoptons une approche délibérée, typiquement minimaliste et traitons chaque matériau de construction avec respect. »

Geddes Ulinskas Architects lleva orquestando la interacción de la luz, el material y la forma con una visión creativa distinta en el área de la Bahía de San Francisco durante casi quince años. En su refinado trabajo, que incluye proyectos residenciales y comerciales, esta versátil firma combina el amor por el modelado conceptual con una profunda reverencia por el contexto del lugar y la experiencia humana, dando como resultado obras atemporales. Una serie única de encargos de trabajo ha demostrado la capacidad de la firma de utilizar artesanos y artistas locales de maneras únicas que redefinen la lengua vernácula regional de San Francisco. "Más allá de su función estructural, los materiales definen la calidad emocional de una casa", dice el Sr. Ulinskas. "Hay un arte en resaltar y enmarcar los materiales correctamente. Adoptamos un enfoque deliberado, típicamente minimalista y tratamos cada material de construcción con respeto".

When a couple from Chicago purchased the 11th floor of a prestigious residential tower located at the crown of San Francisco's Russian Hill, they sought to recreate the mid-western elegance and tradition familiar to them in their new California home. After walking the space, it was apparent that the vistas toward downtown San Francisco and the Bay had to be framed with a distinctive design sensibility. The floor was completely gutted save for the exterior walls, the windows, and some interior columns to create a unique home. The new open plan allowed the light and views to penetrate every space with the layout centered on a gracious central gallery space that made art the focus of the home.

Als ein Paar aus Chicago den 11. Stock eines repräsentativen Wohnturms kaufte, der sich an der Krone des Russischen Hügels von San Francisco befindet, versuchte es, die ihm vertraute mittelwestliche Eleganz und Tradition in ihrem neuen kalifornischen Zuhause wiederherzustellen. Nach dem Spaziergang durch den Raum war klar, dass die Ausblicke in Richtung Innenstadt von San Francisco und der Bay von einer ausgeprägten Design-Sensibilität umrahmt werden mussten. Der Boden wurde komplett ausgeweidet, bis auf die Außenwände, die Fenster und einige Innensäulen, um ein einzigartiges Zuhause zu schaffen. Der neue, offene Plan ermöglicht es dem Licht und der Aussicht, jeden Raum zu durchdringen, wobei sich das Layout auf einen großzügigen zentralen Galerieraum konzentriert, der die Kunst zum Mittelpunkt des Hauses macht.

Lorsqu'un couple de Chicago a acheté le 11e étage d'une prestigieuse tour résidentielle située à la couronne de la Russian Hill de San Francisco, ils ont cherché à recréer l'élégance et la tradition du Midwest qui leur était familière dans leur nouvelle maison californienne. Après avoir parcouru l'espace, il était évident que les vues vers le centre-ville de San Francisco et la baie de San Francisco devaient être encadrées avec une sensibilité de conception distinctive. Le plancher a été complètement éviscéré à l'exception des murs extérieurs, des fenêtres et de quelques colonnes intérieures pour créer une maison unique. Le nouveau plan ouvert a permis à la lumière et aux vues de pénétrer dans chaque espace avec la disposition centrée sur un espace central gracieux de galerie qui a fait l'art le foyer de la maison.

Cuando una pareja de Chicago compró el piso 11 de una prestigiosa torre residencial ubicada en la parte alta de la Russian Hill de San Francisco, buscaron recrear la elegancia y tradición del medio oeste que les era familiar en su nueva casa de California. Después de recorrer el espacio, se hizo evidente que las vistas hacia el centro de San Francisco y la Bahía tenían que ser enmarcadas con una sensibilidad de diseño distintiva. El piso se derribó completamente, excepto las paredes exteriores, las ventanas y algunas columnas interiores para crear una casa única. La nueva planta abierta permitió que la luz y las vistas penetraran en todos los espacios con el diseño centrado en un elegante espacio de galería central que hizo del arte el centro de la casa.

Floor plan

1. Entry vestibule
2. Living room
3. Bar
4. Dining room
5. Kitchen
6. Family room
7. Office
8. Gallery
9. Laundry room
10. Guest bedroom
11. Guest bathroom
12. Master bedroom
13. Master closet
14. Master bathroom

This home was originally constructed in 1950 and designed by San Francisco master architect Joseph Esherick. It features classic midcentury modern ideals: simplicity of volumes, large planes of glass and minimal structure. In renovating the structure which had been untouched for almost sixty years, Geddes Ulinskas and his firm were careful to preserve the humble nature of the design, understanding that it was that quiet quality of the house that allowed it to blend so well into its hillside setting. The basic courtyard layout was preserved and enhanced with subtle changes such as restructuring the stair as a floating, open stair and relocating the dining room to the courtyard. Custom materials include walnut paneling and brass hardware pulls.

Dieses Haus wurde ursprünglich vom San Franciscoer Meisterarchitekten Joseph Esherick entworfen und 1950 erbaut. Es zeigt klassische moderne Ideale aus der Mitte des Jahrhunderts: Einfachheit der Räume, große Glasflächen und minimale Struktur. Bei der Renovierung des seit fast sechzig Jahren unangetasteten Gebäudes achteten Geddes Ulinskas und seine Firma darauf, die bescheidene Natur des Entwurfs zu bewahren, da es diese ruhige Qualität des Hauses war, die es ermöglichte, sich so gut in seine Hanglage einzufügen. Die grundlegende Hofgestaltung wurde beibehalten und durch subtile Änderungen ergänzt, wie z. B. die Umgestaltung der Treppe in eine schwimmende, offene Treppe und die Verlegung des Speisesaals in den Innenhof. Kundenspezifische Materialien umfassen Nussbaumverkleidungen und Messingbeschläge.

Cette maison a été construite en 1950 et conçue par le maître architecte Joseph Esherick de San Francisco. Il se caractérise par des idéaux modernes classiques du milieu du siècle : simplicité des volumes, grands plans de verre et structure minimale. En rénovant la structure intacte depuis près de soixante ans, Geddes Ulinskas et son entreprise ont pris soin de préserver l'humilité de la conception, comprenant que c'est la qualité tranquille de la maison qui lui a permis de s'intégrer si bien dans son environnement en pente. L'aménagement de base de la cour a été préservé et amélioré grâce à de subtils changements tels que la restructuration de l'escalier en un escalier ouvert flottant et le déménagement de la salle à manger dans la cour. Les matériaux sur mesure comprennent des panneaux de noyer et des tirettes de quincaillerie en laiton.

Esta casa fue construida originalmente en 1950 y diseñada por el maestro arquitecto de San Francisco Joseph Esherick. Se caracteriza por sus ideales clásicos de mediados de siglo: simplicidad de volúmenes, grandes planos de vidrio y estructura mínima. Al renovar la estructura, que había permanecido intacta durante casi sesenta años, Geddes Ulinskas y su empresa se preocuparon por preservar la naturaleza sencilla del diseño, entendiendo que era esa cualidad de la casa la que le permitía integrarse tan bien en su entorno de ladera. La distribución básica del patio se mantuvo y se mejoró con cambi os sutiles, como la reestructuración de la escalera como escalera flotante y abierta y la reubicación del comedor en el patio. Los materiales personalizados incluyen paneles de nogal y tiradores de latón.

Third floor plan

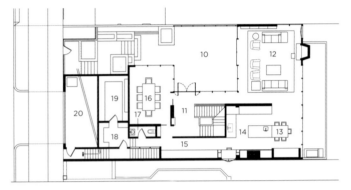

Second floor plan

First floor plan

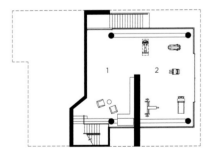

Gym level floor plan

1. Lounge
2. Gym
3. Office
4. Bedroom
5. Bathroom
6. Wine room
7. Laundry room
8. Art storage
9. Mechanical room
10. Courtyard
11. Entry
12. Living room
13. Breakfast room
14. Kitchen
15. Pantry
16. Dining room
17. Powder room
18. Mud room
20. Garage
21. Master bedroom
22. Master bathroom
23. Master dressing
24. Family room

Constructed in the open courtyard of a historic San Francisco Mediterranean home, this modern pool building is a fitting counterpoint to the traditional design of the main residence that it serves. Many of the materials of the main house, such as the limestone floors and the steel windows, are used in the pool building but expressed with different scales and proportions. The new pool building also expresses its structure toward the courtyard and carefully modulates light over the pool through a series of skylights. The infinity spill edge detail of the lap pool abstracts the water, making it appear as a solid, elevated object in space, while light reflections pattern the sloped ceiling that frames the view to the bay.

Erbaut im offenen Innenhof eines historischen mediterranen Hauses in San Francisco, ist dieses moderne Poolgebäude ein passender Kontrapunkt zum traditionellen Design der Hauptwohnung, der es dient. Viele der Materialien des Haupthauses, wie die Kalksteinböden und die Stahlfenster, werden im Poolgebäude verwendet, aber in unterschiedlichen Maßstäben und Proportionen ausgedrückt. Das neue Poolgebäude drückt auch seine Struktur zum Innenhof hin aus und moduliert das Licht über dem Pool durch eine Reihe von Oberlichtern vorsichtig. Das unendliche Auslaufkantendetail des Beckens abstrahiert das Wasser und lässt es als massives, erhöhtes Objekt im Raum erscheinen, während Lichtreflexionen die schräge Decke strukturieren, die den Blick auf die Bucht umrahmt.

Construit dans la cour ouverte d'une maison historique méditerranéenne de San Francisco, ce bâtiment de piscine moderne est un contrepoint approprié au design traditionnel de la résidence principale qu'il dessert. De nombreux matériaux de la maison principale, tels que les planchers de calcaire et les fenêtres en acier, sont utilisés dans le bâtiment de la piscine mais sont exprimés à des échelles et des proportions différentes. Le nouveau bâtiment de la piscine exprime également sa structure vers la cour et module soigneusement la lumière au-dessus de la piscine à travers une série de lucarnes. Le détail du bord de déversement à l'infini de la piscine à débordement fait abstraction de l'eau, la faisant apparaître comme un objet solide et surélevé dans l'espace, tandis que des reflets de lumière modèlent le plafond en pente qui encadre la vue sur la baie.

Construido en el patio abierto de una histórica casa mediterránea de San Francisco, este moderno edificio de la piscina es un contrapunto adecuado al diseño tradicional de la residencia principal a la que sirve. Muchos de los materiales de la casa principal, como los suelos de piedra caliza y las ventanas de acero, se utilizan en el edificio de la piscina, pero se expresan con diferentes escalas y proporciones. El nuevo edificio de la piscina también expresa su estructura hacia el patio y modula cuidadosamente la luz sobre la piscina a través de una serie de tragaluces. El detalle del borde de derrame infinito de la piscina extrae el agua, haciéndola aparecer como un objeto sólido y elevado en el espacio, mientras que los reflejos de la luz adornan al techo inclinado que enmarca la vista hacia la bahía.

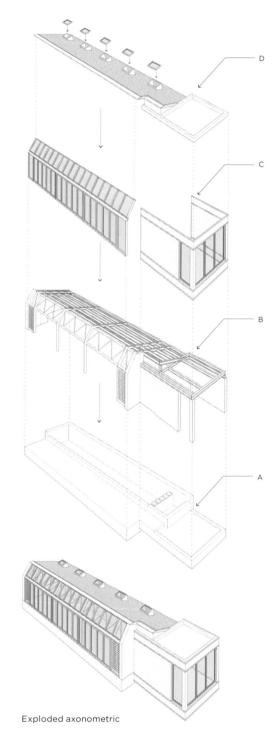

Exploded axonometric

A. Pool, spa, and foundations
B. Structural system
C. Curtain wall and metal cladding
D. Roof system and skylights

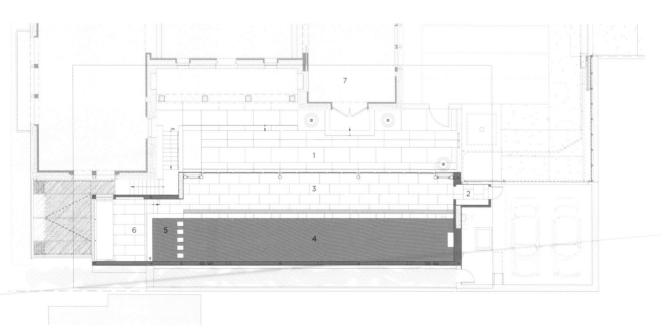

Floor plan

1. Entry courtyard
2. Pool vestibule
3. Pool deck
4. Lap pool
5. Spa
6. Lounge
7. Main house

GUSTAVE CARLSON
DESIGN

CANYON HOUSE

Photography: **Paul Dyer**
Location: **Berkeley, California**
Area: **4,652 Sq. Ft.**
Design Team: **Gustave Carlson, Joan Kiang, and Daniel Tiraschi**
General Contractor: **Ryan Construction and Kokalis Construction**
Landscape Architect: **Hendrikus Group Garden Architecture**
Interior Design: **Carolyn Lawrence and Glenn Bunting**
Structural Engineering: **Jason Campbell**
Lighting Design: **Keena Lucas**
Audio Consultant: **Sound Vision**

CARTER ACRES HOUSE

Photography: **Paul Dyer**
Location: **Martinez, California**
Area: **6,450 Sq. Ft.**
Design Team: **Gustave Carlson, Joan Kiang, and Daniel Tiraschi**
General Contractor: **Cerami Builders**
Landscape Architect: **Garden Architecture**
Stylist: **Yedda Morrison**
Structural Engineering: **Jason Campbell**
Lighting Design: **Keena Lucas**
Audio Consultant: **Matthew Stahnik**

INVERNESS HOUSE

Photography: **Paul Dyer**
Location: **Inverness, California**
Area: **2,673 Sq. Ft.**
Design Team: **Gustave Carlson and Joan Kiang**
General Contractor: **Finn Port Construction**
Structural Engineering: **Jason Campbell**

Gustave Carlson Design is an award-winning boutique architectural and interior design firm specializing in custom home renovation and new house construction. Following a decade of architectural work in New York, Los Angeles, and the San Francisco Bay Area, Gustave Carlson founded the firm in Berkeley, California in 1999. Since then, he has designed renovation, addition, and new construction projects for more than thirty private homes, ranging from craftsman to contemporary styles in San Francisco, Marin County, the Peninsula, and Sonoma County. The firm's architectural inspiration comes from notable architects such as Joseph Esherick, William Wurster, and William Turnbull, while its design principles support the use of green and sustainable materials and technologies. Gustave Carlson is a member of the American Institute of Architects, The National Trust of Historic Preservation, Build It Green, and the National Association of Remodeler's Industry.

Gustave Carlson Design ist ein preisgekröntes Architektur- und Innenarchitekturbüro, das sich auf die Renovierung von Eigenheimen und den Neubau von Häusern spezialisiert hat. Nach zehn Jahren Architekturarbeit in New York, Los Angeles und der San Francisco Bay Area gründete Gustave Carlson 1999 das Büro in Berkeley, Kalifornien. Seitdem hat er Renovierungs-, Erweiterungs- und Neubauprojekte für mehr als dreißig Privathäuser entworfen, die vom handwerklichen Stil bis zum zeitgenössischen Stil in San Francisco, Marin County, der Halbinsel und Sonoma County reichen. Die architektonische Inspiration des Unternehmens stammt von namhaften Architekten wie Joseph Esherick, William Wurster und William Turnbull, während seine Designprinzipien den Einsatz von grünen und nachhaltigen Materialien und Technologien unterstützen. Gustave Carlson ist Mitglied des American Institute of Architects, des National Trust of Historic Preservation, Build It Green und der National Association of Remodeler's Industry.

Gustave Carlson Design est un cabinet primé d'architecture de boutique et de design d'intérieur spécialisé dans la rénovation et la construction de maisons neuves sur mesure. Après une décennie de travail architectural à New York, Los Angeles et dans la région de la baie de San Francisco, Gustave Carlson a fondé le cabinet à Berkeley, Californie, en 1999. Depuis, il a conçu des projets de rénovation, d'ajout et de construction neuve pour plus d'une trentaine de maisons privées, allant de l'artisan au style contemporain à San Francisco, Marin County, la péninsule et Sonoma County. L'inspiration architecturale du cabinet provient d'architectes de renom tels que Joseph Esherick, William Wurster et William Turnbull, tandis que ses principes de conception favorisent l'utilisation de matériaux et de technologies écologiques et durables. Gustave Carlson est membre de l'American Institute of Architects, du National Trust of Historic Preservation, de Build It Green et de la National Association of Remodeler's Industry.

Gustave Carlson Design es una galardonada firma de arquitectura e interiorismo especializada en la renovación de casas a medida y en la construcción de casas de nueva planta. Después de una década de trabajo en Nueva York, Los Ángeles y el área de la Bahía de San Francisco, Gustave Carlson fundó el estudio en Berkeley, California, en 1999. Desde entonces, ha diseñado proyectos de renovación, extensión y nueva construcción para más de treinta casas privadas, desde estilos de base más artesanal hasta estilos contemporáneos en San Francisco, el Condado de Marin, y la Península y el Condado de Sonoma. La inspiración arquitectónica de la firma proviene de arquitectos notables como Joseph Esherick, William Wurster y William Turnbull, mientras que sus principios de diseño apoyan el uso de materiales y tecnologías verdes y sostenibles. Gustave Carlson es miembro del American Institute of Architects, The National Trust of Historic Preservation, Build It Green y de la National Association of Remodeler's Industry.

The Canyon House is an equation of materiality and mindfulness that factors several continents, historical timelines, disciplines, and cultures. It was an orchestration of master craftsmen, artists, designers, and the uniquely visionary homeowners, all working simultaneously with a wealth of skills, knowledge, and thoughtful dedication. A steep canyon and narrow creek setting was the framework for the design of a home that is both functional and aesthetically pleasing from so many different levels in the landscape. The design challenge was to make something look beautiful. We were mindful in the design of what the occupants look out to from each room, as well as what they see looking back at the house when they are outside in the landscape.

Das Canyon House ist eine Gleichung von Materialität und Achtsamkeit, die mehrere Kontinente, historische Zeitlinien, Disziplinen und Kulturen berücksichtigt. Es war eine Orchestrierung von Meistern, Künstlern, Designern und den einzigartig visionären Hausbesitzern, die alle gleichzeitig mit einer Fülle von Fähigkeiten, Wissen und durchdachtem Engagement arbeiteten. Ein steiler Canyon und eine schmale Bachlandschaft waren der Rahmen für die Gestaltung eines Hauses, das sowohl funktional als auch ästhetisch von so vielen verschiedenen Ebenen der Landschaft aus ansprechend ist. Die gestalterische Herausforderung bestand darin, etwas schön aussehen zu lassen. Wir haben höchste ästhetische Maßstäbe angesetzt, sowohl bei der Gestaltung dessen, was die Bewohner von jedem Raum aus sehen, sowie beim Blick zurück auf das Haus, wenn sie sich draußen in der Landschaft befinden.

La Canyon House est une équation de matérialité et d'attention qui tient compte de plusieurs continents, échéances historiques, disciplines et cultures. Il s'agissait d'une orchestration de maîtres artisans, d'artistes, de designers et de propriétaires d'une vision unique, tous travaillant simultanément avec une richesse de compétences, de connaissances et de dévouement réfléchi. Un canyon escarpé et un ruisseau étroit ont servi de cadre à la conception d'une maison qui est à la fois fonctionnelle et esthétique à partir de tant de niveaux différents dans le paysage. Le défi du design était de rendre quelque chose de beau. Nous avons été attentifs à ce que les occupants regardent de chaque pièce, ainsi qu'à ce qu'ils voient lorsqu'ils regardent la maison de l'extérieur dans le paysage.

The Canyon House es una ecuación de materialidad y atención al detalle que tiene en cuenta conceptos geográficos, temporales, distintas disciplinas y culturas. El diseño resultó ser una orquestación de trabajos de maestros artesanos, artistas, diseñadores y propietarios con una visión única, todos ellos trabajando simultáneamente con una gran cantidad de habilidades, conocimientos y dedicación reflexiva. Un cañón escarpado y un estrecho arroyo fueron el marco para el diseño de una casa que es a la vez funcional y estéticamente agradable. El reto consistía en hacer que todo se viera hermoso, prestando atención al diseño tanto de los elementos a la vista de los ocupantes como de lo que ven en el paisaje exterior.

North elevation

East elevation

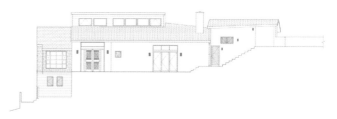

South elevation

West elevation

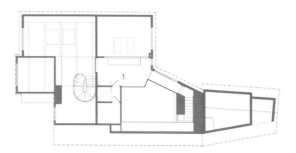

Loft floor plan

Main floor plan

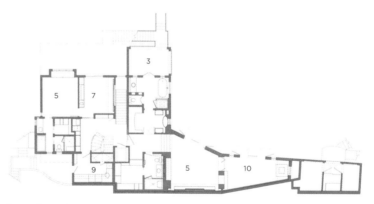

Lower floor plan

Ground floor plan

1. Loft
2. Kitchen
3. Living
4. Dining
5. Bedroom
6. Deck
7. Lounge
8. Wine room
9. Laundry
10. Yoga/meditation room
11. Mechanical room

0   5   15 ft

The Carter Acres House commands an overwhelming view of the Briones Regional Park's rolling hillside. Two existing California native oak trees were protected and saved to frame a distant view while the house rests framing the existing oaks to form a courtyard. The California weather lends itself to living an outdoor lifestyle, so from practically every room in the house borrows a view and has an outdoor veranda. The house was designed to take full advantage of the terrain, which led us to expand from one level—as originally planned—into a two-level home. The house experience was devised to capture the distant view of Mount Diablo so that all the main rooms have a mountain view and the occupants are "transformed" by the environment, as they feel the mountain weather inside their home.

Das Carter Acres House bietet einen überwältigenden Blick auf die sanften Hügel des Regionalparks Briones. Zwei bestehende kalifornische Eichen wurden geschützt und erhalten, um einen weiten Blick zu ermöglichen, während das Haus ruht und die bestehenden Eichen in einem Innenhof zusammenfasst. Das kalifornische Wetter bietet sich für einen Outdoor-Lebensstil an, so dass praktisch jeder Raum im Haus einen Blick auf den Innenhof hat und über eine Veranda verfügt. Das Haus wurde so konzipiert, dass es das Gelände optimal ausnutzt, was dazu führte, dass wir den ursprünglichen Plan nur eines Stockwerks zugunsten eines zweistöckigen Hauses aufgaben. Das Hauserlebnis wurde entwickelt, um die Fernsicht auf den Mount Diablo einzufangen, so dass alle Haupträume einen Blick auf die Berge haben und die Bewohner von der Umgebung „verwandelt" werden, während sie das Bergwetter in ihrem Zuhause spüren.

La maison Carter Acres offre une vue imprenable sur les collines vallonnées du parc régional Briones. Deux chênes californiens existants ont été protégés et sauvegardés pour encadrer une vue de loin tandis que la maison repose sur les chênes existants pour former une cour. Le climat californien se prête à un style de vie en plein air, de sorte que pratiquement toutes les pièces de la maison empruntent une vue et ont une véranda extérieure. La maison a été conçue pour tirer pleinement parti du terrain, ce qui nous a amenés à passer d'un niveau - comme prévu à l'origine - à une maison à deux niveaux. L'expérience de la maison a été conçue pour capturer la vue lointaine du Mont Diablo afin que toutes les pièces principales aient une vue sur la montagne et que les occupants soient « transformés » par l'environnement, car ils sentent le temps de la montagne dans leur maison.

La Casa Carter Acres disfruta de unas vistas abrumadoras a la ladera ondulada del Parque Regional Briones. Dos robles nativos de California fueron protegidos para enmarcar las vistas, mientras que la casa rodea unos robles existentes para formar un patio exterior. El clima de California se presta a un estilo de vida al aire libre, por lo que desde prácticamente todas las habitaciones de la casa, casi todas ellas con terraza exterior, se disfruta de vistas al paisaje. La casa fue diseñada para Todas las habitaciones principales gozan de vistas a la montaña y sus ocupantes, al sentir el clima de la montaña en el interior de su hogar, quedan impresionados por el entorno.

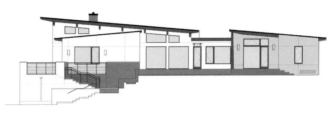

North elevation

East elevation

South elevation

West elevation

Main floor plan

Lower floor plan

N   0   5   15 ft

1. Kitchen
2. Living area
3. Family room
4. Dining area
5. Bedroom
6. Terrace
7. Office
8. Laundry
9. Meditation room
10. Exercise room
11. Home theater
12. Mechanical room
13. Garage
14. Storage

The Inverness house was a wonderful opportunity for indoor and outdoor spaces coming together. The project started as a remodel of a Shingle-style cabin. The homeowners needed more space but did not want an over-scaled, over-built home on the 3-acre property. They also wanted to focus on a sustainable, well-built, and well-crafted design so that it would withstand the elements and thus be "green" in its approach to the earth and its long-term incarnation. The indoor and outdoor meadow spaces reflect a sense of uncluttered natural beauty highlighted by expressed laminated glulam beams and a stained clear Douglas fir wood ceiling. The project's materials were discussed from a point of view of both in keeping to the neighborhood and context to rural West Marin, as well as maintenance and long term care.

Das Inverness Haus war eine wunderbare Gelegenheit, um Innen- und Außenräume zusammenzubringen. Das Projekt begann als Umbau einer Hütte im Schindel-Stil. Die Hausbesitzer benötigten mehr Platz, wollten aber kein überdimensionales, überbordendes Haus auf dem 1,2 Hektar großen Grundstück. Sie wollten sich auch auf ein nachhaltiges, gut ausgebautes und gut verarbeitetes Design konzentrieren, dass den Elementen standhält und somit in seinem Umgang mit der Erde und ihrer langfristigen Inkarnation „grün" ist. Die Innen- und Außenwiese spiegelt ein Gefühl von natürlicher Schönheit wider, das durch ausgeprägte laminierte Brettschichtholzträger und eine gebeizte, klare Douglasien-Decke gesteigert wird. Die Materialien des Projekts wurden unter dem Gesichtspunkt der Nachbarschaft und des Kontextes zum ländlichen Westmarin sowie der Instandhaltung und Langzeitpflege ausgewählt.

La maison d'Inverness a été une merveilleuse occasion de réunir des espaces intérieurs et extérieurs. Le projet a commencé par la rénovation d'une cabane de style bardeau. Les propriétaires avaient besoin de plus d'espace, mais ne voulaient pas d'une maison surdimensionnée et surconstruite sur la propriété de 1,2 hectares. Ils voulaient aussi mettre l'accent sur une conception durable, bien construite et bien conçue qui résiste aux éléments et soit ainsi « verte » dans son approche de la terre et son incarnation à long terme. Les espaces intérieurs et extérieurs des prairies reflètent un sentiment de beauté naturelle épurée mise en valeur par des poutres lamellées lamellées-collées exprimées et un plafond en sapin Douglas clair teinté. Les matériaux du projet ont été discutés du point de vue du respect du quartier et du contexte de la zone rurale de West Marin, ainsi que de l'entretien et des soins de longue durée.

La casa de Inverness fue una oportunidad maravillosa para reunir los espacios interiores y exteriores. El proyecto comenzó como una remodelación de una cabaña estilo "Shingle". Los propietarios necesitaban más espacio, pero no querían una casa ni sobredimensionada ni sobreconstruida en un terreno de 1,2 hectáreas. También querían centrarse en un diseño sostenible que resistiera a los elementos, ecológico en su ajuste con la tierra y su proyección a largo plazo. Los espacios interiores y exteriores reflejan una sensación de belleza natural resaltada por las expresivas vigas de madera laminada y un techo de madera de abeto Douglas transparente y teñido. Los materiales del proyecto fueron discutidos desde el punto de vista de respetar el entorno y el contexto del oeste de la población de Marín, así como su mantenimiento y el cuidado a largo plazo.

North elevation

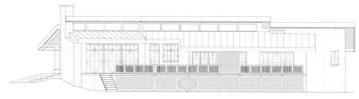

East elevation

West elevation

South elevation

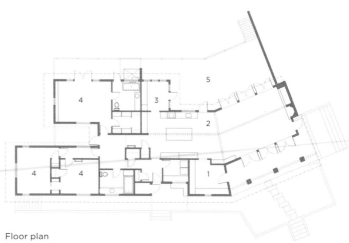

Floor plan

1. Entry
2. Kitchen/living
3. Dining
4. Bedroom
5. Deck

0 5   15 ft   N

JMJ STUDIOS

SAN FRANCISCO REMODEL

Photography: Catherine Nguyen
Location: SanFrancisco, California
Area: 2,500 Sq. Ft.
General Contractor: Fontana Construction
Structural Engineering: STC Design and
Engineering
Planning Consultant: Mike Larkin

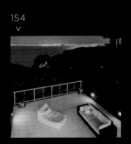

SAUSALITO REMODEL

Photography: Catherine Nguyen
Location: Sausalito, California
Area: 2,400 Sq. Ft.
General Contractor: Jerry James Construction
Structural Engineering: TormeyEngineering
Metal Fabricator: The Urban Lab

MILL VALLEY REMODEL

Renderings: JMJ Studios
Location: Mill Valley, California
Area: 3,250 Sq. Ft.
Structural Engineering: Strandberg Engineers

⊕ www.jmj-studios.com

JMJ Studios is a boutique, all-female design firm recognized for creating smart, inspiring, flexible spaces. Founder Julie M. Johnson brings strong commercial design and construction experience to private practice. We rely on rigorous space planning and constant collaboration to achieve success. We are modernists in form and function and celebrate each client's individual and unique style. We believe that architecture should be designed for a specific client, on a specific site, and for a specific purpose.

JMJ Studios ist eine Boutique, ein rein weibliches Designunternehmen, das für seine intelligenten, inspirierenden und flexiblen Räume bekannt ist. Die Gründerin Julie M. Johnson bringt reiche Erfahrung im Bereich des kommerziellen Designs und des Bauwesens in die Privatpraxis ein. Wir setzen auf eine rigorose Raumplanung und ständige Zusammenarbeit, um erfolgreich zu sein. Wir sind Modernisten in Form und Funktion und feiern den individuellen und einzigartigen Stil jedes Kunden. Wir sind der Meinung, dass Architektur für einen bestimmten Kunden, auf einem bestimmten Standort und für einen bestimmten Zweck entworfen werden sollte.

JMJ Studios est une firme de design boutique entièrement féminine reconnue pour créer des espaces intelligents, inspirants et flexibles. La fondatrice Julie M. Johnson apporte une solide expérience en conception commerciale et en construction à la pratique privée. Nous comptons sur une planification rigoureuse de l'espace et une collaboration constante pour réussir. Nous sommes des modernistes dans la forme et la fonction et célébrons le style individuel et unique de chaque client. Nous croyons que l'architecture doit être conçue pour un client spécifique, sur un site spécifique et dans un but spécifique.

JMJ Studios es una boutique, una firma de diseño totalmente femenina reconocida por crear espacios inteligentes, inspiradores y flexibles. La fundadora Julie M. Johnson aporta a la práctica privada una sólida experiencia en diseño comercial y construcción. Contamos con una rigurosa planificación del espacio y una colaboración constante para lograr el éxito. Somos modernistas en forma y función y celebramos el estilo individual y único de cada cliente. Creemos que la arquitectura debe ser diseñada para un cliente específico, en un sitio específico y para un propósito específico.

This was our very first project as a firm. The original house was built in 1939 and was remodeled by a local ship's captain in 1980 using various nautical features. The shingle-cladded exterior had not performed well in a neighborhood nicknamed Hurricane Gulch. The program was to modernize the home and add more livable space. The existing house was positioned on a small, steep lot that would only allow an additional 250 square feet per the lot's floor area ratio. We proposed to excavate for a new basement, build an enclosed, connected garage, and completely overhaul the home's exterior. Sustainable long-lasting materials were important to withstand the heavy winds and fog. The staircase was one of the limited opportunities for light, so we installed floor-to-ceiling glass to provide indirect light to the basement.

Dies war unser allererstes Projekt als Firma. Das ursprüngliche Haus wurde 1939 erbaut und 1980 von einem ortsansässigen Schiffskapitän mit verschiedenen nautischen Merkmalen umgebaut. Die schindelverkleidete Außenseite hatte sich in einem Viertel, das den Spitznamen „Hurricane Gulch" trägt, nicht gut bewährt. Das Programm bestand darin, das Haus zu modernisieren und mehr Lebensraum zu schaffen. Das bestehende Haus ist auf einem kleinen, steilen Grundstück positioniert, das nur 23 Quadratmeter Grundfläche zusätzlich zum Bau zuließ. Wir schlugen daher vor, für ein neues Untergeschoss zu graben, eine geschlossene, zusammenhängende Garage zu bauen und die Außenseite des Hauses komplett zu überholen. Nachhaltige, langlebige Materialien waren wichtig, um den starken Winden und dem Nebel standzuhalten. Die Treppe war eine der begrenzenden Möglichkeiten für das Licht, deshalb haben wir raumhohes Glas installiert, um das Untergeschoss indirekt zu beleuchten.

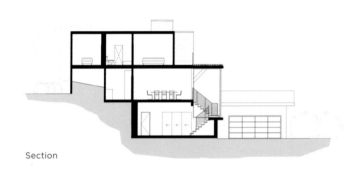

Section

C'était notre tout premier projet en tant que cabinet. La maison originale a été construite en 1939 et a été remodelée par un capitaine de navire local en 1980 en utilisant divers éléments nautiques. L'extérieur revêtu de bardeaux n'avait pas donné de bons résultats dans un quartier surnommé Hurricane Gulch. Le programme visait à moderniser la maison et à ajouter plus d'espace habitable. La maison existante était située sur un petit terrain escarpé qui ne permettrait qu'une superficie supplémentaire de 23 mètres carrés par rapport à la surface du terrain. Nous avons proposé d'excaver pour un nouveau sous-sol, de construire un garage fermé et raccordé et de rénover complètement l'extérieur de la maison. Des matériaux durables étaient importants pour résister aux vents violents et au brouillard. L'escalier était l'une des possibilités limitées de lumière, c'est pourquoi nous avons installé du verre du sol au plafond pour fournir une lumière indirecte au sous-sol.

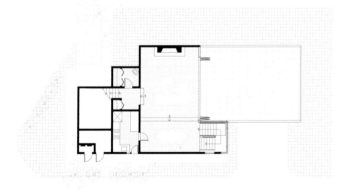

Upper floor plan

Este fue nuestro primer proyecto como empresa. La casa original fue construida en 1939 y fue remodelada por el capitán de un barco local en 1980 usando varios elementos náuticos. El exterior cubierto de tejas no había dado buenos resultados en un barrio apodado Hurricane Gulch. El programa era modernizar la casa y añadir más espacio habitable. La casa original estaba ubicada en un pequeño y empinado terreno que solo permitiría 23 metros cuadrados adicionales por la proporción de área de suelo del terreno. Propusimos excavar un nuevo sótano, construir un garaje cerrado y conectado, y renovar completamente el exterior de la casa. Los materiales sostenibles y duraderos eran importantes para resistir los fuertes vientos y la niebla. La escalera era una de las limitadas oportunidades para conseguir más luz, así que instalamos cristal del suelo al techo para proporcionar luz indirecta al sótano.

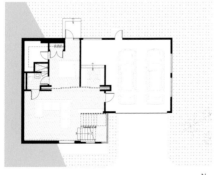

Basement floor plan

0   4   8   16 ft

N

The Bay Area housing market is very competitive. Like so many families in the Bay Area, our client was looking for a single-family home but was priced out of the neighborhood's they desired. This project was the first of several in San Francisco, where we worked with clients to redesign a flat such that their space felt like a single-family home. We honed in on a newly renovated two-bedroom flat near Pacific Heights. The flat had some key attributes that were essential in our vision. We knew that if we could extend the structure even modestly, it would allow for an internal interconnecting stair, full usability of the garage bonus room and a direct connection to the rear yard. Moreover, the remodel would result in a usable deck area for the upper tenant – which gave them much needed outdoor space.

Der Wohnungsmarkt der Bay Area ist sehr wettbewerbsintensiv. Wie so viele Familien in der Bay Area suchte unser Kunde ein Einfamilienhaus, was aber innerhalb der von ihm gewünschten Nachbarschaft nicht bezahlbar war. Dieses Projekt war das erste von mehreren in San Francisco, bei dem wir gemeinsam mit dem Kunden eine Wohnung so umgestaltet haben, dass sie sich wie ein Einfamilienhaus anfühlt. Wir haben eine neu renovierte Zwei-Schlafzimmer-Wohnung in der Nähe von Pacific Heights gefunden. Die Wohnung hatte einige wichtige Eigenschaften, die für unsere Vision wesentlich waren. Wir wussten, dass, wenn wir die Struktur auch nur geringfügig erweitern könnten, eine interne Verbindungstreppe, die volle Nutzbarkeit des Garagenbonusraums und eine direkte Verbindung zum Hinterhof möglich würden. Außerdem würde der Umbau eine nutzbare Dachfläche liefern – was den dringend benötigten Außenraum verschaffte.

Le marché de l'habitation de la région de Bay Area est très concurrentiel. Comme tant d'autres familles de la région de la baie, notre client recherchait une maison unifamiliale, mais son prix ne correspondait pas à celui de son quartier. Ce projet a été le premier d'une série à San Francisco, où nous avons travaillé avec des clients pour redessiner un appartement de façon à ce que leur espace ressemble à une maison unifamiliale. Nous nous sommes installés dans un appartement de deux chambres à coucher récemment rénové près de Pacific Heights. L'appartement possédait quelques attributs clés qui étaient essentiels à notre vision. Nous savions que si nous pouvions agrandir la structure, même modestement, cela nous permettrait d'avoir un escalier d'interconnexion interne, une utilisation complète de la salle de bonus du garage et une connexion directe avec la cour arrière. De plus, le remodelage se traduirait par une surface de pont utilisable pour le locataire supérieur - ce qui leur offrirait un espace extérieur dont ils avaient grandement besoin.

El mercado inmobiliario del Área de la Bahía de San Francisco es muy competitivo. El cliente buscaba una casa unifamiliar de ciertas características pero no tenía el presupuesto necesario para ello. Este proyecto fue el primero de varios en San Francisco, donde se trabajó junto a los clientes para rediseñar un piso de manera que su espacio se pareciera a una casa unifamiliar. El proyecto ha consistido en perfeccionar un apartamento de dos dormitorios recientemente renovado cerca del barrio de Pacific Heights. El piso tenía algunos atributos clave que eran esenciales en la visión de los arquitectos. Ampliar la estructura original, incluso modestamente, permitiría una escalera interna, el uso completo del garaje y una conexión directa con el patio trasero. Además, la remodelación resultaría en un zona cubierta utilizable para el inquilino del piso superior.

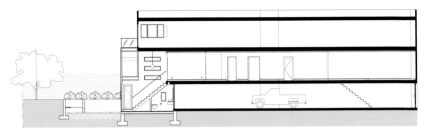

Section

Upper floor plan

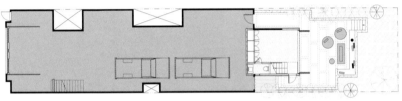

Lower floor plan

0 4 8 16 ft

This project is an expansion of a classic Mill Valley bungalow that had been renovated and expanded upon over time. The existing home enjoys a relatively large, flat lot on the valley floor. The project program was to create more livable area and expand the master bedroom. The local codes allowed for a mere 752-square-foot addition, which was just enough to meet the client's goals, including an unfinished basement. A rear three-story addition mirrors the form of the original house while adding a modern twist. The addition expands off the main kitchen area and creates a working hub. A new outdoor deck area is intimate, with fixed bench seating, a built-in bbq, and a master bedroom deck with rear yard views.

Bei diesem Projekt handelt es sich um eine Erweiterung eines klassischen Bungalows im Mühltal, der im Laufe der Zeit renoviert und erweitert worden war. Das Bestandshaus verfügt über ein relativ großes, flaches Grundstück im Talboden. Das Projektprogramm sah vor, mehr Wohnfläche zu schaffen und das Hauptschlafzimmer zu erweitern. Die lokalen Vorschriften erlaubten einen Zubau von nur 70 Quadratmetern, was gerade genug war, um die Ziele des Kunden zu erreichen, einschließlich eines unvollendeten Kellers. Ein dreistöckiger Anbau im Heck spiegelt die Form des ursprünglichen Hauses wider und verleiht ihm einen modernen Touch. Der Anbau erweitert den Bereich der Hauptküche und schafft eine Arbeitsfläche. Der neue Außenbereich ist intim, mit fester Sitzbank, einem eingebauten Grillplatz und einem Hauptschlafzimmer mit Blick auf den Hinterhof.

Ce projet est l'agrandissement d'un bungalow classique de Mill Valley qui a été rénové et agrandi au fil du temps. La maison existante jouit d'un terrain relativement grand et plat au fond de la vallée. Le programme du projet consistait à créer plus d'espace habitable et à agrandir la chambre des maîtres. Les codes locaux ne permettaient qu'un ajout de 70 mètres carrés, ce qui était juste suffisant pour atteindre les objectifs du client, y compris un sous-sol non aménagé. Un ajout de trois étages à l'arrière reprend la forme de la maison d'origine tout en y ajoutant une touche de modernité. L'ajout agrandit la zone de la cuisine principale et crée un centre de travail. Une nouvelle terrasse extérieure est intime, avec des banquettes fixes, un barbecue intégré et une chambre principale avec vue sur la cour arrière.

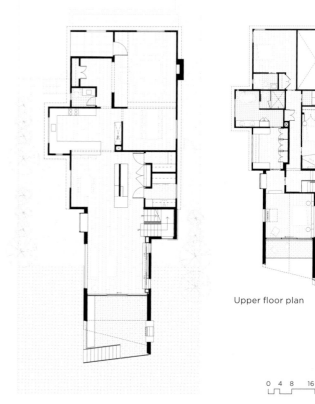

Este proyecto es una extensión de un *bungalow* clásico de Mill Valley que ha sido renovado y ampliado a través del tiempo. La casa existente goza de un terreno relativamente grande y plano. El programa consistió en crear un área más habitable y ampliar el dormitorio principal. Los códigos locales permitían una mera adición de 70 metros cuadrados, lo cual era suficiente para cumplir con las metas del cliente, incluyendo un sótano inacabado. Un anexo trasero de tres pisos recuerda la forma de la casa original, al mismo tiempo que le da un toque moderno. La ampliación permite agrandar el área de la cocina principal y crear una zona de trabajo. La intervención se completa con una nueva área cubierta al aire libre, con asientos de obra, una barbacoa y un dormitorio principal con vistas al patio trasero.

Upper floor plan

0 4 8   16 ft

N

Lower floor plan

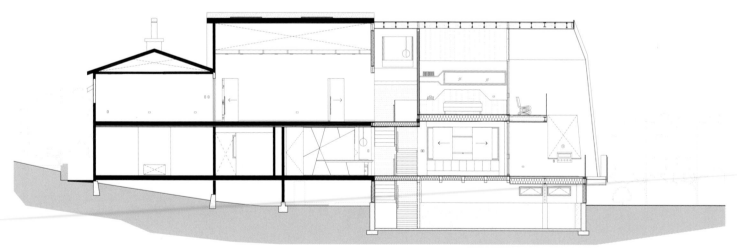

Building section

0 4 8 16 ft

JOHN MANISCALCO
ARCHITECTURE

DOLORES HEIGHTS RESIDENCE I

Photography: **Joe Fletcher Photography**
Drone Photography: **Blake Marvin Photography**
Location: **San Francisco, California**
General Contractor: **Design Line Construction**
Landscape Architect: **Surface Design**
Structural Engineer: **Strandberg Engineering**

MARTIS CAMP RESIDENCE I

Photography: **Joe Fletcher Photography**
Location: **Martis Camp, California**
General Contractor: **Crestwood Construction**
Landscape Architect: **Lichtfield Design + Consulting**
Interior Design: **Dovetail Designworks**
Structural Engineering: **Colovitch Fettig Bjur Engineers**
Civil Engineering: **Gary Davis Group**
Mechanical Engineering: **Weld Fickel**
Lighting Design: **Hiram Banks Lighting Design**
Energy Consultant: **Denise Kowal**

TANK HILL RESIDENCE II

Photography: **Bernard Andre Photography and Jacob Elliot Photography**
Location: **San Francisco, California**
General Contractor: **Hugues and Co Construction**
Landscape Architect: **John Maniscalco Architecture**
Interior Design: **Studio Collins Weir**
Landscape Planting: **Whilborg Design**
Structural Engineering: **Holmes Structures**
Lighting Design: **Hiram Banks Lighting Design**
Energy Consultant: **Gilleran Energy Management**

John Maniscalco Architecture produces work that is analytical in approach, artful in design, rigorous in execution, and wholly informed by the specifics of client and environment. It takes the particular needs, desires, and personality of each client, and through deep collaboration, synthesizes them with the culture and character of the natural context to create a unique architectural solution that is entirely site and client-specific. Working in a variety of natural environments, the studio endeavors to enhance the experience of these places by creating an architecturally quiet framework for users to observe and understand the physical world in unexpected ways. Unique views, spatial sequences, and use rituals are informed by architecture that is innovative, honest, and well-crafted with a focus on the fundamental elements of architecture: materiality, light, space, and clarity of design from concept to detailing.

John Maniscalco Architecture produziert Arbeiten, die analytisch im Ansatz, kunstvoll im Design, rigoros in der Ausführung und vollständig durch die Besonderheiten des Kunden und der Umgebung informiert sind. Es werden die besonderen Bedürfnisse, Wünsche und die Persönlichkeit jedes Kunden berücksichtigt und durch intensive Auseinandersetzung mit der Kultur und dem Charakter des natürlichen Kontextes zu einer einzigartigen architektonischen Lösung kombiniert, die vollständig standort- und kundenspezifisch ist. Das Studio arbeitet in einer Vielzahl von natürlichen Umgebungen und versucht, das Erlebnis dieser Orte zu verbessern, indem es einen architektonisch ruhigen Rahmen schafft, in dem die Benutzer die physische Welt auf unerwartete Weise beobachten und verstehen können. Einzigartige Ansichten, Raumfolgen und Nutzungsrituale werden durch eine innovative, ehrliche und gut gestaltete Architektur geprägt, die sich auf die grundlegenden Elemente der Architektur konzentriert: Materialität, Licht, Raum und Klarheit des Designs vom Konzept bis zur Detaillierung.

John Maniscalco Architecture produit un travail qui est analytique dans son approche, astucieux dans sa conception, rigoureux dans son exécution et entièrement éclairé par les spécificités du client et de son environnement. Il tient compte des besoins particuliers, des désirs et de la personnalité de chaque client et, grâce à une collaboration approfondie, les synthétise avec la culture et le caractère du contexte naturel pour créer une solution architecturale unique qui est entièrement propre au site et au client. Travaillant dans une variété d'environnements naturels, le studio s'efforce d'améliorer l'expérience de ces lieux en créant un cadre architectural calme qui permet aux utilisateurs d'observer et de comprendre le monde physique d'une manière inattendue. Des vues uniques, des séquences spatiales et des rituels d'utilisation sont éclairés par une architecture innovatrice, honnête et bien conçue qui met l'accent sur les éléments fondamentaux de l'architecture : matérialité, lumière, espace et clarté du design, du concept au détail.

John Maniscalco Arquitectura produce un trabajo de enfoque analítico, ingenioso en el diseño, riguroso en la ejecución, y totalmente informado por las especificidades del cliente y el entorno. Tiene en cuenta las necesidades particulares, los deseos y la personalidad de cada cliente y, a través de una profunda colaboración, los sintetiza con la cultura y el carácter del contexto natural para crear una solución arquitectónica única que es totalmente específica para el sitio y el cliente. Trabajando en una variedad de ambientes naturales, el estudio se esfuerza por mejorar la experiencia de estos lugares mediante la creación de un marco arquitectónico silencioso para que los usuarios observen y comprendan el mundo físico de maneras inesperadas. Las vistas únicas, las secuencias espaciales y los rituales de uso se basan en una arquitectura innovadora, honesta y bien elaborada, centrada en los elementos fundamentales de la arquitectura: la materialidad, la luz, el espacio y la claridad del diseño, desde el concepto hasta los detalles.

On an atypically-configured sloping double lot in San Francisco, this new home takes advantage of rare siting to maximize the experience of changing daylight and sweeping city views. The use of deep overhangs and angular cedar forms carefully frames horizon views while gently responding to the corner siting. Spaces and functions are arranged to pair with varied site experiences. A two-story glazed volume clad in cedar slats defines the entry as a bent-steel stair descends to create a connection to the living level. Flow and extension of interior spaces to exterior gathering areas are achieved through an open floor plan. A restrained palette of subtle organic materials unifies the visual language of the exterior landscape with the internal architecture of the home, creating a serenity not often found in the center of this busy city.

Auf einem atypisch konfigurierten, schrägen Doppelgrundstück in San Francisco nutzt dieses neue Zuhause die Vorteile seltener Standorte, um das Erlebnis von wechselndem Tageslicht und weitreichenden Stadtansichten zu maximieren. Die Verwendung von tiefen Überhängen und eckiger Zeder bildet einen sorgfältigen Rahmen für den Blick auf den Horizont und reagiert sanft auf die Ecklage. Räume und Funktionen sind so organisiert, dass der Ort auf unterschiedliche Weise erlebt wird. Ein zweigeschossiges, verglastes Volumen, das mit Zedernholzlamellen verkleidet ist, definiert den Eingang, während eine gebogene Stahltreppe hinabführt, um eine Verbindung zum Wohnniveau herzustellen. Die Durchströmung und Ausdehnung der Innenräume auf die äußeren Sammelflächen werden durch einen offenen Grundriss erreicht. Eine zurückhaltende Palette subtiler organischer Materialien vereint die visuelle Sprache der Außenlandschaft mit der Innenarchitektur des Hauses und schafft eine Ruhe, die man nur selten im Zentrum dieser geschäftigen Stadt findet.

Sur un terrain en pente atypique à San Francisco, cette nouvelle maison profite d'un emplacement rare pour maximiser l'expérience de changer la lumière du jour et de balayer les vues de la ville. L'utilisation de porte-à-faux profonds et de formes angulaires en cèdre permet d'encadrer soigneusement les vues à l'horizon tout en répondant doucement à l'emplacement des coins. Les espaces et les fonctions sont organisés de telle sorte que le lieu est vécu de différentes manières. Un volume vitré de deux étages recouvert de lattes de cèdre définit l'entrée comme un escalier en acier coudé qui descend pour créer un lien avec le niveau de vie. L'écoulement et l'extension des espaces intérieurs vers les aires de rassemblement extérieures s'effectuent au moyen d'un plan d'étage ouvert. Une palette sobre de matériaux organiques subtils unifie le langage visuel du paysage extérieur avec l'architecture intérieure de la maison, créant une sérénité que l'on ne retrouve pas souvent dans le centre de cette ville animée.

En una parcela doble, inclinada y atípicamente configurada en San Francisco, esta nueva casa aprovecha una ubicación poco común para maximizar la experiencia de cambiar la luz del día y contemplar las vistas de la ciudad. El uso de voladizos profundos y formas angulares de cedro enmarca cuidadosamente las vistas del horizonte mientras responde suavemente a la posición en esquina. Los espacios y las funciones se organizan de manera que el lugar es experimentado en diversas formas. Un volumen acristalado de dos pisos revestido con listones de cedro define la entrada mientras que una escalera de acero curvado desciende para crear una conexión con el nivel de la zona de estar. El flujo y la extensión de los espacios interiores a las áreas de reunión exteriores se logran a través de un plano abierto. Una sobria paleta de sutiles materiales orgánicos unifica el lenguaje visual del paisaje exterior con la arquitectura interior de la casa, creando una serenidad poco frecuente en el centro de esta ajetreada ciudad.

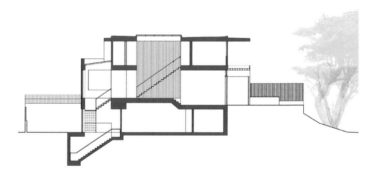

Longitudinal section

Cross section

Roof plan

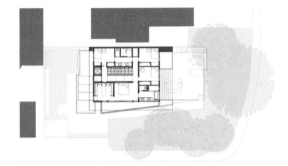

Level 3 floor plan

Level 2 floor plan

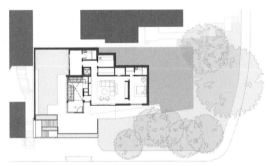

Level 1 floor plan

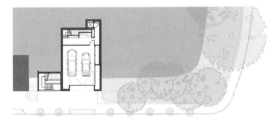

Level 0 floor plan

This home on a down-sloping wooded site carves a serpentine form in the topography that simultaneously provides privacy toward the street while opening toward the panoramic meadow and Pacific Crest mountain views beyond. The primary forms are sited to create a seamless blending of indoor and outdoor spaces beneath a single planar roof, which gently slopes upward to open toward the mountain peaks and the expansive sky. The public and private spaces are developed as distinct wings maintaining privacy and separation while creating varied perspectives on the surrounding landscape. The programmatic elements are organized by the solar movement across the site. A simple palette of site-defined materials—stained cedar, zinc roofing, and board-form concrete—allows for a quiet dialogue between the house and its environment.

Dieses Haus auf einem abfallenden Waldgrundstück schneidet eine Serpentinenform in die Topographie, die gleichzeitig Privatsphäre gegenüber der Straße bietet und sich für einen Panoramablick vom Kamm über Wiesen und den Pazifik öffnet. Die primären Formen sind so angeordnet, dass sie eine nahtlose Mischung aus Innen- und Außenräumen unter einem einzigen ebenen Dach schaffen, das sanft nach oben abfällt und sich zu den Berggipfeln und dem weiten Himmel öffnet. Die Gemeinschafts- und privaten Räume werden als eigenständige Flügel entwickelt, die Privatsphäre und Trennung wahren und gleichzeitig vielfältige Perspektiven auf die umgebende Landschaft schaffen. Die programmatischen Elemente werden vom Sonnenverlauf über dem Standort organisiert. Eine einfache Palette von standortdefinierten Materialien – gefärbte Zeder, Zinkdachdeckung und plattenförmiger Beton – ermöglicht einen ruhigen Dialog zwischen dem Haus und seiner Umgebung.

Cette maison sur un site boisé en pente descendante sculpte une forme serpentine dans la topographie qui offre à la fois une intimité vers la rue tout en s'ouvrant vers la prairie panoramique et les montagnes de Pacific Crest vues au-delà. Les formes primaires sont placées de façon à créer un mélange harmonieux d'espaces intérieurs et extérieurs sous un seul toit plan qui s'incline doucement vers le haut pour s'ouvrir vers les sommets de la montagne et le ciel étendu. Les espaces publics et privés sont aménagés comme des ailes distinctes qui préservent l'intimité et la séparation tout en créant des perspectives variées sur le paysage environnant. Les éléments programmatiques sont organisés par le mouvement solaire à travers le site. Une palette simple de matériaux définis par le site - cèdre teinté, toiture en zinc et béton en planches - permet un dialogue tranquille entre la maison et son environnement.

Esta casa en un terreno boscoso en pendiente descendente dibuja una forma serpenteante en la topografía que simultáneamente proporciona privacidad hacia la calle mientras se abre hacia la pradera panorámica y las vistas de las montañas de Pacific Crest y más allá. Las formas primarias están ubicadas para crear una mezcla perfecta de espacios interiores y exteriores bajo un solo tejado plano, que se inclina suavemente hacia arriba para abrirse hacia los picos de las montañas y el cielo expansivo. Los espacios públicos y privados se desarrollan como alas distintas, manteniendo la privacidad y la separación, a la vez que crean perspectivas variadas sobre el paisaje circundante. Los elementos programáticos están organizados por el movimiento solar a través del sitio. Una paleta simple de materiales definidos por el lugar —cedro teñido, tejados de zinc y hormigón en forma de tabla— permite un diálogo tranquilo entre la casa y su entorno.

Section

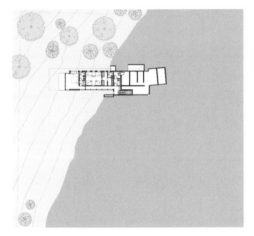

Lower floor plan

Upper floor plan

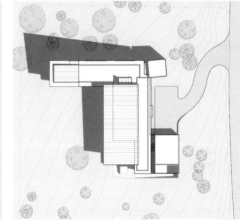

Roof plan

On an atypically wide, steeply sloped urban lot, this new home creates deep and varied connections to the immediately surrounding landscape and the city beyond. In response to the flow of landforms in and around the house, we created a spatial center that spans over its entire height. This gesture creates a core that brings light deep into the home, reflects an internalization of the site's slope, and reorients the users towards the variety of site connections that anchor the home to the site. In the broadest sense, the house is continually changing how one relates to the site. A rich palette of organic materials is utilized, carefully detailed throughout both interior and exterior, to further reinforce the natural ties of the home to the site.

Auf einem atypisch breiten, steil abfallenden Stadtgrundstück schafft dieses neue Zuhause tiefe und vielfältige Verbindungen zur unmittelbar angrenzenden Landschaft und zur Stadt dahinter. Als Reaktion auf den Fluss der Landformen im und um das Haus herum haben wir ein räumliches Zentrum geschaffen, das sich über seine gesamte Höhe erstreckt. Diese Geste schafft einen Kern, der Licht tief in das Haus bringt, eine Verinnerlichung der Neigung des Grundstücks widerspiegelt und die Nutzer auf die Vielfalt der Standortverbindungen ausrichtet, die das Haus in der Örtlichkeit verankern. Im weitesten Sinne modifiziert das Haus ständig die Beziehungen der Menschen zum Ort. Eine reiche Palette von organischen Materialien wird verwendet, die sowohl im Innen- als auch im Außenbereich sorgfältig ausgeführt wurden, um die natürlichen Verbindungen des Hauses zum Standort weiter zu verstärken.

Sur un terrain urbain d'une largeur atypique et d'une pente abrupte, cette nouvelle maison crée des liens profonds et variés avec le paysage environnant immédiat et la ville au-delà. En réponse au flux de formes de relief à l'intérieur et autour de la maison, nous avons créé un centre spatial qui s'étend sur toute sa hauteur. Ce geste crée un noyau qui apporte de la lumière en profondeur dans la maison, reflète une intériorisation de la pente du site et réoriente les utilisateurs vers la variété des connexions du site qui ancrent la maison au site. Au sens le plus large, la maison change continuellement la façon dont on se rattache au site. Une riche palette de matériaux organiques est utilisée, soigneusement détaillée à l'intérieur comme à l'extérieur, pour renforcer les liens naturels de la maison avec le site.

En un terreno urbano atípicamente ancho y con pendientes pronunciadas, esta nueva casa crea profundas y variadas conexiones con el paisaje circundante y con la ciudad más allá. En respuesta al flujo de formas del terreno dentro y alrededor de la casa, creamos un centro espacial que se extiende a lo largo de toda su altura. Este gesto crea un núcleo que lleva la luz a las profundidades de la casa, refleja una internalización de la pendiente del lugar y reorienta a los usuarios hacia la variedad de conexiones del sitio que anclan la casa al lugar. En el sentido más amplio, la casa está cambiando continuamente la forma en que uno se relaciona con el sitio. Se utiliza una rica paleta de materiales orgánicos, cuidadosamente detallados tanto en el interior como en el exterior, para reforzar aún más los lazos naturales de la casa con el lugar.

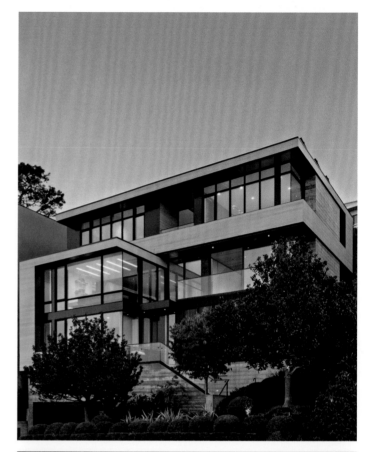

Section

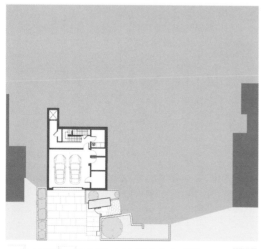

Level 0 floor plan

Level 1 floor plan

Level 2 floor plan

Level 3 floor plan

Roof Plan

MARK ENGLISH
ARCHITECTS

172
ˇ

HILLTOP HOUSE

Photography: Joe Fletcher Photography
Location: Los Gatos, California
Lot area: 1.17 acres
Built area: 3,400 Sq. Ft. (habitable) +
500 Sq. Ft. (garage)
Project team: Mark English, Brian Person,
and Samantha Senn
General Contractor: De Mattei Construction
Structural Engineering: GFDS Structural
Engineers

174
ˇ

TŌRŌ HOUSE

Photography: Bruce Damonte
Location: Woodside, California
Lot area: 29,310 Sq. Ft.
Built area: 2,563 Sq. Ft. (habitable) +
300 Sq. Ft. (garage)
Project team: Mark English and Greg Corbett
General Contractor: Golobic Construction
Structural Engineering: Dominic Chu
Structural Engineer

178
ˇ

COW HOLLOW RESIDENCE

Photography: Joe Fletcher Photography
Location: San Francisco, California
Lot area: 6,664 Sq. Ft.
Built area: 2,702 Sq. Ft. (habitable) +
359 Sq. Ft. (garage)
Project team: Mark English and Greg Corbett
General Contractor: De Mattei Construction
Structural Engineering: GFDS Structural
Engineers
Acoustical Consultant: West Coast
Sound Solutions
Geotechnical Engineering:
Earth Systems Pacific
Historic Research: Page & Turnbull

Mark English Architects is located in the North Beach neighborhood of San Francisco, in the 1940 former studio of sculptors Robert Howard and Adaline Kent. The building is perfect for the practice, full of natural light, logical, and beautifully sculpted for its use. The firm provides design that is sustainable because it is sensible, flexible, and built to last. With a special interest in building in the urban context, it has been creating beautifully tailored homes, work, and entertainment spaces throughout California, Texas, and Mexico since 1992, with half of its work in San Francisco. A Bay Area native, Mark English offers a designer's sense of artistry supported by practical knowledge gained from years of direct, hands-on building experience. Mark English is the editor of The Architects' Take, a respected online magazine featuring original interviews and commentary.

Mark English Architects befindet sich im North-Beach-Viertel von San Francisco, im ehemaligen Atelier der Bildhauer Robert Howard und Adaline Kent. Das Gebäude ist perfekt für die Praxis, voller natürlichem Licht, logisch und schön gestaltet für seine Nutzung. Das Unternehmen bietet ein Design, das nachhaltig ist, weil es sinnvoll, flexibel und auf Langlebigkeit ausgelegt ist. Mit einem besonderen Interesse am Bauen im urbanen Kontext schafft es seit 1992 in Kalifornien, Texas und Mexiko maßgeschneiderte Wohn-, Arbeits- und Unterhaltungsräume, die zur Hälfte in San Francisco entstehen. Mark English, gebürtig in der Bay Area, besitzt den Sinn eines Designers für Kunstfertigkeit, unterstützt durch praktisches Wissen, das aus jahrelanger direkter, praktischer Bauerfahrung gewonnen wurde. Mark English ist Herausgeber von *The Architects' Take*, einem angesehenen Online-Magazin mit Originalinterviews und Kommentaren.

Mark English Architects est situé dans le quartier North Beach de San Francisco, dans l'ancien atelier des sculpteurs Robert Howard et Adaline Kent en 1940. Le bâtiment est parfait pour la pratique, plein de lumière naturelle, logique et magnifiquement sculpté pour son utilisation. L'entreprise offre une conception durable parce qu'elle est sensée, flexible et construite pour durer. Avec un intérêt particulier pour la construction en milieu urbain, elle crée depuis 1992 des maisons, des espaces de travail et de divertissement sur mesure en Californie, au Texas et au Mexique, la moitié de son travail étant à San Francisco. Originaire de la région de la Baie, Mark English offre le sens artistique d'un concepteur, appuyé par des connaissances pratiques acquises au fil des années d'expérience directe et pratique dans le domaine de la construction. Mark English est le rédacteur en chef de *The Architects' Take*, un magazine en ligne respecté qui présente des entrevues et des commentaires originaux.

Mark English Architects está ubicado en el barrio de North Beach de San Francisco, en el antiguo estudio de los escultores Robert Howard y Adaline Kent de 1940. El edificio es perfecto, lleno de luz natural, lógico y bellamente esculpido para su uso. La empresa proporciona un diseño que es sostenible porque es sensible, flexible y construido para que sea duradero. Con un interés especial en la construcción en el contexto urbano, ha estado creando casas bellamente diseñadas, espacios de trabajo y entretenimiento en California, Texas y México desde 1992, con la mitad de su trabajo en San Francisco. Mark English, nativo del Área de la Bahía de San Francisco, ofrece el sentido artístico de un diseñador apoyado por el conocimiento práctico adquirido a lo largo de años de experiencia directa y práctica en la construcción. Mark English es el editor de *The Architects' Take*, una respetada revista *online* que ofrece entrevistas y comentarios originales.

The project is a renovation and addition to an existing single-family, mid-century hillside home. The challenge focused on taking a wonderfully conceived, but woefully realized home and help it reach its potential. The entry has an existing, wonderful cast glass translucent window. We added a 21st-century companion piece made of cold-rolled steel featuring a wave pattern with adjustable hued LED lamps. The wave theme is echoed in the in situ painting on the living room wall by Momoko Sudo. Hot-rolled steel is used to match two existing fireplaces and the entry screen between them. The steel hearth for the family room fireplace steps up to the laundry and guest bedroom wing of the house. All of the cabinet wood veneer in the kitchen and family room is made of reclaimed Eucalyptus felled at the Presidio in San Francisco.

Das Projekt ist eine Renovierung und Ergänzung eines bestehenden Einfamilienhauses aus der Mitte des Jahrhunderts. Die Herausforderung bestand darin, einem wunderbar konzipierten, aber erbärmlich realisierten Zuhause zur Entfaltung seines Potenzials zu verhelfen. Der Eingang hat ein bestehendes, wunderschönes, lichtdurchlässiges Fenster aus Gussglas. Wir haben ein Begleiterstück aus kaltgewalztem Stahl aus dem 21. Jahrhundert mit einem Wellenmuster und verstellbaren farbigen LED-Lampen hinzugefügt. Das Wellenmotiv spiegelt sich in der in Situ-Malerei von Momoko Sudo an der Wohnzimmerwand wider. Warmgewalzter Stahl wird verwendet, um zwei vorhandene Kamine und die Zwischenwand anzupassen. Der Stahlkamin für die Familienzimmer-Feuerstelle führt zur Waschküche und zum Gästezimmerflügel des Hauses. Alle Schrankholzfurniere in der Küche und im Familienzimmer bestehen aus recyceltem Eukalyptus, der im Presidio in San Francisco gefällt wurde.

Le projet consiste en la rénovation et l'agrandissement d'une maison unifamiliale existante à flanc de colline datant du milieu du siècle. Le défi consistait à prendre un foyer merveilleusement conçu, mais malheureusement réalisé, et à l'aider à atteindre son plein potentiel. L'entrée possède une magnifique fenêtre en verre moulé translucide. Nous avons ajouté une pièce d'accompagnement du 21e siècle en acier laminé à froid avec un motif ondulé et des lampes à DEL à tonalité réglable. Le thème des vagues est repris dans la peinture in situ sur le mur du salon par Momoko Sudo. L'acier laminé à chaud est utilisé pour faire correspondre deux cheminées existantes et l'écran d'entrée qui les sépare. Le foyer en acier pour le foyer de la salle familiale s'élève jusqu'à l'aile de la buanderie et de la chambre d'amis de la maison. Tout le placage de bois de la cuisine et de la salle familiale est fait d'eucalyptus récupéré et abattu au Presidio de San Francisco.

El proyecto es una renovación y una adición a una casa unifamiliar existente en la ladera de una colina a mediados de siglo. El desafío se centró en tomar un hogar maravillosamente concebido, pero deplorablemente realizado y ayudarlo a aprovechar todo su potencial. La entrada tiene una maravillosa ventana translúcida de vidrio fundido. Añadimos una pieza complementaria del siglo XXI hecha de acero laminado en frío con un patrón de olas con luces LED de tonalidad ajustable. El tema de las olas se refleja en la pintura *in situ* en la pared de la sala de estar de Momoko Sudo. El acero laminado en caliente se utiliza para combinar dos chimeneas existentes y la pantalla de entrada que las separa. La chimenea de acero para la chimenea de la habitación familiar da paso a la lavandería y al ala de la habitación de invitados de la casa. Toda la chapa de madera de los armarios de la cocina y la sala de estar está hecha de eucalipto recuperado talado en el Presidio de San Francisco.

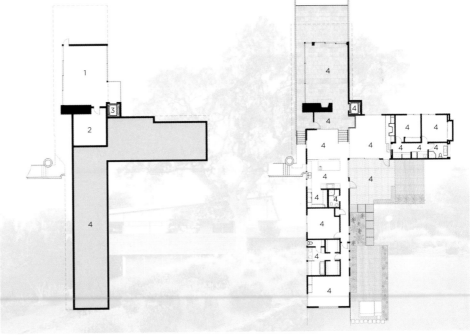

Basement floor plan

Main floor plan

 0 8 16 ft N

1. Carport
2. Mechanical room
3. Elevator
4. Crawl space
5. Entry

6. Living room
7. Dining room
8. Kitchen
9. Pantry
10. Bathroom

11. Master bathroom
12. Master bedroom
13. Bedroom
14. Family room
15. Laundry room

16. Storage
17. Deck
18. Backyard

The project is a renovation and addition to an existing single-family home. The house is perched on a hillside, marking the interface between a redwood forest and a deciduous grove and meadow. The original mid-century home was laid out in an "L" plan around a central terrace facing a monumental lone redwood tree. The buildable area left for an addition and a pool was a narrow triangular shape bisected by an unbuildable steep slope. Our client is a true renaissance man: a designer, software engineer, product designer, and playwright. He loves the site and the choreography of moving through it. A love for the essence of all things Japanese directs his design aesthetic. Our shared brief was to create a home that added the necessary program and accentuated the feeling of being perched in the trees.

Das Projekt ist eine Renovierung und Ergänzung eines bestehenden Einfamilienhauses. Das Haus liegt auf einem Hügel und markiert die Schnittstelle zwischen einem Mammutwald, einem Laubwald und einer Wiese. Das ursprüngliche Haus aus der Mitte des Jahrhunderts wurde in einem „L"-Plan um eine zentrale Terrasse herum angelegt, die auf einen monumentalen, einsamen Mammutbaum zeigt. Die bebaubare Fläche, die für einen Anbau und einen Pool zur Verfügung stand, war eine schmale dreieckige Form, die von einem nicht baubaren Steilhang halbiert wurde. Unser Kunde ist ein wahrer Mann der Renaissance: ein Designer, Softwareentwickler, Produktdesigner und Dramatiker. Er liebt den Ort und die Choreographie, sich durch ihn zu bewegen. Die Liebe zur Essenz aller Dinge des Japanischen lenkt seine Designästhetik. Unser gemeinsames Ziel war es, ein Zuhause zu schaffen, das das notwendige Programm hinzufügt und das Gefühl hervorruft, in den Bäumen zu sitzen.

Le projet consiste en une rénovation et un ajout à une maison unifamiliale existante. La maison est perchée sur un flanc de colline, marquant l'interface entre une forêt de séquoias et une forêt de feuillus et de prairies. La maison d'origine du milieu du siècle a été aménagée en « L » autour d'une terrasse centrale face à un séquoia solitaire et monumental. La zone constructible laissée pour un agrandissement et une piscine était une forme triangulaire étroite coupée en deux par une pente abrupte non constructible. Notre client est un véritable homme de la renaissance : un concepteur, un ingénieur logiciel, un concepteur de produits et un dramaturge. Il adore le site et la chorégraphie de se déplacer à travers lui. L'amour de l'essence de tout ce qui est japonais dirige l'esthétique de son design. Notre mission commune était de créer une maison qui ajoutait le programme nécessaire et accentuait le sentiment d'être perché dans les arbres.

El proyecto es una renovación y una adición a una casa unifamiliar existente. La casa está encaramada en una ladera, marcando el punto de contacto entre un bosque de secuoyas y una arboleda y pradera de hoja caduca. La casa original de mediados de siglo estaba dispuesta en forma de "L" alrededor de una terraza central frente a una monumental y solitaria secuoya. El área edificable dejada para una adición y una piscina era una forma triangular estrecha dividida por una pendiente empinada no edificable. Nuestro cliente es un verdadero hombre renacentista: diseñador, ingeniero de software, diseñador de productos y dramaturgo. Le encanta el sitio y la coreografía de moverse a través de él. El amor por la esencia de todas las cosas japonesas dirige su estética de diseño. Nuestro objetivo común era crear una casa que añadiera el programa necesario y acentuara la sensación de estar encaramado en los árboles.

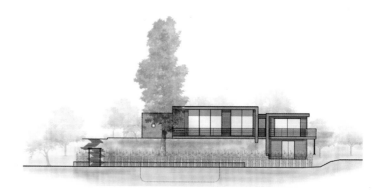

East elevation

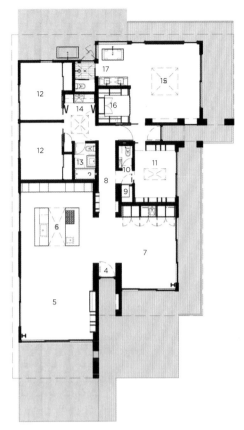

Main floor plan

Lower floor plan

0   30 ft   N

1. Media room
2. Mechanical room
3. Crawl space
4. Entry
5. Family room
6. Kitchen
7. Dining room
8. Hall
9. Pantry
10. Powder room
11. Office
12. Bedroom
13. Bathroom
14. Laundry room
15. Master bedroom
16. Master closet
17. Master bathroom

The Cow Hollow Residence consists of a remodel and small addition to the existing two-story, single-family residence originally built in 1917. The original owners, P.J. Martin Estates, hired architect Elizabeth Austin—one of the Bay Area's first female architects—to design the home. Our project consisted of a complete interior remodel, including the conversion of the existing crawl space into habitable square footage, and additions at the first and second levels. The finished design not only maintained the historic facade and materials but also created a modern, open household. This project displays elements of the First Bay Tradition, a Bay Area adaption of the East Coast Shingle style. This is shown through the wood shingle siding, brick chimney, asymmetrical facades, varied eave lines, and numerous roof gables.

Die Cow Hollow Residence besteht aus einem Umbau und einer kleinen Erweiterung eines bestehenden zweistöckigen Einfamilienhauses, das ursprünglich 1917 erbaut worden war. Die ursprüngliche Eigentümerin, P.J. Martin Estates, beauftragte die Architektin Elizabeth Austin – eine der ersten weiblichen Architekten der Bay Area – mit der Gestaltung des Hauses. Unser Projekt bestand aus einem kompletten Innenausbau, einschließlich der Umwandlung der vorhandenen Niedrigflächen in bewohnbare Quadratmeter und Ergänzungen auf der ersten und zweiten Ebene. Das fertige Design bewahrte nicht nur die historische Fassade und die Materialien, sondern schuf auch einen modernen, offenen Haushalt. Dieses Projekt zeigt Elemente der First Bay Tradition, einer Anpassung der Bay Area an den East Coast Shingle Stil. Dies zeigt sich an der Holzschindelverkleidung, dem gemauerten Schornstein, den asymmetrischen Fassaden, den unterschiedlichen Traufenlinien und den zahlreichen Dachgiebeln.

La résidence Cow Hollow consiste en une rénovation et un petit ajout à la résidence unifamiliale existante de deux étages, construite en 1917. Les premiers propriétaires, P.J. Martin Estates, ont engagé l'architecte Elizabeth Austin, l'une des premières femmes architectes de la région de la Baie, pour concevoir la maison. Notre projet consistait en un réaménagement intérieur complet, incluant la conversion du vide sanitaire existant en superficie habitable, ainsi que des ajouts aux premier et deuxième niveaux. Le design fini n'a pas seulement préservé la façade et les matériaux historiques, mais a également créé une maison moderne et ouverte. Ce projet présente des éléments de la First Bay Tradition, une adaptation de la région de la baie du style East Coast Shingle. Le revêtement de bardeaux de bois, la cheminée en brique, les façades asymétriques, les lignes d'avant-toit variées et les nombreux pignons de toit en témoignent.

La residencia Cow Hollow Residence consiste en una remodelación y una pequeña adición a la residencia unifamiliar existente de dos pisos, construida originalmente en 1917. Los propietarios originales, P.J. Martin Estates, contrataron a la arquitecta Elizabeth Austin —una de las primeras arquitectas del área de la Bahía— para diseñar la casa. Nuestro proyecto consistió en una remodelación interior completa, incluyendo un semisótano existente en metros cuadrados habitables, y adiciones en el primer y segundo nivel. El diseño acabado no solo mantuvo la fachada histórica y los materiales, sino que también creó un hogar moderno y abierto. Este proyecto muestra elementos de la First Bay Tradition, una adaptación del estilo East Coast Shingle del área de la Bahía. Esto se muestra a través del revestimiento de tejas de madera, chimenea de ladrillo, fachadas asimétricas, líneas de aleros variadas y numerosos hastiales de tejado.

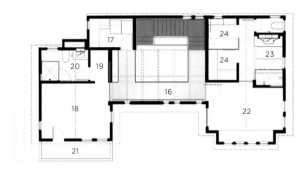

Upper floor plan

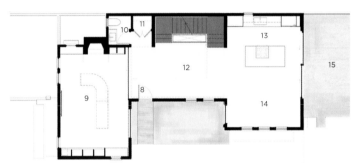

Main floor plan

Basement floor plan

0   30 ft   N⊕

1. Driveway   9. Home Office   17. Laundry room
2. Garage   10. Powder room   18. Guest bedroom
3. Powder room   11. Closet   19. Closet
4. Mech./Storage   12. Dining atrium   20. Guest bathroom
5. Server room   13. Kitchen   21. Balcony
6. Storage   14. Living room   22. Master bedroom
7. Media room   15. Patio   23. Master bathroom
8. Entry   16. Walkway   24. Master closet

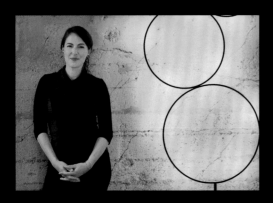

MARTINE PAQUIN
DESIGN

Martine Paquin Design is an award-winning firm established in 2009 in San Francisco. Our interiors are designed to elevate architecture by creating beautiful spaces aligned with the true nature of people who inhabit them. We are a Certified Green Business offering high-level design services with a keen eye for aesthetic and a commitment to promoting healthy environments and sustainable concepts. Born and raised in Montreal, the flair of Martine's French heritage is evident in her design process. She leads a team comprised of international staff with strong creative skills, technical knowledge, and critical thinking. Clients who value quality design will have an advocate they can trust to make the best decision when creating timeless interior spaces.

Martine Paquin Design ist ein preisgekröntes Unternehmen, das 2009 in San Francisco gegründet wurde. Unsere Innenräume sind so konzipiert, dass sie die Architektur hervorheben, indem sie schöne Räume schaffen, die auf die wahre Natur der Menschen ausgerichtet sind, die sie bewohnen. Wir sind ein zertifiziertes Green Business, das hochwertige Design-Dienstleistungen mit einem scharfen Blick für Ästhetik und dem Engagement für gesunde Umwelt und nachhaltige Konzepte anbietet. Geboren und aufgewachsen in Montreal, zeigt sich das Flair von Martines französischem Erbe in ihrem Gestaltungsprozess. Sie leitet ein Team aus internationalen Mitarbeitern mit ausgeprägten kreativen Fähigkeiten, technischem Wissen und kritischem Denken. Kunden, die Wert auf hochwertiges Design legen, haben hier einen Anwalt, dem sie vertrauen können, um die beste Entscheidung bei der Schaffung zeitloser Innenräume zu treffen.

Martine Paquin Design est une firme primée fondée en 2009 à San Francisco. Nos intérieurs sont conçus pour rehausser l'architecture en créant de beaux espaces en harmonie avec la vraie nature des gens qui les habitent. Nous sommes une Entreprise Verte Certifiée offrant des services de design de haut niveau avec un sens aigu de l'esthétique et un engagement à promouvoir des environnements sains et des concepts durables. Née et élevée à Montréal, le flair de l'héritage français de Martine est évident dans son processus de création. Elle dirige une équipe composée d'employés internationaux possédant de solides compétences créatives, des connaissances techniques et une pensée critique. Les clients qui accordent de l'importance à un design de qualité auront un avocat en qui ils peuvent avoir confiance pour prendre la meilleure décision lors de la création d'espaces intérieurs intemporels.

Martine Paquin Design es una empresa galardonada establecida en 2009 en San Francisco. Nuestros interiores están diseñados para elevar la arquitectura creando hermosos espacios alineados con la verdadera naturaleza de las personas que los habitan. Somos una empresa ecológica certificada que ofrece servicios de diseño de alto nivel con una gran visión estética y un compromiso con la promoción de entornos saludables y conceptos sostenibles. Nacida y criada en Montreal, el encanto de la herencia francesa de Martine es evidente en su proceso de diseño. Dirige un equipo compuesto por personal internacional con fuertes habilidades creativas, conocimientos técnicos y pensamiento crítico. Los clientes que valoran el diseño de calidad tendrán un abogado en quien confiar para tomar la mejor decisión al crear espacios interiores atemporales.

Nestled into a hillside in the Martis Camp development near Lake Tahoe, this mountain home offers sweeping views and a feeling of seclusion within nature. The design is decidedly minimal with warm touches and low maintenance materials. Wood floors and ceilings invite coziness while skylights maximize natural light. The great room boasts a window wall connecting to outdoor gathering space, effortlessly bringing the beauty of the surrounding forest indoors. Whimsically modern light fixtures are clustered in communal spaces to encourage conversation. The materials are durable, sustainable, and the lighting is high-efficiency. The story of this home is warm from start to finish – it was a pleasure to design and bring to life.

Eingebettet in einen Hang in der Martis-Camp-Siedlung in der Nähe des Lake Tahoe, bietet dieses Berghaus einen weiten Blick und ein Gefühl der Abgeschiedenheit in der Natur. Das Design ist ausgesprochen minimalistisch, mit warmen Akzenten und pflegeleichten Materialien. Holzböden und -decken vermitteln Behaglichkeit, während Oberlichter das natürliche Licht maximieren. Der große Raum verfügt über eine Fensterwand, die mit dem Außenbereich verbunden ist und die Schönheit des umgebenden Waldes mühelos in den Innenraum bringt. Launisch moderne Leuchten sind konversationsfördernd in Gemeinschaftsräumen zusammengefasst. Die Materialien sind langlebig, nachhaltig und die Beleuchtung ist hocheffizient. Die Geschichte dieses Hauses ist von Anfang bis Ende warm – es war ein Vergnügen, es zu gestalten und zum Leben zu erwecken.

Nichée à flanc de colline dans le développement du camp Martis près du lac Tahoe, cette maison de montagne offre une vue imprenable et un sentiment d'isolement dans la nature. Le design est résolument minimal avec des touches chaudes et des matériaux nécessitant peu d'entretien. Les planchers et les plafonds en bois invitent au confort, tandis que les puits de lumière maximisent la lumière naturelle. La grande salle est dotée d'un mur-fenêtre relié à un espace de rassemblement extérieur, ce qui permet de profiter sans effort de la beauté de la forêt environnante à l'intérieur. Les luminaires modernes et fantaisistes sont regroupés dans des espaces communs pour encourager la conversation. Les matériaux sont durables et l'éclairage est très efficace. L'histoire de cette maison est chaleureuse du début à la fin - ce fut un plaisir de la concevoir et de lui donner vie.

Enclavada en una colina en el desarrollo de Martis Camp cerca de Lake Tahoe, esta casa de montaña ofrece vistas impresionantes y una sensación de aislamiento dentro de la naturaleza. El diseño es decididamente minimalista, con toques cálidos y materiales de bajo mantenimiento. Los suelos y techos de madera invitan a la calidez, mientras que los tragaluces maximizan la luz natural. La gran sala cuenta con una pared de ventana que se conecta con un espacio de reunión exterior, que trae la belleza del bosque circundante en el interior. Las luminarias modernas y caprichosas se agrupan en espacios comunes para fomentar la conversación. Los materiales son duraderos, sostenibles y la iluminación es de alta eficiencia. La historia de esta casa es cálida de principio a fin –fue un placer diseñar y dar vida.

In this 5,000 square foot custom home, Martine Paquin Design created a showcase retreat of natural beauty. The residence can be classified as modern alpine architecture, bringing natural surrounding materials with modern textures and forms. Martine Paquin Design envisioned and designed several custom pieces, including the fireplace, cabinetry, casework, and feature walls. Materials, such as wood, stone, metal, and glass, were selected carefully for each area of the house, bringing the outside in. Focusing on the clean lines and size of the structure, Martine Paquin Design chose furniture and lighting that would complement the serenity of the large spaces and exist as sophisticated elements.

In diesem 464 Quadratmeter großen Custom Home schuf Martine Paquin Design ein Paradies voll natürlicher Schönheit. Die Residenz kann als moderne alpine Architektur eingestuft werden, die natürliche Umgebungsmaterialien mit modernen Texturen und Formen bietet. Martine Paquin Design entwarf mehrere Sonderanfertigungen, darunter Kamin, Schrank, Gehäuse und Feature-Wände. Materialien wie Holz, Stein, Metall und Glas wurden für jeden Bereich des Hauses sorgfältig ausgewählt und bringen die Außenseite nach innen. Martine Paquin Design konzentrierte sich auf die klaren Linien und die Größe der Struktur und wählte Möbel und Leuchten, die die Ruhe der großen Räume ergänzen und als anspruchsvolle Elemente existieren.

Dans cette maison sur mesure de 464 mètres carrés, Martine Paquin Design a créé une vitrine d'une beauté naturelle. La résidence peut être classée dans la catégorie de l'architecture alpine moderne, apportant des matériaux naturels environnants avec des textures et des formes modernes. Martine Paquin Design a imaginé et conçu plusieurs pièces sur mesure, y compris la cheminée, les armoires, les coffrets et les murs. Les matériaux, comme le bois, la pierre, le métal et le verre, ont été choisis avec soin pour chaque partie de la maison, en faisant entrer l'extérieur. Mettant l'accent sur les lignes épurées et la taille de la structure, Martine Paquin Design a choisi un mobilier et un éclairage qui s'harmonisent avec la sérénité des grands espaces et qui existent comme éléments sophistiqués.

En esta casa de 464 metros cuadrados, Martine Paquin Design creó un refugio de belleza natural. La residencia se puede clasificar como arquitectura alpina moderna, aportando materiales naturales al entorno con texturas y formas modernas. Martine Paquin Design concibió y diseñó varias piezas a medida, incluyendo la chimenea, los armarios, la carpintería y las paredes decorativas. Los materiales, como madera, piedra, metal y vidrio, se seleccionaron cuidadosamente para cada área de la casa, llevando el exterior hacia adentro. Centrándose en las líneas limpias y el tamaño de la estructura, Martine Paquin Design eligió muebles e iluminación que complementaran la serenidad de los grandes espacios y existieran como elementos sofisticados.

This new construction in Palo Alto expresses the ultimate indoor/outdoor California lifestyle. Creating a connection from the central living space to the backyard, the living room's plaster fireplace relates to the outdoor concrete fire pit through tall glazed doors. The kitchen's focal point is a polished calacatta d'oro marble backsplash that complements the oak cabinets' golden tone. The kitchen windows maximize the entry of natural light and view of the garden. The focal entry closet is cladded with a rich western red cedar, creating warmth and texture to enhance a cozy feeling, while subtly dividing the entrance from the living space. This inviting home received special attention for the selection of quality material and ties to the architectural lines.

Dieses neue Gebäude in Palo Alto steht für den ultimativen kalifornischen Lebensstil im Innen- und Außenbereich. Der Gipskamin des Wohnzimmers, der eine Verbindung vom zentralen Wohnraum zum Hinterhof herstellt, bezieht sich durch hohe verglaste Türen auf die Betonfeuerstelle im Freien. Im Mittelpunkt der Küche steht eine polierte Aufkantung aus Calacatta-d'oro-Marmor, die den Goldton der Eichenschränke ergänzt. Die Küchenfenster maximieren den Eintritt von natürlichem Licht und den Blick auf den Garten. Der fokale Eingangsschrank ist mit westlicher roter Zeder verkleidet, die Wärme und Textur erzeugt, um ein gemütliches Gefühl zu verstärken, während sie den Eingang subtil vom Wohnraum trennt. Dieses einladende Haus erhielt besondere Aufmerksamkeit bei der Auswahl des hochwertigen Materials und der Verbindung zu den architektonischen Linien.

Cette nouvelle construction à Palo Alto exprime le style de vie intérieur/extérieur ultime de la Californie. En créant un lien entre l'espace de vie central et l'arrière-cour, le foyer en plâtre du salon est relié à la fosse à feu extérieure en béton par de hautes portes vitrées. Le point central de la cuisine est un dosseret en marbre calacatta d'oro poli qui complète le ton doré des armoires en chêne. Les fenêtres de la cuisine maximisent l'entrée de la lumière naturelle et la vue sur le jardin. Le placard d'entrée central est recouvert d'un riche cèdre rouge de l'Ouest, ce qui crée de la chaleur et de la texture propageant une atmosphère chaleureuse, tout en divisant subtilement l'entrée de l'espace de vie. Cette maison accueillante a fait l'objet d'une attention particulière pour le choix de matériaux de qualité et les liens avec les lignes architecturales.

Esta nueva construcción en Palo Alto expresa el último estilo de vida de California en interiores y exteriores. La chimenea de yeso de la sala de estar, que crea una conexión entre el espacio central de la vivienda y el patio trasero, se relaciona con la chimenea de hormigón exterior a través de altas puertas acristaladas. El punto central de la cocina es un aplacado de mármol calacatta d'oro pulido que complementa el tono dorado de los armarios de roble. Las ventanas de la cocina maximizan la entrada de luz natural y la vista al jardín. El armario de la entrada está revestido con un rico cedro rojo del oeste, aportando calidez y textura para realzar una sensación acogedora, mientras que divide sutilmente la entrada del la zona de estar. En este acogedor hogar se prestó una atención especial a la selección de materiales de calidad y su vinculación con las líneas arquitectónicas.

ODS
ARCHITECTURE

196
v

200
v

204
v

ATHERTON RESIDENCE

Photography: John Sutton and Philip Liang
Location: Atherton, California
Area: 4,538 Sq. Ft. main house + 1,098 Sq. Ft.
6-car garage including 2-car elevators +
640 Sq. Ft. detached pool house + 700 Sq. Ft.
detached studio + swimming pool
Site Master Planning: ODS Architecture
General Contractor: Exact Builders
Structural Engineering: Gregory Paul Wallace
Structural Engineer
Landscape Architect: Shades of Green
Landscape Architecture

KENTFIELD RESIDENCE

Photography: Paul Dyer and Philip Liang
Location: Kentfield, California
Area: 3,825 Sq. Ft. major remodel, including
225 Sq. Ft. addition + 825 Sq. Ft. garage
Site Master Planning: ODS Architecture
General Contractor: Eden Roc
Structural Engineering: Gregory Paul Wallace
Structural Engineer
Landscape Architect: Pedersen Associates

ORINDA RESIDENCE

Photography: Paul Dyer, Russel Abraham,
and Philip Liang
Location: Kentfield, California
Area: 4,784 Sq. Ft., including a 3-car garage
Site Master Planning: ODS Architecture
General Contractor: JDR Builder
Structural Engineering: Gregory Paul Wallace
Structural Engineer
Landscape Architect: Huettl Landscape
Architecture

ODS Architecture is an architectural design firm that specializes in custom residential homes. We create buildings and spaces for living and working that are simple, efficient, and unique to the owners and their lives. The solution is the coming together of all these elements in a modern, creative way. Services include extensive 3D modeling, planning and building department coordination, color, materials and lighting design, and construction supervision through project completion. With over twenty years of experience, we have developed a system that ensures that design, permit, bid, and construction guides an efficient start to completion process. Our knowledge of materials, fixtures, and space form a result tailored to the owner's exact needs.

ODS Architecture ist ein Architekturbüro, das sich auf individuelle Wohnhäuser spezialisiert hat. Wir schaffen Gebäude und Räume zum Leben und Arbeiten, die einfach, effizient und einzigartig für die Eigentümer und ihr Leben sind. Die Lösung ist das Zusammenkommen all dieser Elemente auf eine moderne, kreative Weise. Die Dienstleistungen umfassen umfangreiche 3D-Modellierung, Planung und Koordination der Bauarbeiten, Farb-, Material- und Lichtdesign sowie die Bauüberwachung bis zur Fertigstellung des Projekts. In über zwanzig Jahren Erfahrung haben wir ein System entwickelt, das sicherstellt, dass Planung, Genehmigung, Angebot und Bau einen effizienten Start bis zur Fertigstellung begleiten. Unsere Kenntnisse über Materialien, Einbauten und Räume schaffen ein Ergebnis, das genau auf die Bedürfnisse des Bauherrn zugeschnitten ist.

ODS Architecture est une firme de conception architecturale qui se spécialise dans la conception de maisons résidentielles sur mesure. Nous créons des bâtiments et des espaces de vie et de travail qui sont simples, efficaces et uniques pour les propriétaires et leurs vies. La solution consiste à réunir tous ces éléments d'une manière moderne et créative. Les services comprennent la modélisation 3D, la planification et la coordination du service de construction, la conception des couleurs, des matériaux et de l'éclairage, ainsi que la supervision de la construction jusqu'à l'achèvement du projet. Avec plus de vingt ans d'expérience, nous avons développé un système qui assure que la conception, les permis, les soumissions et la construction guident un processus efficace du début à la fin. Notre connaissance des matériaux, de l'agencement et de l'espace forme un résultat adapté aux besoins exacts du propriétaire.

ODS Architecture es una firma de arquitectura que se especializa en casas personalizadas. Crean edificios y espacios para vivir y trabajar de concepto simple, eficiente y único para los propietarios y sus estilos de vida. La solución es la unión de todos estos elementos de una manera moderna y creativa. Los servicios incluyen un amplio modelado 3D, planificación y coordinación del departamento de construcción, selección de colores, materiales e iluminación, y supervisión de la construcción hasta la finalización del proyecto. Con más de veinte años de experiencia, han desarrollado un sistema que asegura que el diseño, los permisos, las ofertas y la construcción guíen un proceso eficiente desde el inicio hasta la finalización. Su conocimiento de los materiales, los accesorios y el espacio forman un resultado adaptado a las necesidades exactas del propietario.

Our clients purchased an existing home on a one-acre flag-shaped lot and asked us to design a new dream home for them. Given the rectangular shape of the lot, we angled the house to incoming visitors slightly to more dramatically present itself. Angles and alignments guided the placement of buildings and their layouts to favor visual connections among them as well as between each building and the surrounding landscape. The result is a compound of buildings, where Feng Shui principles were used to optimize circulation, light, and a balance of form and function.

Unsere Kunden kauften ein bestehendes Haus auf einem ein Hektar großen Grundstück und baten uns, ein neues Traumhaus für sie zu entwerfen. Angesichts der rechteckigen Form des Grundstücks haben wir das Haus leicht an die ankommenden Besucher angepasst, um es dramatischer zu präsentieren. Winkel und Ausrichtungen führten die Platzierung von Gebäuden und deren Grundrissen zu visuellen Verbindungen untereinander sowie zwischen jedem Gebäude und der umgebenden Landschaft. Das Ergebnis ist ein Gebäudekomplex, in dem Feng-Shui-Prinzipien zur Optimierung von Durchblutung, Licht und Balance von Form und Funktion eingesetzt wurden.

Nos clients ont acheté une maison existante sur un terrain d'un acre en forme de drapeau et nous ont demandé de concevoir une nouvelle maison de rêve pour eux. Étant donné la forme rectangulaire du terrain, nous avons incliné la maison pour qu'elle s'adresse aux visiteurs entrants légèrement à se présenter de façon plus spectaculaire. Les angles et les alignements ont guidé l'emplacement des bâtiments et leur disposition afin de favoriser les liens visuels entre eux ainsi qu'entre chaque bâtiment et le paysage environnant. Le résultat est un ensemble de bâtiments où les principes du Feng Shui ont été utilisés pour optimiser la circulation, la lumière, et un équilibre de forme et de fonction.

Nuestros clientes compraron una casa en un terreno de un acre con forma de bandera y nos pidieron que diseñáramos una nueva casa de ensueño para ellos. Dada la forma rectangular de la parcela, hemos orientado la casa hacia los visitantes para que cuando entren se presente de forma más espectacular. Los ángulos y alineaciones guiaron la colocación de los edificios y sus disposiciones para favorecer las conexiones visuales entre ellos, así como entre cada edificio y el paisaje circundante. El resultado es un conjunto de edificios, donde los principios del Feng Shui se utilizaron para optimizar la circulación, la luz y el equilibrio de forma y función.

Site plan

1. Kitchen	8. Den	15. Pool house
2. Living area	9. Bathroom	16. Studio
3. Dining area	10. Bedroom	17. Garage
4. Family room	11. Master suite	18. Driveway
5. Powder room	12. Lounge	19. Firepit
6. Foyer	13. Veranda	20. Barbeque
7. Laundry room	14. Pool	

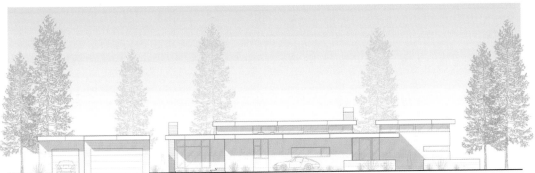

Elevation

The first day we met our clients at their home in Kentfield, we were surprised at how nondescript the front yard was, versus the all-glass backyard with great views of the San Francisco Bay. Wanting to balance the house and open it up, we were asked to raise the ceilings and provide more glass and views to the entry front yard. The house was already large, so adding square footage was not a necessity. It just needed an architectural facelift. The effect of lifting the roof three feet and opening the house views up is dramatic. The house reflects the owners' interests and lifestyle, which involves sports and entertaining. A new concrete patio was designed outside the kitchen for outdoor cooking and dining. Overlooking the pool and the Bay view, it is a perfect setting.

Am ersten Tag, an dem wir unsere Kunden in ihrem Haus in Kentfield trafen, waren wir überrascht, wie unscheinbar der Vorgarten im Gegensatz zum Ganzglas-Hof mit herrlichem Blick auf die San Francisco Bay war. Um das Haus auszugleichen und zu öffnen, wurden wir gebeten, die Decken anzuheben und mehr Glas und Ausblicke auf den Eingangsvorplatz zu bieten. Das Haus war bereits groß, so dass das Hinzufügen von Quadratmetern keine Notwendigkeit war. Es brauchte nur ein architektonisches Facelifting. Der Effekt, wenn man das Dach einen Meter hochhebt und die Aussicht auf das Haus öffnet, ist dramatisch. Das Haus spiegelt die Interessen und den Lebensstil der Eigentümer wider, der Sport und Unterhaltung beinhaltet. Außerhalb der Küche wurde eine neue Betonterrasse für das Kochen und Essen im Freien entworfen. Mit Blick auf den Pool und die Bucht ist es ein perfekter Wohnort.

Le premier jour où nous avons rencontré nos clients chez eux à Kentfield, nous avons été surpris de constater à quel point la cour avant était indescriptible par rapport à la cour arrière entièrement vitrée avec une vue magnifique sur la baie de San Francisco. Souhaitant équilibrer la maison et l'ouvrir, on nous a demandé de surélever les plafonds et de fournir plus de vitres et de vues sur la cour d'entrée. La maison était déjà grande, il n'était donc pas nécessaire d'ajouter de la superficie en mètres carrés. Elle avait juste besoin d'un lifting architectural. L'effet de soulever le toit d'un mètre et d'ouvrir la vue de la maison est dramatique. La maison reflète les intérêts et le style de vie des propriétaires, ce qui implique le sport et le divertissement. Un nouveau patio en béton a été conçu à l'extérieur de la cuisine pour la cuisine et la salle à manger extérieures. Surplombant la piscine et la vue sur la baie, c'est un cadre parfait.

El primer día que nos reunimos con nuestros clientes en su casa en Kentfield, nos sorprendió lo anodino que era el patio delantero, en comparación con el patio trasero totalmente acristalado con excelentes vistas de la bahía de San Francisco. Con el fin de equilibrar la casa y abrirla, se nos pidió que eleváramos los techos y proporcionáramos más vidrio y vistas al patio de entrada. La casa ya era grande, por lo que no era necesario añadir metros cuadrados. Sólo necesitaba una mejora arquitectónica. El efecto de levantar el tejado un metro y abrir las vistas de la casa es espectacular. La casa refleja los intereses de los propietarios y su estilo de vida, que incluye deportes y recibir visitas. Un nuevo patio de hormigón fue diseñado en el exterior de la cocina para cocinar y cenar al aire libre. Con vistas a la piscina y a la bahía, es un lugar perfecto.

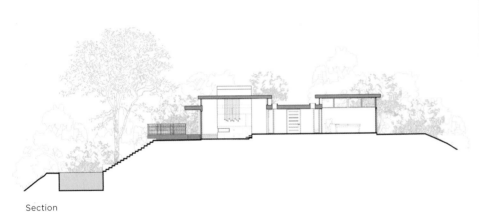

Section

Site plan

1. Garage
2. Mudroom
3. Bathroom
4. Bedroom
5. Kitchen
6. Family room
7. Dining room
8. Living room
9. Foyer
10. Game room
11. Wet bar
12. Gym/bedroom
13. Walk-in-closet
14. Master bathroom
15. Master bedroom
16. Hot tub
17. Pool
18. Outdoor patio
19. Zen garden
20. Bocce court
21. Court

The clients asked us to investigate whether they should purchase an empty lot and whether building a new home would be feasible before completing the sale. After doing some design studies, meeting with Orinda City Planning, Fire, and Building departments, the one-acre lot was purchased. It was the last one available in this planned development in Orinda. Part of our work was to design a new access driveway serving the new 5,000-square-foot, two-story, three-bedroom home. We were also asked to explore roof forms such as butterfly shapes that would maximize the views. It soon became clear that the steep hillside made placing the living space on the second floor the best solution. Every room and the wrap-around decks have spectacular views of the valley.

Die Kunden baten uns zu prüfen, ob sie ein leeres Grundstück kaufen sollten und ob der Entwurf eines neuen Hauses vor Abschluss des Verkaufs möglich sei. Nach einigen Designstudien und einem Treffen mit den Abteilungen Stadtplanung, Feuerwehr und Bauwesen von Orinda wurde das ein Hektar große Grundstück gekauft. Es war das letzte, das für diese geplante Entwicklung in Orinda verfügbar war. Ein Teil unserer Arbeit bestand darin, eine neue Zufahrtsstraße zu entwerfen, die das neue dreistöckige Haus mit drei Schlafzimmern auf einer Fläche von 460 Quadratmetern versorgt. Wir wurden auch gebeten, Dachformen wie Schmetterlingsformen zu erforschen, die die Aussicht maximieren. Schnell wurde klar, dass der steile Hang die Platzierung des Wohnraums im zweiten Stockwerk zur besten Lösung machte. Alle Zimmer und die Wrap-Around-Decks bieten einen spektakulären Blick auf das Tal.

Les clients nous ont demandé de vérifier s'ils devaient acheter un terrain vide et s'il était possible de construire une nouvelle maison avant de conclure la vente. Après avoir fait quelques études de conception, rencontré les services d'urbanisme, d'incendie et de construction d'Orinda, le terrain d'un acre a été acheté. C'était le dernier disponible dans ce projet de développement à Orinda. Une partie de notre travail consistait à concevoir une nouvelle allée d'accès desservant la nouvelle maison de 460 mètres carrés, de deux étages et de trois chambres à coucher. On nous a également demandé d'explorer des formes de toit telles que des formes de papillons qui maximiseraient la vue. Il s'est vite avéré que la pente abrupte de la colline faisait de l'aménagement de l'espace de vie au deuxième étage la meilleure solution. Toutes les chambres et les terrasses panoramiques ont des vues spectaculaires sur la vallée.

Los clientes nos pidieron que investigáramos si debían comprar un terreno vacío y si sería factible construir una casa nueva antes de completar la venta. Después de hacer algunos estudios de diseño, reuniéndose con los departamentos de planificación urbana, bomberos y construcción de Orinda, se compró el terreno de un acre. Fue el último disponible en esta urbanización prevista en Orinda. Parte de nuestro trabajo fue diseñar una nueva entrada de acceso que sirviera a la nueva casa de 460 metros cuadrados, de dos pisos y tres dormitorios. También nos pidieron que exploráramos formas de tejado tales como formas de mariposas que maximizaran las vistas. Enseguida se hizo evidente que la empinada ladera hacía que la mejor solución fuera la colocación del espacio habitable en el segundo piso. Cada habitación y las terrazas envolventes tienen vistas espectaculares del valle.

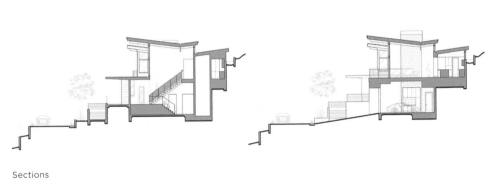

Sections

Elevation

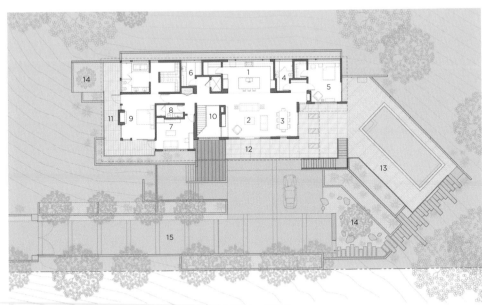

Site plan

1. Kitchen
2. Living area
3. Dining area
4. Powder room
5. Bedroom
6. Laundry room
7. Den/guest bedroom
8. Bathroom
9. Master suite
10. Stairs
11. Master deck
12. Living deck
13. Pool deck
14. Gardens
15. Driveway

N

PAULETT TAGGART
ARCHITECTS

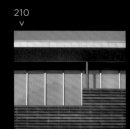

210
v

FOLSOM

Photography: **Jane Lidz**
Location: **San Francisco, California**
Area: **4,920 Sq. Ft. (housing) +
4,150 Sq. Ft. (commercial)**
Landscape Consultant: **Arcadia Landscape**
Structural Engineer: **Endres Ware**
Mechanical Engineer: **Lefler Engineering**

212
v

HUNTERS VIEW 5&6

Photography: **Bruce Damonte**
Location: **San Francisco, California**
Area: **65,780 Sq. Ft.; 53 units**
Density: **55 units/acre**
Client: **Hunters View Associates**
General Contractor: **Cahill/Nibbi Joint Venture**
Landscape Consultant: **GLS Landscape
Architecture**
Structural Engineer: **Structural Design Engineers**
Lighting Consultant: **Auerbach Glasow French**
Electrical Engineer: **FW Associates**
Mechanical Engineer: **Timmons Design Engineers**

216 ·
v

901 FAIRFAX

Photography: **Bruce Damonte, Marion Brenner**
Location: **San Francisco, California**
Area: **92,587 Sq. Ft.; 72 units; 60 units/acre**
Client: **Hunters View Partners LP**
Architects: **Paulett Taggart Architects/David
Baker Architects joint venture**
General Contractor: **Cahill/Nibbi Joint Venture**
Landscape Consultant: **Andrea Cochran
Landscape Architecture**
Structural Engineer: **KPFF Consulting Engineers**
Lighting Consultant: **Horton Lees Brogden
Lighting Design**
Mechanical Engineer: **Emerald City Engineers**

Paulett Taggart Architects is a mission-driven firm that believes good design can make a real difference in people's lives, and that those with less can benefit most from it. The firm, which is best known for designing affordable housing, has been shaping the built environment in San Francisco and the Bay Area since 1986. Its portfolio varies as much in type—from community pools to office interiors and private homes—as it does in scale—from multi-block housing to the renovation of the Golden Gate Park's iconic windmills. The firm's designs emerge from a deep understanding of the Bay Area's unique architecture, topography, and quality of light. Whether or not a given project targets certification, energy efficiency and environmental sensitivity are first concerns at Paulett Taggart Architects.

Paulett Taggart Architects ist ein aufgabenorientiertes Unternehmen, das glaubt, dass gutes Design das Leben der Menschen entscheidend verändern kann und dass diejenigen mit weniger Ressourcen mehr davon profitieren können. Das Studio, bekannt für die Entwicklung erschwinglicher Wohnungen, prägt seit 1986 die gebaute Umgebung von San Francisco und der Bay Area. Seine Arbeiten variieren ebenso stark in seiner Art – von Gemeinschaftspools über Büroeinrichtungen und Privathäuser – wie auch in seiner Größe, vom Multiblockgehäuse bis hin zur Renovierung der legendären Windmühlen des Golden Gate Park. Die Entwürfe des Studio gehen aus einem tiefen Verständnis der einzigartigen Architektur, Topographie und Lichtqualität der Bay Area hervor. Unabhängig davon, ob ein Projekt auf Zertifizierung abzielt, sind Energieeffizienz und Umweltverträglichkeit bei Paulett Taggart Architects ein wichtiges Anliegen.

Paulett Taggart Architects est un bureau axé sur la mission qui croit qu'un bon design peut faire une grande différence dans la vie des gens et que ceux qui ont moins de ressources peuvent en profiter davantage. Le studio, connu pour la conception de logements abordables, façonne l'environnement bâti de San Francisco et dans la région de la baie depuis 1986. Son oeuvre varie autant en termes de type - des piscines communautaires aux intérieurs de bureaux et de maisons privées - qu'en termes d'échelle - des logements multibloc à la rénovation des moulins à vent iconiques du Golden Gate Park. Les conceptions du studio émergent d'une profonde compréhension de l'architecture, de la topographie et de la qualité de la lumière uniques de la région de la baie. Qu'un projet vise la certification ou non, l'efficacité énergétique et la sensibilité environnementale sont des préoccupations majeures chez Paulett Taggart Architects.

Paulett Taggart Architects es una empresa impulsada por una misión que cree que un buen diseño puede marcar una verdadera diferencia en la vida de las personas, y que aquellas con menos recursos pueden beneficiarse más de ello. El estudio, conocido por el diseño de viviendas asequibles, ha estado dando forma al entorno construido de San Francisco y el Área de la Bahía desde 1986. Sus trabajos varían tanto en el tipo —desde piscinas comunitarias a interiores de oficinas y casas privadas— como en la escala —desde bloques de viviendas hasta la renovación de los emblemáticos molinos de viento del Golden Gate Park. Los diseños del estudio surgen de un profundo entendimiento de la arquitectura, topografía y calidad de la luz del Área de la Bahía. Independientemente de si un proyecto se centre o no en la certificación, la eficiencia energética y la sensibilidad medioambiental son las principales inquietudes de Paulett Taggart Architects.

Set within an established residential area of San Francisco's Mission neighborhood on the site of a former commercial building, the Folsom project consists of a new "Kitchen Incubator" and three townhouses around a new landscaped courtyard. The nonprofit organization, La Cocina, formed to help low-income women develop their small cooking/catering businesses into economically viable enterprises. The firm worked with the client to develop the kitchen program, then and evaluate the remainder of the site, ultimately designing three townhouses. The challenge was to design buildings to house this mixed-use program while respecting the scale and texture of the surrounding residential neighborhood and reflecting a contemporary and inherently San Francisco expression.

In einer etablierten Wohngegend des Mission-Viertels von San Francisco auf dem Gelände eines ehemaligen Geschäftshauses das Folsom-Projekt besteht aus einem neuen „Kitchen Incubator" und drei Stadthäusern rund um einen neu gestalteten Innenhof. Die gemeinnützige Organisation La Cocina wurde gegründet, um einkommensschwachen Frauen zu helfen, ihre kleinen Koch- und Cateringunternehmen zu wirtschaftlich rentablen Unternehmen auszubauen. Die Firma arbeitete mit dem Kunden zusammen, um das Küchenprogramm zu entwickeln, dann den Rest des Geländes zu bewerten und schließlich drei Reihenhäuser zu entwerfen. Die Herausforderung bestand darin, Gebäude zu entwerfen, die dieses gemischt genutzte Programm beherbergen, wobei die Größe und Struktur des umgebenden Wohnquartiers respektieren werden sollte und ein zeitgenössischer und inhärenter San Francisco Ausdruck widerzuspiegeln.

Situé dans un quartier résidentiel établi du quartier Mission de San Francisco, sur le site d'un ancien immeuble commercial, le projet Folsom consiste d'un nouveau « incubateur de cuisine » et trois maisons de ville autour d'une nouvelle cour paysagée. L'organisation à but non lucratif, La Cocina, a été créée pour aider les femmes à faibles revenus à transformer leurs petites entreprises de cuisine et de restauration en projets économiquement viables. Le bureau a travaillé avec le client pour élaborer le programme de cuisine, puis pour évaluer le reste du site et finalement fiare construire trois maisons de ville. Le défi consistait à concevoir des bâtiments pour abriter ce programme polyvalent tout en respectant l'échelle et la texture du quartier résidentiel environnant et en reflétant une expression contemporaine et inhérente à San Francisco.

Situado en una zona residencial establecida del barrio de la Misión de San Francisco y en el sitio de un antiguo edificio comercial, el proyecto Folsom consiste en una nueva "Incubadora de Cocina" y tres casas adosadas alrededor de un nuevo patio ajardinado. La organización sin fines de lucro, La Cocina, se formó para ayudar a las mujeres de bajos ingresos a transformar sus pequeños negocios de cocina y *catering* en empresas económicamente viables. El estudio colaboró con el cliente para desarrollar el programa de cocina, luego, evaluar el resto del terreno para finalmente diseñar tres casas adosadas. El desafío fue diseñar edificios para albergar este programa de uso mixto, respetando la escala y la textura del barrio residencial circundante y reflejando una expresión contemporánea e inherente a San Francisco.

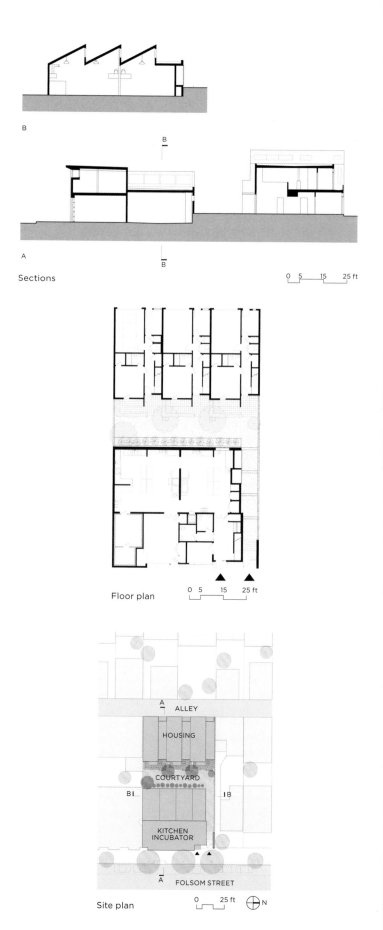

Sections

Floor plan

Site plan

Paulett Taggart Architects designed two blocks with 53 units of new affordable family housing at Hunters View as part of the first phase of San Francisco's ambitious three-phase HOPE SF program—a plan to revitalize the worst of San Francisco's crime-ridden and forgotten low-income neighborhoods. Each of the two blocks has a pair of L-shaped buildings that form continuous street frontages and surround two courtyards, providing shared, secure open space. The buildings also step down along the streets in patterns typical of traditional San Francisco row housing. Each building, designed to look like a grouping of individual houses with private or shared entry stoops, contains stacked multilevel units, which are sited to take advantage of steep grade changes. Hunters View 5&6 is certified LEED for Neighborhood Design, GreenPoint Rated (GPR).

Die Paulett-Taggart-Architekten entwarfen zwei Blöcke mit 53 Einheiten neuer erschwinglicher Familienwohnungen in Hunters View als erste Phase von San Franciscos ehrgeizigem dreiphasigem HOPE SF Programm – einem Plan, um die benachteiligsten unter den kriminellen und vergessenen einkommensschwachen Stadtvierteln San Franciscos wiederzubeleben. Jeder der beiden Blöcke besteht aus einem Paar L-förmiger Gebäude, die durchgehende Straßenfronten bilden und zwei geschützte Innenhöfe umgeben, die einen gemeinsamen, sicheren Freiraum bieten. Die Gebäude treten auch entlang der Straßen in typischen Mustern der traditionellen Reihenhäuser San Franciscos auf. Jedes dieser Gebäude, die so konzipiert sind, dass sie wie Gruppen von Einzelhäusern mit privatem oder gemeinsamem Eingangsbereich aussehen, enthält gestapelte mehrstöckige Einheiten, die so angeordnet sind, dass sie die Vorteile steiler Gefällewechsel nutzen. Hunters View 5&6 ist LEED-zertifiziert für Neighborhood Design, GreenPoint Rated (GPR).

Paulett Taggart Architects a conçu deux blocs de 53 logements familiaux abordables à Hunters View dans le cadre de la première phase de l'ambitieux programme en trois phases de San Francisco HOPE SF - un plan pour revitaliser les quartiers à faibles revenus les plus touchés par la criminalité et oubliés de San Francisco. Chacun des deux blocs a une paire de bâtiments en forme de L qui forment des façades de rue continues et entourent deux cours sécurisées, offrant un espace ouvert partagé et sécurisé. Les bâtiments descendent également le long des rues selon des modèles typiques des maisons en rangée traditionnelles de San Francisco. Chaque bâtiment, conçu pour ressembler à des groupes de maisons individuelles avec des perrons d'entrée privés ou partagés, contient des unités empilées à plusieurs niveaux, qui sont situées de façon à profiter des changements de pente abrupts. Hunters View 5&6 est certifié LEED for Neighborhood Design, GreenPoint Rated (GPR).

Paulett Taggart Architects diseñó dos bloques con 53 unidades de nuevas viviendas familiares asequibles en Hunters View como la primera fase del ambicioso programa de tres fases de San Francisco HOPE SF, un plan para revitalizar los peores barrios de bajos ingresos de San Francisco asolados por el crimen y olvidados. Cada uno de los dos bloques tiene un par de edificios en forma de L que forman fachadas de calle continuas y rodean dos patios, proporcionando un espacio abierto compartido y seguro. Los edificios también bajan a lo largo de las calles en patrones típicos de las viviendas en hilera tradicionales de San Francisco. Cada edificio, diseñado para parecerse a grupos de casas individuales con entradas privadas o compartidas, contiene unidades apiladas en varios niveles, las cuales están ubicadas para aprovechar los cambios de pendiente. Hunters View 5&6 tiene certificación LEED for Neighborhood Design, GreenPoint Rated (GPR).

Site plan

0 5 10 20   50 ft   N

BLOCK 5

BLOCK 6

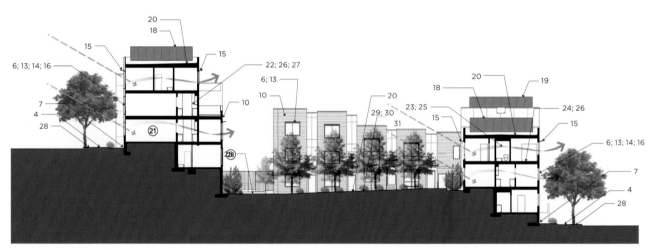

Sustainability section

NEIGBORHOOD DESIGN
1. Urban infill increases density/efficiency land use
2. Reduced surface parking - only street parking
3. Public transit: close vicinity to public bus routes
4. 5' wide sidewalks to encourage pedestrian traffic
5. Accessible central courtyards for community gatherings and children's play
6. Building safety: windows create "eyes on the street" and increase visibility
7. Durable materials deter vandalism and graffiti

BUILDING MATERIALS AND SYSTEMS
8. Concrete elements utilize 35% FLYASH
9. Structural framing utilizes engineered wood beams and headers
10. Durable exterior cladding materials
11. Projected energy efficiency >18% above standard

CONSTRUCTION PRACTICES
12. 89% of construction waste diverted

UNITS
13. Large, operable windows maximize daylighting, views
14. Natural cross ventilation in every unit

15. Sunshades control heat gain
16. Insulated, low-E windows for energy efficiency
17. Central mechanical system provides radiant heat and hot water
18. Rooftop solar thermal with 70% solar fraction reduces energy use for hot water
19. PV system provides energy for 74% of total demand
20. Low albedo roofing
21. Acoustic design minimizes noise and vibration between units
22. Energy Star appliances and light fixtures
23. Low-flow plumbing fixtures
24. Low-emitting, durable floor finishes
25. Moisture-resistant finishes in wet areas
26. Low- and no-VOC finishes for indoor air quality
27. Solid WD/PLYWD casework for durability

LANDSCAPING
28. Permeable landscaping to reduce runoff
29. Hardy, low-water plantings of native plant varieties
30. Minimized turf landscaping
31. High efficiency irrigation
32. Storm water collected and stored for use as needed in tank under adjacent park

Located at the crest of a hill, 901 Fairfax is the social heart of the Hunters View community. Part of the second phase of a comprehensive master plan, the project replaced existing dilapidated public housing with a new mixed-income community, including 72 residences, a child development center, a community room, offices, a lounge, a wellness center, a fitness room, and a recording studio. To break down the building's scale, the structure is set into the hillside and organized into two wings: one a playful composition of ribbon windows, the other a serrated façade reinforcing the curve of Fairfax Avenue. The wings create a public plaza to foster community while providing access to the uses within. The project emphasizes sustainability strategies that benefit residents' health and well-being. The project is certified LEED for Neighborhood Design, LEED Gold.

901 Fairfax liegt auf dem Kamm eines Hügels und ist das soziale Herz der Hunters View Community. Als Teil der zweiten Phase eines umfassenden Masterplans ersetzte das Projekt bestehende baufällige öffentliche Wohnungen durch eine neue Gemeinde mit gemischtem Einkommen, darunter 72 Wohnungen, ein Kinderentwicklungszentrum, ein Gemeinschaftsraum, Büros, eine Lounge, ein Wellnesszentrum, ein Fitnessraum und ein Aufnahmestudio. Um den Maßstab des Gebäudes zu brechen, ist die Struktur in den Hang eingelassen und in zwei Flügel gegliedert: einer eine spielerische Komposition von Bandfenstern, der andere eine gezackte Fassade, die die Kurve der Fairfax Avenue verstärkt. Die Flügel bilden einen öffentlichen Platz, um die Gemeinschaft zu fördern und gleichzeitig den Zugang zu den Nutzräumen im Inneren zu ermöglichen. Das Projekt legt den Schwerpunkt auf Nachhaltigkeitsstrategien, die der Gesundheit und dem Wohlbefinden der Bewohner dienen. Das Projekt ist LEED-zertifiziert für Neighborhood Design, LEED Gold.

Situé au sommet d'une colline, le 901 Fairfax est le cœur social de la communauté de Hunters View. Dans le cadre de la deuxième phase d'un plan directeur global, le projet a remplacé les logements sociaux délabrés existants par une nouvelle communauté à revenus mixtes, comprenant 72 résidences, un centre de développement de l'enfant, une salle communautaire, des bureaux, un salon, un centre de bien-être, une salle de fitness et un studio d'enregistrement. Pour décomposer l'échelle du bâtiment, la structure est intégrée au flanc de la colline et organisée en deux ailes : l'une une composition ludique de fenêtres en ruban, l'autre une façade dentelée renforçant la courbe de l'avenue Fairfax. Les ailes créent une place publique pour favoriser la communauté tout en donnant accès aux usages qui s'y trouvent. Le projet met l'accent sur des stratégies de durabilité qui favorisent la santé et le bien-être des résidents. Le projet est certifié LEED for Neighborhood Design, LEED Gold.

Situado en la cima de una colina, 901 Fairfax es el corazón social de la comunidad de Hunters View. Como parte de la segunda fase de un plan maestro integral, el proyecto reemplazó las viviendas públicas deterioradas existentes por una nueva comunidad de ingresos mixtos, que incluye 72 residencias, un centro de desarrollo infantil, una sala comunitaria, oficinas, un salón, un centro de bienestar, un gimnasio y un estudio de grabación. Para romper la escala del edificio, la estructura está colocada en la ladera y organizada en dos alas: una de ellas es una composición de bandas de ventanas y la otra es una fachada serrada que refuerza la curva de la Avenida Fairfax. Las alas crean una plaza pública para fomentar la comunidad al mismo tiempo que proporcionan acceso a los usos internos. El proyecto hace hincapié en las estrategias de sostenibilidad que benefician la salud y el bienestar de los residentes. El proyecto está certificado LEED para Neighborhood Design, LEED Gold.

LEED GOLD U.S. GREEN BUILDING COUNCIL · LEED GOLD

SITE			WATER				MATERIALS				ENERGY		
1	2	3	4	5	6	7	8	9	10	11	12	13	14
INCREASE DENSITY	BIKE STORAGE	PUBLIC TRANSIT	EFFICIENT IRRIGATION	STORM WATER CONTROL	LOW FLOW FIXTURES	DROUGHT TOLERANT PLANTS	LOW/ NO VOC PAINTS	COOL ROOF	LOW-E GLAZING	RECYCLED MATERIALS	SOLAR THERMAL INSTALLED	HIGH EFFICIENCY EQUIPMENT	ENERGY EFFICIENCY EXCEEDS CODE BY 21%

Ground floor plan

Second floor plan

N

RED DOT STUDIO

DOGPATCH

Photography: Joe Fletcher Photography
Location: San Francisco, California
Original year built: 1890 Water tap Turn-on
Area: 1,780 Sq. Ft. including a 300 Sq. Ft. garage
General Contractor: CHTSF and
Kotas Construction
Structural Engineering: Toft DeNevers and
Lee Structural Engineers
Cabinetry: J. Spix Fine Cabinets
Metal Fabrication: The urban Lab

BANKS

Photography: Joe Fletcher Photography
Location: San Francisco, California
Area: 1,253 Sq. Ft.
General Contractor: Aaron Gordon
Construction
Structural Engineering: Toft DeNevers and
Lee Structural Engineers

HAWKS

Photography: John Lee
Location: San Francisco
Area: 1,944 Sq. Ft.
General Contractor: MT
Development
Structural Engineering:
Cabinetry: Shada Build
Landscape Architect: Fl

www.reddotstudio.com reddotstudio

Karen Curtiss is the Founder of Red Dot Studio. Born and raised on the East Coast of the United States, Karen Curtiss studied in Scotland, and then lived in Hungary, before settling in San Francisco. Her cultural explorations, intellectual pursuits, and participation in competitive fencing eventually led her to architecture and inform her unconventional approach to the practice. Since founding Red Dot Studio in 2005, Karen has championed a design thinking and engagement based on a belief in the profoundness of the prosaic in elevating the human experience and creating spaces imbued with the feeling of good design. What's in a name? Red dots are ubiquitous, from a Bindi to a sold sign for artwork, each one a simple "solution" to complex requirements. Our design approach, akin to the simplicity of a red dot, looks for everyday beauty and meaning, drawing from the Bay Area Tradition, the natural world, and an appreciation of craft.

Karen Curtiss ist die Gründerin des Red Dot Studio. Geboren und aufgewachsen an der Ostküste der Vereinigten Staaten, studierte Karen Curtiss in Schottland und lebte dann in Ungarn, bevor sie sich in San Francisco niederließ. Ihre kulturellen Erkundungen, intellektuellen Bestrebungen und die Teilnahme am Wettkampffechten führten sie schließlich zur Architektur und ermöglichten einen unkonventionellen Zugang zur Praxis. Seit der Gründung des Red Dot Studio im Jahr 2005 setzt sich Karen für ein Design-Denken und -Engagement ein, das auf dem Glauben an die Tiefe des Prosaischen basiert, indem sie die menschliche Erfahrung erhöht und Räume schafft, die mit dem Gefühl von gutem Design erfüllt sind. Was der Name bedeutet? Rote Punkte sind allgegenwärtig, von einem Bindi bis zu einem „Verkauft"-Zeichen für Kunstwerke, jeder einzelne eine einfache „Lösung" für komplexe Anforderungen. Unser Designansatz, der der Einfachheit eines roten Punktes ähnelt, sucht nach alltäglicher Schönheit und Bedeutung und bezieht sich auf die Tradition der Bay Area, die Natur und die Wertschätzung des Handwerks.

Karen Curtiss est la fondatrice de Red Dot Studio. Née et élevée sur la côte est des États-Unis, Karen Curtiss a étudié en Écosse, puis a vécu en Hongrie, avant de s'installer à San Francisco. Ses explorations culturelles, ses recherches intellectuelles et sa participation à des compétitions d'escrime l'ont finalement menée à l'architecture et l'ont amenée à adopter une approche non conventionnelle de la pratique. Depuis la fondation de Red Dot Studio en 2005, Karen s'est fait la championne d'une réflexion et d'un engagement en matière de design fondés sur la croyance en la profondeur de la prosaïque pour élever l'expérience humaine et créer des espaces empreints du sentiment d'un bon design. Qu'y a-t-il dans un nom ? Les points rouges sont omniprésents, d'un Bindi à une enseigne vendue pour une œuvre d'art, chacun étant une « solution » simple à des exigences complexes. Notre approche du design, proche de la simplicité d'un point rouge, recherche la beauté et le sens du quotidien, en s'inspirant de la tradition de la région de la baie, du monde naturel et d'une appréciation de l'artisanat.

Karen Curtiss es la fundadora de Red Dot Studio. Nacida y criada en la costa este de los Estados Unidos, estudió en Escocia y luego vivió en Hungría, antes de establecerse en San Francisco. Sus exploraciones culturales, sus búsquedas intelectuales y su participación en competiciones de esgrima la llevaron finalmente a la arquitectura, accediendo a esta con un enfoque poco convencional. Desde la fundación de Red Dot Studio en 2005, Karen ha defendido un pensamiento claro de diseño y el compromiso basado en la creencia de lo prosaico, en la elevación de la experiencia humana y la creación de espacios imbuidos con la sensación de un buen diseño. ¿Qué hay en un nombre? Los puntos rojos son omnipresentes, desde un Bindi hasta un letrero vendido para obras de arte, cada uno de ellos conforman una simple "solución" a requisitos complejos. El enfoque del diseño, similar a la simplicidad de un punto rojo, busca la belleza y el significado cotidiano, basándose en la tradición del Área de la Bahía de San Francisco, el mundo natural y un reconocimiento por la artesanía.

This historic Pelton Cottage survived the 1906 San Francisco earthquake and fires, only to be almost completely destroyed by a fire in 2013. Into this near blank slate, Red Dot designed a house within a house, creating a two-story volume and light shelf to bounce southern daylight between levels of the residence. This strategy allowed to keep the traditional center room of a railroad Victorian while still maintaining an open view from the front living room to the kitchen at the rear.

Dieses historische Pelton Cottage überlebte das Erdbeben und die Brände von 1906 in San Francisco, wurde aber 2013 durch einen Brand fast vollständig zerstört. In diesen fast leeren Schiefer entwarf Red Dot ein Haus in einem Haus entworfen, das ein zweistöckiges Volumen und ein Lichtbrett schafft, um das südliche Tageslicht zwischen den Ebenen der Residenz zu reflektieren. Diese Strategie ermöglichte es, das traditionelle Zentrum einer viktorianischen Eisenbahn zu erhalten und gleichzeitig einen offenen Blick vom vorderen Wohnzimmer auf die Küche im hinteren Teil zu bewahren.

Cette maisonnette historique Pelton a survécu au tremblement de terre et aux incendies de San Francisco en 1906, avant d'être presque entièrement détruit par un incendie en 2013. Dans cette ardoise presque vierge, Red Dot a conçu une maison à l'intérieur d'une maison, créant un volume de deux étages et une étagère lumineuse pour faire rebondir la lumière du jour du sud entre les niveaux de la résidence. Cette stratégie a permis de conserver la salle centrale traditionnelle d'une maison victorienne tout en conservant une vue dégagée du salon avant vers la cuisine à l'arrière.

Esta histórica casa de campo Pelton sobrevivió al terremoto y a los incendios de 1906 en San Francisco, antes de ser destruida casi por completo por un incendio en 2013. En esta pizarra casi en blanco, Red Dot diseñó una casa dentro de una casa, creando un volumen de dos pisos y un estante de luz para hacer rebotar la luz del día del sur entre los niveles de la residencia. Esta estrategia permitió mantener la tradicional habitación central de una casa victoriana mientras manteníamos una vista abierta desde la sala de estar de la parte delantera hasta la cocina en la parte trasera.

This neighborhood home was owned by one family for four generations. The new owners honored that past, exposing much of the framing and recycling what couldn't be salvaged into the board form for the exterior concrete walls. A southern-facing side yard created a new entry sequence and sun-filled urban oasis.

Dieses Nachbarschaftshaus war vier Generationen lang im Besitz einer Familie. Die neuen Besitzer würdigten diese Vergangenheit und enthüllten einen Großteil der Rahmen und recycelten das, was nicht in die Brettform für die äußeren Betonwände gerettet werden konnte. Ein nach Süden ausgerichteter Seitenhof schuf eine neue Eingangssequenz und eine sonnengefüllte Stadtoase.

Cette maison de quartier appartenait à une famille depuis quatre générations. Les nouveaux propriétaires ont honoré ce passé en exposant une grande partie de l'ossature et en recyclant ce qui ne pouvait pas être récupéré dans le coffrage en planches pour les murs extérieurs en béton. Une cour latérale orientée vers le sud a créé une nouvelle séquence d'entrée et une oasis urbaine ensoleillée.

Esta casa fue propiedad de una familia durante cuatro generaciones. Los nuevos propietarios honraron ese pasado, exponiendo gran parte de la estructura y reciclando lo que no pudo ser recuperado en forma de tablones para las paredes exteriores de hormigón. Un patio lateral orientado al sur creó una nueva secuencia de entrada y un oasis urbano lleno de sol.

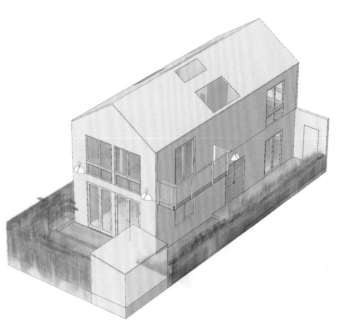

Axonometric view of the house

Perspective section

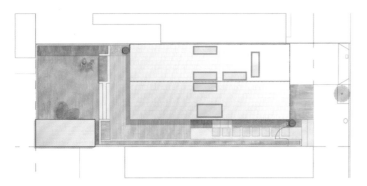

Roof plan

Second floor plan

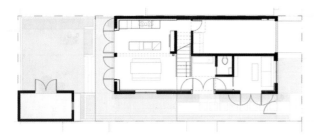

Ground floor plan

N

This traditional rear yard cottage was transformed into an airy, light-filled home with a natural connection to the outdoors on multiple levels. Starting at the entry gate, moving through a drought-tolerant garden to the home's interior, the sequence progresses from an urban setting to a private personal space.

Dieses traditionelle Hinterhofhäuschen wurde in ein luftiges, licht-durchflutetes Haus mit einer natürlichen Verbindung zur Außenwelt auf mehreren Ebenen verwandelt. Vom Eingangstor über einen tro-ckentoleranten Garten bis ins Innere des Hauses geht die Sequenz von einem urbanen Umfeld zu einem privaten persönlichen Raum über.

Ce chalet traditionnel à l'arrière de la cour a été transformé en une maison aérée et lumineuse avec une connexion naturelle à l'extérieur sur plusieurs niveaux. En commençant par le portail d'entrée, en pas-sant par un jardin tolérant à la sécheresse jusqu'à l'intérieur de la mai-son, la séquence passe d'un cadre urbain à un espace personnel privé.

Esta tradicional casa de campo con patio trasero se transformó en un hogar espacioso y luminoso con una conexión natural con el exterior en varios niveles. Desde la puerta de entrada, pasando por un jardín resistente a la sequía hasta el interior de la casa, la secuencia pasa de un entorno urbano a un espacio personal privado.

ROBERT FREAR
ARCHITECTS

🌐 **www.robertfrear.com**   ⊡ **frear.kennedy.group**

Robert Frear Architects is a small, San Francisco-based architectural and design firm that specializes in demanding residential, commercial, furniture, and graphic design projects. Established in 1986, the firm has completed a wide range of projects, from the renovations of landmark residences to the designs of corporate headquarter facilities. Clients include start-up companies and large corporations, business executives, and private homeowners. The firm's design philosophy rests on the belief that meaningful architecture comes from solutions that respond to the needs of a specific place and a particular client. The firm designs well-crafted projects throughout the Bay Area for clientele that expects a detailed level of creativity and service.

Robert Frear Architects ist ein kleines, in San Francisco ansässiges Architektur- und Designbüro, das sich auf anspruchsvolle Wohn-, Geschäfts-, Möbel- und Grafikprojekte spezialisiert hat. Das 1986 gegründete Unternehmen hat eine Vielzahl von Projekten abgeschlossen, von der Renovierung denkmalgeschützter Wohnungen bis hin zur Gestaltung von Einrichtungsgegenständen der Unternehmenszentrale. Zu den Kunden gehören Start-up-Unternehmen und Großkonzerne, Unternehmer und private Hausbesitzer. Die Designphilosophie des Büros basiert auf dem Glauben, dass sinnvolle Architektur aus Lösungen entsteht, die auf die Bedürfnisse eines bestimmten Ortes und eines bestimmten Kunden eingehen. Das Unternehmen entwirft in der gesamten Bay Area gut durchdachte Projekte für Kunden, die ein detailliertes Maß an Kreativität und Service erwarten.

Robert Frear Architects est une petite firme d'architecture et de design basée à San Francisco qui se spécialise dans les projets résidentiels, commerciaux, de mobilier et de design graphique exigeants. Fondée en 1986, l'entreprise a réalisé une vaste gamme de projets, allant de la rénovation de résidences historiques à la conception de sièges sociaux d'entreprises. Nos clients comprennent des entreprises en démarrage et de grandes sociétés, des dirigeants d'entreprise et des propriétaires de maisons privées. La philosophie de conception du cabinet repose sur la croyance que l'architecture significative provient de solutions qui répondent aux besoins d'un lieu spécifique et d'un client particulier. La firme imagine des projets bien conçus dans toute la région de la Baie pour une clientèle qui s'attend à un niveau détaillé de créativité et de service.

Robert Frear Architects es una pequeña firma de arquitectura y diseño con sede en San Francisco que se especializa en proyectos exigentes de diseño residencial, comercial, mobiliario y gráfico. Establecida en 1986, la firma ha llevado a cabo una amplia gama de proyectos, desde la renovación de residencias emblemáticas hasta el diseño de las instalaciones de la sede corporativa. Entre sus clientes se encuentran empresas de nueva creación y grandes corporaciones, ejecutivos de negocios y propietarios de viviendas privadas. La filosofía de diseño de la firma se basa en la creencia de que la arquitectura significativa proviene de soluciones que responden a las necesidades de un lugar específico y de un cliente en particular. La firma diseña proyectos bien hechos en toda el área de la bahía para una clientela que espera un nivel detallado de creatividad y servicio.

On a ten-acre farm in wine country lies the part-time residence of two empty nesters from San Francisco who love to garden. The couple wanted a potting shed near their raised planting beds, which are about 100 feet from the main house. Robert Frear saw an opportunity to design the potting shed as a centerpiece to tie the other structures on the property together. This 9'x18'x10' potting shed can be described as an updated version of a 19th-century farm building with a modern, functional plan. Stone was used for the foundation and low walls, wood-framed with board and batten siding. The angled roof, designed with rainwater collection in mind, is comprised of redwood decking and corrugated steel. Stone pavers and gravel make up the floor of the potting shed for easy cleanup.

Auf einem 4 Hektar großen Bauernhof im Weinland liegt die Teilzeitresidenz zweier Menschen aus San Francisco, deren Kinder aus dem Haus sind und die gerne im Garten arbeiten. Das Paar wollte einen Topfschuppen in der Nähe ihrer erhöhten Pflanzbeete, die etwa 30 Meter vom Haupthaus entfernt liegen. Robert Frear sah die Möglichkeit, den Topfschuppen als Herzstück zu entwerfen, um die anderen Strukturen auf dem Grundstück miteinander zu verbinden. Dieser 3 x 6 x 3 m große Topfschuppen kann als eine aktualisierte Version eines Bauernhauses aus dem 19. Jahrhundert mit einem modernen, funktionalen Plan beschrieben werden. Für das Fundament und die niedrigen Wände wurde Stein verwendet, der mit Brett und Lattenverkleidung holzgerahmt ist. Das abgewinkelte Dach, das unter Berücksichtigung der Regenwassersammlung entworfen wurde, besteht aus Rotholzdielen und Wellblech. Steinpflaster und Kies bilden den Boden des Blumenschuppens für eine einfache Reinigung.

Dans une ferme de 4 hectares au pays du vin se trouve la résidence à temps partiel dún couple avec des enfants plus âgés de San Francisco qui aiment jardiner. Le couple voulait un abri de jardin près de leurs plates-bandes surélevées, qui se trouvent à environ 30 mètres de la maison principale. Robert Frear a vu l'occasion de concevoir l'atelier de rempotage comme une pièce maîtresse pour relier les autres structures de la propriété entre elles. Ce hangar de 3 x 6 x 3 m peut être décrit comme une version mise à jour d'un bâtiment agricole du 19ème siècle avec un plan moderne et fonctionnel. La fondation et les murets étaient en pierre, encadrés de bois avec des planches et un parement de lattes. Le toit en angle, conçu pour recueillir l'eau de pluie, est composé d'une terrasse en séquoia et d'un toit en tôle d'acier ondulée. Des pavés de pierre et du gravier composent le plancher de l'atelier de rempotage pour faciliter le nettoyage.

En una finca de 4 hectáreas en la región vinícola se encuentra la residencia a tiempo parcial de una pareja con hijos ya mayores de San Francisco a quienes les encanta trabajar en el jardín. La pareja quería un cobertizo para sus trabajos de jardinería cerca de sus jardineras elevadas, que están a unos 30 metros de la casa principal. Robert Frear vio la oportunidad de diseñar el cobertizo como una pieza central que sirviera de unión con las otras estructuras de la propiedad. Este cobertizo de 3 x 6 x 3 m puede ser descrito como una versión actualizada de un edificio agrícola del siglo XIX con un plan moderno y funcional. La piedra se utilizó para los cimientos y las paredes bajas, con marco de madera y revestimiento de tablas y listones. El tejado en ángulo, diseñado pensando en la recolección de agua de lluvia, está compuesto por una cubierta de madera roja y acero corrugado. Los adoquines de piedra y la grava forman el suelo del cobertizo para facilitar la limpieza.

South elevation

North elevation

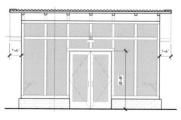

East elevation

This project began with the client's desire to renovate the property to bring it up to par with the landscape. New construction included a workshop, a guesthouse, and a pool house, all nestled in the landscape and framed by a terrace below and an orchard above. The main house was reworked in a refined Northern Italian aesthetic, eliminating the home's original inconsistency of styles. Additionally, the new structures took on vernacular features appropriate to the hillside setting. Materials include integral-color plaster, terra cotta roof tiles, dry-stack stone, bronze, and mahogany. The interior details and color palette of the changing room for the pool house were carefully chosen. Frear designed a custom shelving unit and a teak stool with hand-carved details to match.

Dieses Projekt begann mit dem Wunsch des Bauherrn, die Immobilie zu renovieren und mit der Landschaft in Einklang zu bringen. Der Neubau umfasste eine Werkstatt, ein Gästehaus und ein Poolhaus, die sich alle in die Landschaft einfügen und von einer Terrasse darunter und einem Obstgarten darüber eingerahmt werden. Das Haupthaus wurde in einer raffinierten norditalienischen Ästhetik überarbeitet, wodurch die ursprüngliche Inkonsistenz der Stile des Hauses beseitigt wurde. Darüber hinaus erhielten die neuen Strukturen landestypische Merkmale, die der Hanglage angemessen sind. Zu den Materialien gehören einfarbiger Putz, Terrakotta-Dachziegel, Trockenbaustein, Bronze und Mahagoni. Die Inneneinrichtung und die Farbpalette der Umkleide für das Poolhaus wurden sorgfältig ausgewählt. Frear entwarf ein individuelles Regal und einen Teakhocker mit handgeschnitzten Details.

Ce projet est né de la volonté du client de rénover la propriété pour l'adapter au paysage. La nouvelle construction comprenait un atelier, une maison d'hôtes et un pool house, tous nichés dans le paysage et encadrés par une terrasse en contrebas et un verger au-dessus. La maison principale a été retravaillée dans une esthétique raffinée du nord de l'Italie, éliminant ainsi l'incohérence des styles d'origine de la maison. De plus, les nouvelles structures ont acquis des caractéristiques vernaculaires adaptées à la situation à flanc de colline. Les matériaux comprennent du plâtre monochrome, des tuiles en terre cuite, de la pierre sèche, du bronze et de l'acajou. Les détails intérieurs et la palette de couleurs du vestiaire du pool house ont été soigneusement choisis. Frear a conçu une étagère sur mesure et un tabouret en teck avec des détails sculptés à la main.

Este proyecto comenzó con el deseo del cliente de renovar la propiedad para adaptarla paisaje. La nueva construcción incluía un taller, una casa de huéspedes y una casa de la piscina, todo ello enclavado en el paisaje y enmarcado por una terraza en la parte inferior y un huerto en la parte superior. La casa principal fue reformada con una estética refinada del norte de Italia, eliminando la inconsistencia original de los estilos de la casa. Además, las nuevas estructuras adquirieron características vernáculas adecuadas al entorno de la ladera. Los materiales incluyen yeso de color, tejas de terracota, piedra seca, bronce y caoba. Los detalles interiores y la paleta de colores del vestuario de la casa de la piscina fueron cuidadosamente elegidos. Frear diseñó una estantería personalizada y un taburete de teca con detalles tallados a mano a juego.

"Le Verger" was built in 1925 by Arthur Brown Jr., the architect of the San Francisco City Hall. The house was originally designed as the primary residence of Arthur Brown and his wife. The new owner of the home requested a renovation that would finesse the Beaux-Arts exterior and modify the interior to accommodate a growing family with children. On the interior, a warren of closets, pantries, and servant areas were combined to create larger family spaces. On the exterior, a layer of detail was added to the balconies, chimneys and window openings to complete the classical ensemble. Terraces were created to anchor the mass of the house and to provide usable exterior space. The renovation was punctuated with a new pool house, which drew its vocabulary and palette from the existing house.

„Le Verger" wurde 1925 von Arthur Brown Jr., dem Architekten der San Francisco City Hall, erbaut. Das Haus wurde ursprünglich als Hauptwohnsitz von Arthur Brown und seiner Frau entworfen. Der neue Besitzer des Hauses wünschte eine Renovierung, die die äußere Beaux-Arts-Architektur verfeinern und das Innere an eine wachsende Familie mit Kindern anpassen sollte. Im Inneren wurde ein Labyrinth aus Schränken, Vorratskammern und Servicebereichen zu größeren Familienräumen kombiniert. Außen wurden die Balkone, Schornsteine und Fensteröffnungen mit einer Detailschicht versehen, um das klassische Ensemble zu vervollständigen. Es wurden Terrassen angelegt, um die Masse des Hauses zu verankern und nutzbaren Außenraum zu schaffen. Die Renovierung wurde durch ein neues Poolhaus unterbrochen, das sein Vokabular und seine Palette aus dem bestehenden Haus bezieht.

« Le Verger » a été construit en 1925 par Arthur Brown Jr, l'architecte de l'hôtel de ville de San Francisco. La maison a été conçue à l'origine comme résidence principale d'Arthur Brown et de son épouse. Le nouveau propriétaire de la maison a demandé une rénovation qui finaliserait l'extérieur des Beaux-Arts et modifierait l'intérieur pour accommoder une famille grandissante avec enfants. À l'intérieur, un dédale d'armoires, de garde-manger et d'aires de service a été combiné pour créer de plus grands espaces familiaux. À l'extérieur, une couche de détails a été ajoutée aux balcons, aux cheminées et aux ouvertures des fenêtres pour compléter l'ensemble classique. Des terrasses ont été créées pour ancrer la masse de la maison et offrir un espace extérieur utilisable. La rénovation a été ponctuée d'un nouveau pool house, qui a puisé son vocabulaire et sa palette dans la maison existante.

"Le Verger" fue construido en 1925 por Arthur Brown Jr, el arquitecto del Ayuntamiento de San Francisco. La casa fue originalmente diseñada como la residencia principal de Arthur Brown y su esposa. El nuevo propietario de la casa pidió una renovación que arreglara con sutileza el exterior de Beaux-Arts y modificara el interior para acomodar a una creciente familia con niños. En el interior, una laberito de armarios, despensas y áreas de servicio se combinaron para crear espacios familiares más amplios. En el exterior, una capa de ornamentación fue añadida a los balcones, chimeneas y aberturas de ventanas para completar el conjunto clásico. Se diseñaron terrazas para anclar el volumen de la casa y proporcionar espacio exterior utilizable. La renovación añadió además con una nueva casa de la piscina, que extrajo su vocabulario y paleta de la casa original.

ROBERT NEBOLON
ARCHITECTS

ART GALLERY HOUSE

Photography: Bruce Damonte Photography
Location: Hillsborough, California
Area: 4,880 Sq. Ft.
Architect: Robert Nebolon Architects AIA
Interior Design: Urbanism Designs and
Robert Nebolon Architects AIA
General Contractor: W.B. Elmer & Co
Landscape Architect: Imagine Sonoma
Landscape Architects
Structural Engineering: Arnold Engineering

FLOATING HOUSE

Photography: Matthew Millman Photography
Location: San Francisco, California
Area: 2,030 Sq. Ft.
Architect: Robert Nebolon Architects AIA
Interior Design: Owner and
Robert Nebolon Architects AIA
General Contractor: W.B. Elmer & Co
Structural Engineering: Sarmiento Engineering

BROOKSIDE HOUSE

Photography: Pixton Photography
Location: Oakland, California
Area: 2,571 Sq. Ft.
Architect: Robert Nebolon Architects AIA
Interior Design: Owner and
Robert Nebolon Architects AIA
Landscape Architect: Owner (landscape
designer) and Robert Nebolon Architects AIA
General Contractor: W.B. Elmer & Co
Structural Engineering: Manning
Structural Engineering

The Bay Area is distinctive for its blending of geographical, cultural, technological, and ecological influences in home design. Robert Nebolon Architects has had the pleasure of designing many homes amidst all these influences on many beautiful, unique settings in the Bay Area. When working with our clients, we discover solutions that speak of that particular location and create a character that suits our clients' lifestyle. We closely look at site features such as views, sunlight, and climate, which can enrich the clients' daily lives. These features may celebrate the changing play of sunlight in a room, on a terrace or the wall. Our best designs are the results of much thought and merging of many concepts.

Die Bay Area zeichnet sich durch ihre Mischung aus geografischen, kulturellen, technologischen und ökologischen Einflüssen im Wohndesign aus. Robert Nebolon Architects hatte das Vergnügen, viele Häuser inmitten all dieser Einflüsse an vielen schönen, einzigartigen Orten in der Bay Area zu entwerfen. In der Zusammenarbeit mit unseren Kunden finden wir Lösungen, die von diesem speziellen Standort sprechen und einen Charakter schaffen, der zum Lebensstil unserer Kunden passt. Wir betrachten die Standortmerkmale wie Aussicht, Sonnenlicht und Klima, die das tägliche Leben der Kunden bereichern können. Diese Funktionen können das wechselnde Spiel des Sonnenlichts in einem Raum, auf einer Terrasse oder an der Wand feiern. Unsere besten Entwürfe sind das Ergebnis vieler Überlegungen und der Verschmelzung vieler Konzepte.

La région de la Baie se distingue par son mélange d'influences géographiques, culturelles, technologiques et écologiques dans la conception des maisons. Robert Nebolon Architects a eu le plaisir de concevoir de nombreuses maisons au milieu de toutes ces influences sur de nombreux sites magnifiques et uniques dans la région de la Baie. En travaillant avec nos clients, nous découvrons des solutions qui parlent de cet endroit particulier et créent un caractère qui convient au style de vie de nos clients. Nous examinons de près les caractéristiques du site telles que les vues, la lumière du soleil et le climat, qui peuvent enrichir la vie quotidienne des clients. Ces éléments peuvent célébrer le jeu changeant de la lumière du soleil dans une pièce, sur une terrasse ou sur le mur. Nos meilleures conceptions sont le résultat d'une longue réflexion et de la fusion de nombreux concepts.

El área de la Bahía se distingue por su combinación de influencias geográficas, culturales, tecnológicas y ecológicas en el diseño del hogar. Robert Nebolon Architects ha tenido el placer de diseñar muchas casas en medio de todas estas influencias en muchos lugares hermosos y únicos en el área de la Bahía. Al trabajar con nuestros clientes, descubrimos soluciones que hablan de ese lugar en particular y creamos un carácter que se adapta al estilo de vida de nuestros clientes. Observamos de cerca las características del sitio, como las vistas, la luz solar y el clima, que pueden enriquecer la vida diaria de los clientes. Estas características pueden celebrar el juego cambiante de la luz del sol en una habitación, en una terraza o en la pared. Nuestros mejores diseños son el resultado de mucha reflexión y de la fusión de muchos conceptos.

The house design is based on the East Indian planning principle called Vastu Shastra—which was then modified to adapt to California outdoor living for an "East meets West" fusion. The wooded site is triangular-shaped and is squeezed between the street and a creek. To fit on the site and address Vastu Shastra, the final building form evolved into a three-wing solution; the wings skew at a 15-degree angle to each other thus allowing gardens and daylight to penetrate the house in unexpected ways; the center wing, orientated on the cardinal compass points for excellent Vastu Shastra, has large folding glass doors on two opposite sides which allows the terrace to flow thru the house from south to north. Inside, high light monitors provide natural daylighting for optimal lighting for the modern East Indian art collection.

Der Hausentwurf basiert auf dem ostindischen Planungsprinzip Vastu Shastra, das dann modifiziert wurde, um sich dem kalifornischen Outdoor-Leben anzupassen und eine „East-meets-west"-Fusion durchzuführen. Das bewaldete Gelände ist dreieckig und wird von der Straße und einem Bach eingegrenzt. Um zum Grundstück und dem Vastu Shastra zu passen, entwickelte sich die endgültige Gebäudeform zu einer dreiflügeligen Lösung. Die Flügel sind um 15 Grad geneigt, sodass die Sicht auf die Gärten und das Tageslicht unerwartet ins Haus eindringen können. Der mittlere Flügel, der sich an den Himmelsrichtungen orientiert für exzellentes Vastu Shastra, hat große Glastüren auf zwei gegenüberliegenden Seiten, so dass die Terrasse von Süden nach Norden durch das Haus fließen kann. Im Inneren sorgen High-Light-Monitore mit natürlichem Tageslicht für eine optimale Beleuchtung der modernen ostindischen Kunstsammlung.

La conception de la maison est basée sur le principe de planification des Indes orientales appelé *Vastu Shastra* qui a ensuite été modifié pour s'adapter à la vie en plein air californienne pour une fusion « East meets West ». Le site boisé est de forme triangulaire et est serré entre la rue et un ruisseau. Pour s'adapter au site et s'adresser à Vastu Shastra, la forme finale du bâtiment a évolué vers une solution à trois ailes ; les ailes s'inclinent à un angle de 15 degrés l'une par rapport à l'autre permettant ainsi aux jardins et à la lumière du jour de pénétrer dans la maison de manière inattendue ; l'aile centrale, orientée sur les points cardinaux pour un excellent Vastu Shastra, possède deux grandes portes en verre repliables sur les côtés opposés permettant à la terrasse de traverser la maison du sud au nord. À l'intérieur, des moniteurs à haute luminosité fournissent un éclairage naturel pour un éclairage optimal de la collection d'art moderne des Indes orientales.

El diseño de la casa se basa en el principio de planificación de las Indias Orientales llamado *Vastu Shastra*, que luego fue modificado para adaptarse a la vida al aire libre de California para una fusión de "El Este se encuentra con el Oeste". El terreno boscoso tiene forma triangular y está encajonado entre la calle y un arroyo. Para encajar en el sitio y dirigirse a Vastu Shastra, la forma final del edificio evolucionó en una solución de tres alas; las alas se inclinan en un ángulo de 15 grados entre sí, permitiendo así que los jardines y la luz del día penetren en la casa de forma inesperada; el ala central, orientada en los puntos cardinales de la brújula para un excelente Vastu Shastra, tiene grandes puertas plegables de vidrio en dos lados opuestos que permiten que la terraza fluya a través de la casa de sur a norte. En el interior, los monitores de alta luminosidad proporcionan luz natural para una iluminación óptima de la moderna colección de arte de las Indias Orientales.

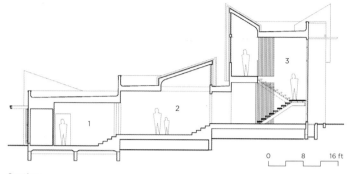

Section

1. Entry Hall
2. Living room
3. Staircase

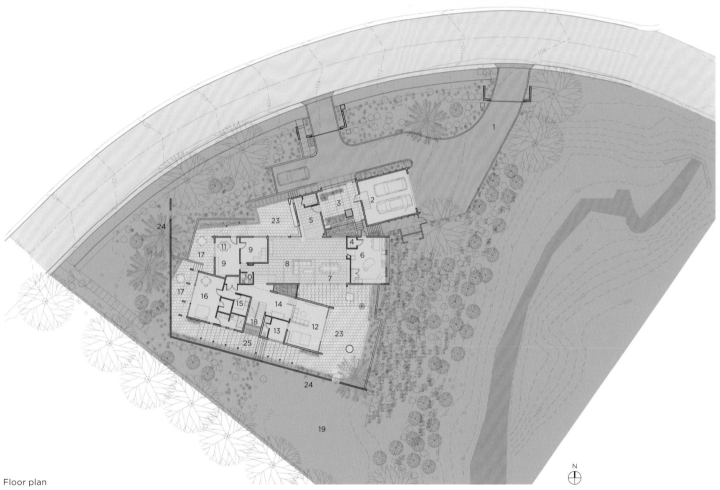

Floor plan

1. Driveway
2. Garage
3. Entry courtyard
4. Puja prayer room
5. Entry hall
6. Kitchen
7. Dining room

8. Living room
9. Office
10. Powder room
11. Den
12. Family room
13. Gym
14. Library

15. Laundry room
16. Guest bedroom
17. Patio
18. Staircase
19. Garden
20. Bedroom
21. Bathroom

22. Play/study
23. Terrace
24. Vastu Shastra
    site wall
25. Walk of Shiva

The clients purchased a water site in a small floating community in San Francisco. The surrounding area was once an industrial area and the final house shape took on that of a saw-toothed factory that once stood nearby. The house is sheathed with durable painted metal siding and roofing reminiscent of modern maritime shipping containers. Large small-paned warehouse-style windows add to the industrial imagery. The clients required a great room on the top floor to take in the views and light. The saw-tooth roof admits natural daylight from above while large windows frame downtown views across the water. Inside, the stair is painted the same orange color as the famous Golden Gate Bridge. Outside, the white forms are reminiscent of sailboats, or crashing waves.

Die Kunden kauften ein Wassergelände in einer kleinen schwimmenden Gemeinde in San Francisco. Die Umgebung war einst ein Industriegebiet und die endgültige Hausform nahm die einer Fabrik an, die einst in der Nähe stand. Das Haus ist mit einem langlebigen lackierten Metallverkleidungsteil und einer Überdachung versehen, die an moderne Seecontainer erinnert. Große, kleinteilige Fenster im Lagerhaus-Stil ergänzen die industrielle Bildsprache. Die Kunden benötigten einen großen Raum im Dachgeschoss, um die Aussicht und das Licht zu genießen. Das Sheddach lässt natürliches Tageslicht von oben herein, während große Fenster den Blick über das Wasser in die Innenstadt freigeben. Im Inneren ist die Treppe im gleichen Orangeton lackiert wie die berühmte Golden Gate Bridge. Draußen erinnern die weißen Formen an Segelboote oder stürzende Wellen.

Les clients ont acheté un site d'eau dans une petite communauté flottante à San Francisco. La zone environnante était autrefois une zone industrielle et la maison a pris la forme finale d'une usine à dents de scie qui se trouvait autrefois à proximité. La maison est recouverte d'un revêtement en métal peint durable et d'une toiture qui rappelle les conteneurs maritimes modernes. De grandes fenêtres à petits carreaux de style entrepôt ajoutent à l'imagerie industrielle. Les clients avaient besoin d'une grande pièce au dernier étage pour profiter de la vue et de la lumière. Le toit en dents de scie laisse entrer la lumière naturelle du jour par le haut, tandis que de grandes fenêtres encadrent les vues du centre-ville sur l'eau. À l'intérieur, l'escalier est peint de la même couleur orange que le célèbre Golden Gate Bridge. À l'extérieur, les formes blanches rappellent les voiliers ou les vagues qui s'écrasent.

Los clientes compraron un terreno en una pequeña comunidad flotante en San Francisco. El área circundante fue una vez un área industrial y la forma final de la casa tomó la forma de una fábrica de dientes de sierra que una vez estuvo cerca. La casa está revestida de metal pintado duradero y un techo que recuerda a los modernos contenedores marítimos. Los grandes ventanales con cuarterones tipo almacén se suman a la imaginería industrial. Los clientes necesitaban una gran sala en el último piso para disfrutar de las vistas y la luz. El techo de dientes de sierra admite la luz natural del día desde arriba, mientras que los grandes ventanales enmarcan las vistas del centro de la ciudad sobre del agua. En el interior, la escalera está pintada del mismo color naranja que el famoso puente Golden Gate. En el exterior, las formas blancas recuerdan a los veleros o a las olas rompientes.

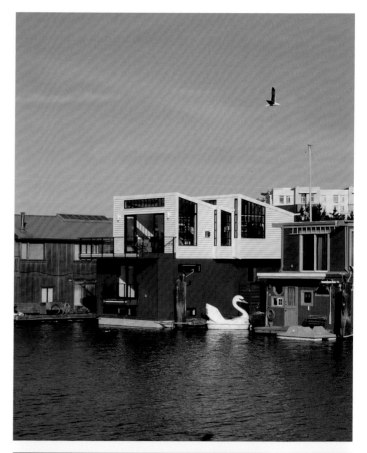

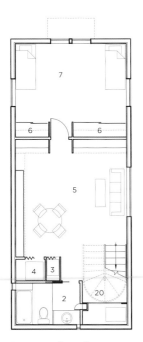

Basement floor plan

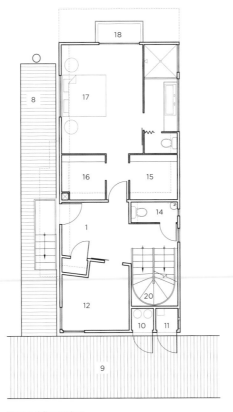

Ground floor plan

Second floor plan

1. Foyer
2. Bathroom
3. Furnace
4. Washer/dryer
5. Family room
6. Closet
7. Bedroom
8. Finger pier
9. Main pier
10. Propane storage
11. Water heater
12. Office
13. Entry
14. Powder room
15. Dressing (his)
16. Dressing (hers)
17. Master bedroom
18. Deck
19. Planter
20. Staircase
21. Kitchen
22. Dining area
23. Living room

In 1989, a fire burned the entire neighborhood including the house that stood on this narrow site of which only two large redwoods survived. The client, a landscape architect, wanted a home that provided an open plan with sunny decks and allowed the largest redwood to coexist with the new home. The house's final form took on that of a slender multi-storied structure with a small footprint well away from the redwood's shallow root system. The large trellis overhead suggests a forest by how the exposed roof structure, supported by tall steel columns acting as steel tree trunks, creates a forest-like canopy over the cantilevered deck below. Inside, the stair rises inside the home with two bridges that span across the stair volume with views to the forest surrounding the home.

1989 zerstörte ein Brand das gesamte Viertel einschließlich des Hauses, das auf dieser engen Stelle stand, wo nur zwei große Mammutbäume überlebten. Der Bauherr, ein Landschaftsarchitekt, wollte ein Haus, das einen offenen Grundriss mit Sonnendecks bietet und die größten Mammutbäume mit dem neuen Haus koexistieren lässt. Die endgültige Form des Hauses nahm die eines schlanken, mehrstöckigen Gebäudes mit kleiner Grundfläche weit weg vom flachen Wurzelsystem des Redwoods an. Das große Überkopf-Spalier deutet auf einen Wald hin, indem die freiliegende Dachkonstruktion, die von hohen Stahlstützen getragen wird, die als Stahlbaumstämme fungieren, ein waldähnliches Vordach über dem freitragenden Deck darunter bildet. Im Inneren des Hauses erhebt sich die Treppe mit zwei Brücken, die sich über das Treppenhausvolumen erstrecken und einen Blick auf den Wald um das Haus herum bieten.

En 1989, un incendie a brûlé tout le quartier, y compris la maison qui se trouvait sur ce site étroit dont seuls deux grands séquoias ont survécu. Le client, un architecte paysagiste, voulait une maison offrant un plan ouvert avec des terrasses ensoleillées et permettant au plus grand séquoia de coexister avec la nouvelle maison. La maison a pris la forme finale d'une structure mince à plusieurs étages avec une faible superficie au sol, bien loin du système racinaire peu profond du séquoia. Le grand treillis au-dessus de la tête suggère une forêt par la façon dont la structure exposée du toit, soutenue par de hautes colonnes d'acier agissant comme des troncs d'arbre en acier, crée une canopée semblable à une forêt au-dessus du pont en porte-à-faux en dessous. À l'intérieur, l'escalier monte à l'intérieur de la maison avec deux ponts qui enjambent le volume de l'escalier avec vue sur la forêt qui entoure la maison.

En 1989, un incendio quemó todo el barrio, incluyendo la casa que estaba en este terreno estrecho en el cual solo sobrevivieron dos grandes secuoyas. El cliente, un arquitecto paisajista, quería una casa que proporcionara un plano abierto con cubiertas soleadas y permitiera que la secuoya más grande coexistiera con la nueva casa. La forma final de la casa tomó la forma de una estructura esbelta de varios pisos con una pequeña huella bien lejos del sistema de raíces poco profundas de la secoya. El gran enrejado en la parte superior sugiere un bosque por la forma en que la estructura expuesta del tejado, sostenida por altas columnas de acero que actúan como troncos de árboles de acero, crea un dosel similar al bosque sobre la cubierta en voladizo que se encuentra debajo. En el interior, la escalera se eleva dentro de la casa con dos puentes que se extienden a través del volumen de la escalera con vistas al bosque que rodea la casa.

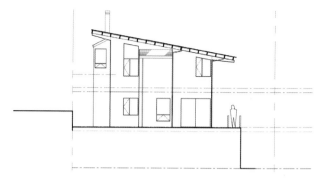

North elevation

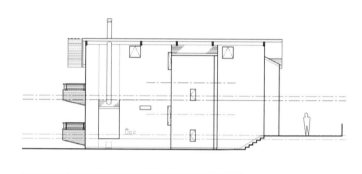

East elevation

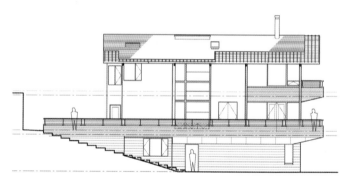

West elevation

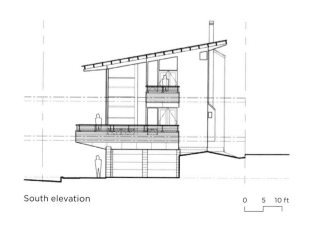

South elevation

0   5   10 ft

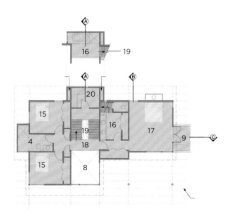

Third floor plan

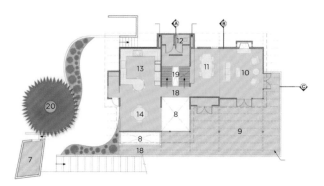

Second floor plan

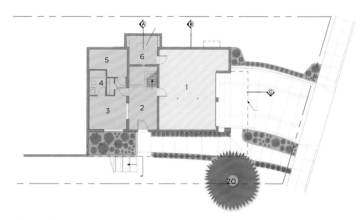

Ground floor plan

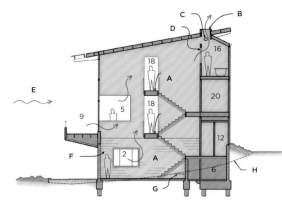

Section A

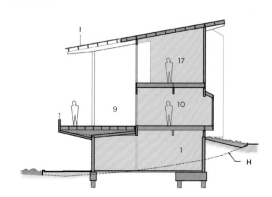

Section B

Section C

1. Garage
2. Foyer
3. Office
4. Bathroom
5. Storage
6. Utility room
7. Old stone ruins
8. Open to below
9. Deck
10. Living area
11. Dining area
12. Powder room
13. Kitchen
14. Family room
15. Bedroom
16. Master bathroom
17. Master bedroom
18. Bridge
19. Staircase
20. Existing tree
21. Laundry

A. Open staircase for natural ventilation
B. Thermostatically operated skylight
C. High return air
D. Operable sliding shoji screens
E. prevailing west breeze
F. Thermal mass: split-face concrete block
G. Low return air
H. Original grade
I. Trellis roof

STUDIO KEITH ANDING
ARCHITECTURE + DESIC

MANZANITA RESIDENCE

Photography: **Michael Hospelt**
Location: **Glen Ellen, California**
Area: **2,100 Sq. Ft.**
General Contractor and Construction
Documents: **FAIRWEATHER modern homes**
Landscape Architect: **Andrea Cochran
Landscape Architecture**
Structural Engineer: **Level Engineering**

SONOMA VINEYARD RESIDENCE

Photography: **Sharon Risedorph**
Location: **Sebastopol, California**
Area: **3,700 Sq. Ft.**
General Contractor: **FAIRWEATHER
modern homes**
Landscape Architect: **Andrea Cochran
Landscape Architecture**
Structural Engineer: **Pivot Structural
Engineering**

WILDLANDS RETREAT

Photography: **Sharon Ri**
Location: **Sebastopol, C**
Area: **2,550 Sq. Ft.**
General Contractor: **FAI
modern homes**
Structural Engineer: **Pivc
Engineering**

⊕ www.studiokeithanding.com ⊙ studiokeithandingarchitectureanddesign

Studio Keith Anding provides architectural design services for intelligently crafted, environmentally responsible, client-driven new homes and residential remodels, as well as small commercial projects. The practice, which began with an equal mix of commercial and residential projects, has evolved to primarily focus on unique modern residences that are intimate, warm, and livable. A deep commitment to clarity of architectural ideas and the logical expression of the inherent nature of materials and construction drives the design practice. Each project is envisioned through the lens of sustainability, addressed not only with environmentally conscious material and technological strategies, but also less obvious holistic decisions such as planning for the future evolution of needs and the longevity of choices.

Studio Keith Anding bietet architektonische Entwürfe für intelligent gestaltete, umweltfreundliche, kundenorientierte Wohnumbauten und den Neubau von Wohnungen sowie für kleine kommerzielle Projekte. Die Praxis, die mit einer gleichmäßigen Mischung aus Geschäfts- und Wohnprojekten begann, hat sich zu einem Schwerpunkt entwickelt, der sich in erster Linie auf einzigartige moderne Wohnräume konzentriert, die intim, warm und wohnlich sind. Ein starkes Engagement für die Klarheit architektonischer Ideen und der logische Ausdruck der Natur von Materialien und Konstruktionen treibt die Entwurfspraxis an. Jedes Projekt wird unter dem Gesichtspunkt der Nachhaltigkeit konzipiert, nicht nur mit umweltbewussten Material- und Technologiestrategien, sondern auch mit weniger offensichtlichen, ganzheitlichen Entscheidungen wie der Planung für die zukünftige Entwicklung der Bedürfnisse und die Langlebigkeit der Entscheidungen.

Studio Keith Anding offre des services de conception architecturale pour des projets de rénovation résidentielle, de construction de nouvelles maisons et de petits projets commerciaux intelligents, respectueux de l'environnement et axés sur le client. La pratique, qui a commencé avec un mélange égal de projets commerciaux et résidentiels, a évolué pour se concentrer principalement sur des résidences modernes uniques qui sont intimes, chaleureuses et agréables à vivre. Un engagement profond à la clarté des idées architecturales et à l'expression logique de la nature inhérente des matériaux et de la construction guide la pratique de la conception. Chaque projet est envisagé sous l'angle de la durabilité, non seulement à l'aide de stratégies matérielles et technologiques soucieuses de l'environnement, mais aussi de décisions holistiques moins évidentes, comme la planification de l'évolution future des besoins et de la longévité des choix.

El estudio Keith Anding provee servicios de diseño arquitectónico para remodelaciones residenciales y construcción de casas nuevas. Trabaja también en pequeños proyectos comerciales, inteligentemente diseñados, ambientalmente responsables y orientados a las necesidades de los clientes. El estudio, que comenzó con una mezcla igual de proyectos comerciales y residenciales, ha evolucionado para enfocarse principalmente en residencias modernas únicas de personalidad íntima, cálida y habitable. Un profundo compromiso con la claridad de las ideas arquitectónicas y la expresión lógica de la naturaleza inherente de los materiales y la construcción impulsa el diseño de este estudio. Cada proyecto se concibe desde el punto de vista de la sostenibilidad, abordado no sólo con material y estrategias tecnológicas conscientes del medio ambiente, sino también con decisiones holísticas menos obvias, como la planificación de la evolución futura de las necesidades y la longevidad de las opciones.

This linear residence stretches out along a ridgeline hidden in an oak and manzanita forest. It opens up to both a park-like grove and expansive views across the valley below. The interior connects with nature through large openings and disappearing glass walls. Circulation is along an open-air walkway lined with repurposed wine barrel wood under a wide, seemingly cantilevered roof. The original program called for a three-bedroom, two-bathroom main home with independent guest accommodation. Early discussions led us to the obvious. A house this large was not required and the program was paired down to a one-bedroom home with a freestanding office and independent guest quarters. Reducing the size of the building had the added benefit of minimizing the environmental impact of the project.

Diese lineare Residenz erstreckt sich entlang eines Reitpfades, der in einem Eichen- und Manzanita-Wald versteckt ist. Sie öffnet sich sowohl zu einem parkähnlichen Hain als auch zu einem weiten Blick über das Tal. Der Innenraum verbindet sich mit der Natur durch große Öffnungen und verschwindende Glaswände. Die Zirkulation erfolgt entlang eines Freiluftganges, der mit umgewandeltem Weinfassholz unter einem breiten, scheinbar freitragenden Dach ausgekleidet ist. Das ursprüngliche Programm sah ein Haupthaus mit drei Schlafzimmern und zwei Badezimmern mit unabhängigen Gästeunterkünften vor. Frühe Diskussionen führten uns zum Offensichtlichen: Ein so großes Haus war nicht erforderlich und das Programm wurde zu einem Ein-Schlafzimmer-Haus mit einem freistehenden Büro und unabhängigen Gästezimmern neukonzipiert. Die Reduzierung der Größe des Gebäudes hatte den zusätzlichen Vorteil, dass die Umweltauswirkungen des Projekts minimiert wurden.

Cette résidence linéaire s'étend le long d'une crête cachée dans une forêt de chênes et de manzanites. Il s'ouvre à la fois sur un bosquet en forme de parc et sur une vue imprenable de la vallée en contrebas. L'intérieur est relié à la nature par de grandes ouvertures et des murs de verre qui disparaissent. La circulation se fait le long d'une allée en plein air bordée d'une barrique de bois recyclé sous un large toit apparemment en porte-à-faux. Le programme original prévoyait une maison principale de trois chambres à coucher et de deux salles de bains avec hébergement indépendant pour les invités. Les premières discussions nous ont menés à l'évidence. Une maison aussi grande n'était pas nécessaire et le programme a été jumelé à une maison d'une chambre à coucher avec un bureau indépendant et des chambres d'invités indépendantes. La réduction de la taille du bâtiment a eu l'avantage supplémentaire de minimiser l'impact environnemental du projet.

Esta residencia lineal se extiende a lo largo de una cordillera escondida en un bosque de robles y manzanos. Se abre a una arboleda parecida a un parque y a amplias vistas del valle en el que se ha construido. El interior se conecta con la naturaleza a través de grandes aberturas y paredes de cristal. La circulación se realiza a lo largo de una pasarela al aire libre revestida de madera de barril de vino reutilizada bajo un techo ancho, aparentemente en voladizo. El programa original preveía una casa de tres dormitorios y dos baños con alojamiento independiente para los huéspedes. Las primeras discusiones llevaron a lo obvio: no era necesario construir una vivienda de dimensiones exageradas y sí ceñirse a un programa más lógico, diseñando una casa de un dormitorio con una oficina independiente y cuartos de huéspedes independientes. La reducción del tamaño del edificio tuvo el beneficio adicional de minimizar el impacto ambiental del proyecto.

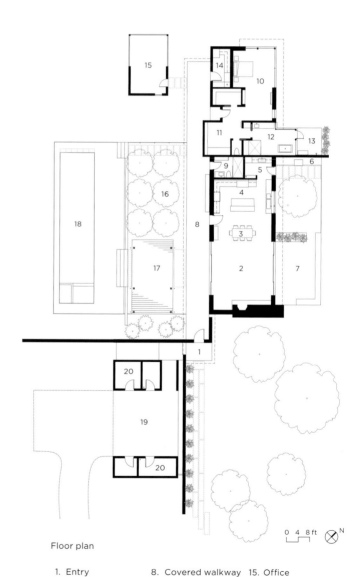

Floor plan

1. Entry
2. Living area
3. Dining area
4. Kitchen
5. Pantry
6. Outdoor kitchen
7. Patio
8. Covered walkway
9. Guest bathroom
10. Master bedroom
11. Dressing
12. Master bathroom
13. Outdoor shower
14. Laundry room
15. Office
16. Gravel Court
17. Trellis
18. Pool
19. Carport
20. Mechanical room

This vineyard residence, located on a knoll near the rim of a small historic farm valley, naturally emerges from the site. The design for a compound of buildings satisfies the desire to engage with the land while reviving the abandoned farm and the owners' resonance with Italian hill towns. Interior and exterior spaces function interchangeably. Some areas of green space open to the sky; others are glass-enclosed or open verandas. These spaces, flowing together effortlessly, are well suited for the owners' frequent community and private vineyard gatherings. Their strong connection—both professionally and personally—to food, wine, and the land informed the program, making the kitchen and dining area the primary public interior spaces in the main building.

Diese Weinbergsresidenz, die auf einer Anhöhe am Rande eines kleinen vernachlässigten Bauerntals liegt, entspringt natürlich aus dem Gelände. Der Entwurf eines rücksichtsvollen Gebäudekomplexes entspricht dem Wunsch, sich mit dem Land zu beschäftigen und gleichzeitig den verlassenen Bauernhof und die Resonanz der Eigentümer auf italienische Hügelstädte wiederzubeleben. Innen- und Außenräume funktionieren austauschbar. Einige Bereiche der Grünfläche sind zum Himmel hin offen, andere sind verglaste oder offene Veranden. Diese Räume, die mühelos zusammenfließen, eignen sich gut für die häufigen Zusammenkünfte der Eigentümer in der Gemeinde und im privaten Weinberg. Ihre starke Verbindung – sowohl beruflich als auch persönlich – zu Essen, Wein und Land prägt das Programm und macht die Küche und den Essbereich zu den wichtigsten Gemeinschaftsräumen im Hauptgebäude.

Cette demeure viticole, située sur un monticule près du bord d'une petite vallée agricole négligée, émerge naturellement du site. La conception d'un ensemble de bâtiments attentionnés satisfait le désir de s'engager avec la terre tout en faisant revivre la ferme abandonnée et la résonance des propriétaires avec les villes italiennes des collines. Les espaces intérieurs et extérieurs sont interchangeables. Certains espaces verts s'ouvrent vers le ciel, d'autres sont des vérandas vitrées ou ouvertes. Ces espaces, qui s'entremêlent sans effort, sont bien adaptés aux fréquents rassemblements communautaires et privés des propriétaires de vignes. Leur lien solide - tant professionnel que personnel - avec la nourriture, le vin et le terrain a inspiré le programme, faisant de la cuisine et de la salle à manger les principaux espaces intérieurs publics du bâtiment principal.

Esta residencia de viñedos, situada en un montículo cerca del borde de un pequeño valle agrícola abandonado, emerge de forma natural. El diseño satisface el deseo de comprometerse con la tierra y revitaliza la granja abandonada y la resonancia de los propietarios con las típicas ciudades italianas de montaña. Los espacios interiores y exteriores funcionan indistintamente. Algunas áreas de espacio verde quedan abiertas al exterior; otras son galerías cerradas con vidrio o abiertas. Estos espacios, que fluyen sin esfuerzo, son ideales para las reuniones de los propietarios. Su fuerte conexión —tanto profesional como personal— con la comida, el vino y la tierra condicionaron el programa, haciendo de la cocina y el comedor los principales espacios públicos interiores del edificio principal.

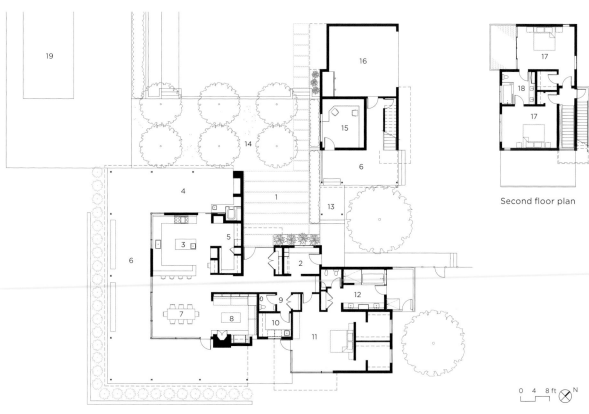

Ground floor plan

Second floor plan

1. Entry court
2. Mudroom
3. Kitchen
4. Outdoor kitchen
5. Pantry
6. Covered porch
7. Dinin area
8. Living area
9. Powder room
10. Laundry room
11. Master bedroom
12. Master bathroom
13. Covered walkway
14. Tree court
15. Office
16. Garage
17. Bedroom
18. Bathroom
19. Pool

0 4 8 ft   N

The site is located above Dry Creek Valley up a dirt road, miles from the nearest power line. It offered an amazing view of wilderness and a prominent ancient oak at the edge of an open grass meadow. The tree spoke to the design of the home, calling for a gathering place. Three rectangular shed-roofed structures forming two wings embrace the tree. Away from the main house is a tiny cabin and deck largely constructed of salvaged and repurposed materials. It was used for camping before the house was built and now is used as overflow art studio space. The independent guest wing at the house and art barn facilitate an Art Residency program that brings three or more artists to live and work on site for several weeks each summer.

Das Grundstück befindet sich oberhalb von Dry Creek Valley auf einem Feldweg, kilometerweit von der nächsten Stromleitung entfernt. Es trug ein bescheidenes, architektonisch unscheinbares Haus und eine markante alte Eiche am Rande einer offenen Graswiese. Der Baum sprach bei der Gestaltung des Hauses mit und rief nach einem Treffpunkt. Drei rechteckige Sheddach-Konstruktionen, die zwei Flügel bilden, umschließen nun den Baum. Abseits des Haupthauses befindet sich eine winzige Hütte und ein Deck, das größtenteils aus erhaltenen und wiederverwendeten Materialien besteht. Es wurde vor dem Bau des Hauses als Campingplatz genutzt und dient heute als Flanierfläche für Künstler. Der unabhängige Gästeflügel im Haus und in der Kunstscheune ermöglicht ein Art Residency-Programm, das drei oder mehr Künstler dazu bringt, jeden Sommer mehrere Wochen lang vor Ort zu leben und zu arbeiten.

Le site est situé au-dessus de Dry Creek Valley, sur une route de terre, à des kilomètres de la ligne électrique la plus proche. Elle abritait une maison modeste, dont l'architecture était indescriptible, et un chêne ancien proéminent au bord d'une prairie herbeuse ouverte. L'arbre parlait de la conception de la maison, appelant à la création d'un lieu de rassemblement. Trois structures rectangulaires coiffées d'un toit en appentis formant deux ailes entourent l'arbre. À l'écart de la maison principale se trouvent une minuscule cabane et un pont en grande partie construits avec des matériaux récupérés et réutilisés. Il a été utilisé pour le camping avant la construction de la maison et est maintenant utilisé comme espace de débordement pour l'usage des artistes. L'aile des invités, indépendante de la maison et de la grange d'art, facilite un programme de résidence d'art qui permet à trois artistes ou plus de vivre et de travailler sur place pendant plusieurs semaines chaque été.

El terreno está ubicado sobre el valle de Dry Creek en un camino de tierra, a kilómetros de la línea eléctrica más cercana. Tenía una casa modesta, que era arquitectónicamente indescriptible, y un roble antiguo prominente al borde de una pradera. El diseño de la casa giró en torno a la figura del árbol, construyendo tres estructuras rectangulares con techo de paja que forman dos alas que lo abrazan. Lejos de la casa principal se ubica una pequeña cabaña construida en gran parte con materiales recuperados y reutilizados. Se utilizó antiguamente como lugar de acampada; ahora es espacio de inspiración artística. La zona de huéspedes independiente de la casa y el granero facilitan un programa de Residencia Artística que aloja a tres o más artistas para vivir y trabajar durante varias semanas cada verano.

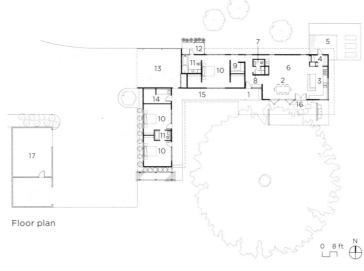

Floor plan

1. Entry
2. Dining area
3. Kitchen
4. Pantry
5. Deck/garden
6. Living area
7. Powder room
8. Coat
9. Office
10. Bedroom
11. Bathroom
12. Shower
13. Carport
14. Laundry/
    mechanical
15. Covered walk
16. Patio/BBQ
17. Art barn

0 8 ft N

STUDIO SARAH WILLMER
ARCHITECTURE

TWO-WAY HOUSE

Photography: Jasper Sanidad
Location: San Francisco, California
Area: Main House Sq. Ft.: 2,600, Second Unit
Sq. Ft.: 800, and share space Sq. Ft.: 1,185.
Design team: Sarah Willmer, Britta Tuschhoff,
Megan Carter, Olya Piskun, and Manon Bertoia
General Contractor: Kasten Builders
Landscape Architect: Inside Out
Structural Engineering: Double-D Engineering

SONOMA RETREAT

Photography: Jasper Sanidad (exterior
photos) and Daniel Bernauer of Henrybuilt
(interior photos)
Location: Healdsburg, California
Area: 2,338 Sq. Ft.
Design team: Sarah Willmer, Britta Tuschhoff,
Megan Carter, and Olya Piskun
General Contractor: Hawkes Construction
Landscape Architect:
Arterra Landscape Architects
Structural Engineering: Vinson Engineering
Civil Engineering: Atterbury & Associates
Cabinetry: Henrybuilt

ATLASSIAN OFFICES

Photography: Jasper Sanidad
Location: San Francisco, California
Area: 42,000 Sq. Ft.
Design team: Sarah Willmer, Doris Guerrero,
Megan Carter, Olya Piskun, and
Josue Munoz-Miramon
General Contractor: Rossi Builders
Structural Engineering:
Pivot Structural Engineering

San Francisco and the Northern California landscape are inextricably linked to the ethos of Studio Sarah Willmer. The work of the studio elegantly integrates a modern townhouse into the vernacular of San Francisco and designs a country retreat in deference to the site and its indigenous California oak trees. The collaborative culture of a tech company is reflected in a fully transparent and open workspace. Three principals guide our design process: the use of structure as a primary expression of space, the control and infusion of natural light, and an environmentally sensitive and simple material palette. Sarah Willmer is Senior Adjunct Professor at California College of the Arts and a lecturer at the University of California, Berkeley.

San Francisco und die nordkalifornische Landschaft sind untrennbar mit dem Ethos des Studio Sarah Willmer verbunden. Die Arbeit des Studios integriert elegant ein modernes Stadthaus in die Eigenart von San Francisco und entwirft einen ländlichen Rückzugsort, der den Platz und seine einheimischen kalifornischen Eichen respektiert. Die kollaborative Kultur eines Technologieunternehmens spiegelt sich in einem völlig transparenten und offenen Arbeitsumfeld wider. Drei Prinzipien leiten unseren Designprozess: die Verwendung von Struktur als primärem Ausdruck des Raumes, die Kontrolle und Infusion von natürlichem Licht und eine umweltfreundliche und einfache Materialpalette. Sarah Willmer ist Senior Adjunct Professor am California College of the Arts und Dozentin an der University of California, Berkeley.

San Francisco et le paysage du nord de la Californie sont inextricablement liés à la philosophie du Studio Sarah Willmer. Le travail de l'atelier intègre élégamment une maison de ville moderne dans la langue vernaculaire de San Francisco et conçoit une retraite champêtre dans le respect du site et de ses chênes de Californie indigènes. La culture de collaboration d'une entreprise de technologie se reflète dans un espace de travail totalement transparent et ouvert. Trois principes guident notre processus de conception : l'utilisation de la structure comme expression primaire de l'espace, le contrôle et l'infusion de la lumière naturelle, et une palette de matériaux simples et respectueux de l'environnement. Sarah Willmer est professeure auxiliaire principale au California College of the Arts et hargée de cours à l'Université de Californie à Berkeley.

San Francisco y el paisaje del norte de California están inextricablemente ligados a la ética del Studio Sarah Willmer. El trabajo del estudio integra elegantemente una casa de pueblo moderna en la lengua vernácula de San Francisco y diseña un retiro en el campo en deferencia al sitio y a sus robles nativos de California. La cultura de colaboración de una empresa tecnológica se refleja en un espacio de trabajo totalmente transparente y abierto. Tres principios guían nuestro proceso de diseño: el uso de la estructura como expresión primaria del espacio, el control y la infusión de la luz natural, y una paleta de materiales simple y sensible al medio ambiente. Sarah Willmer es Profesora Adjunta Senior en el California College of the Arts y es profesora en la Universidad de California, Berkeley.

The Two-way House was conceived around the pairing of the original 1900 Victorian façade and traditional parlor with an open plan and modern two-story backyard addition. A series of interlocking interior spaces, courtyard, and decks create a seamless indoor-outdoor flow. A double-height volume establishes vertical connections shaped by skylights and windows, revealing unexpected views through the residence. Stained white oak and cedar create a soft palette throughout, connecting the floor to the cabinets, the cabinets to the main stair, interior walls to exterior walls, and the historic front to the modern back. The Two-way House bridges recognizable San Francisco architecture to the way today's design-savvy San Franciscans enjoy living in their homes.

Das Zwei-Wege-Haus wurde um die Kombination der ursprünglichen viktorianischen Fassade von 1900 und des traditionellen Salons mit einem offenen Grundriss und einer modernen zweistöckigen Hinterhofzugabe konzipiert. Eine Reihe von ineinandergreifenden Innenräumen, Innenhöfen und Terrassen sorgen für einen reibungslosen Ablauf im Innen- und Außenbereich. Ein doppelhohes Volumen schafft vertikale Verbindungen, die durch Oberlichter und Fenster geformt sind und unerwartete Blicke durch die Residenz freigeben. Gebeizte Weißeiche und Zedernholz bilden eine durchweg weiche Palette, die den Boden mit den Schränken, die Schränke mit der Haupttreppe, die Innenwände mit den Außenwänden und die historische Front mit der modernen Rückseite verbindet. Das Zwei-Wege-Haus verbindet die erkennbare Architektur von San Francisco mit der Art und Weise, wie die heutigen designorientierten San Franciscoer das Leben in ihren Häusern genießen.

La Maison à double sens a été conçue autour de l'association de la façade victorienne d'origine de 1900 et du salon traditionnel avec un plan ouvert et une cour arrière moderne à deux étages. Une série d'espaces intérieurs, de cours et de terrasses imbriqués les uns dans les autres créent un flux intérieur-extérieur continu. Un volume à double hauteur établit des connexions verticales façonnées par des puits de lumière et des fenêtres, révélant des vues inattendues à travers la résidence. Le chêne blanc teinté et le cèdre créent une palette douce qui relie le plancher aux armoires, les armoires à l'escalier principal, les murs intérieurs aux murs extérieurs, et la façade historique à l'arrière moderne. Le Two-way House fait le lien entre l'architecture reconnaissable de San Francisco et la façon dont les franciscains d'aujourd'hui aiment vivre dans leur maison.

La Two-way House fue concebida en torno a la combinación de la fachada victoriana original de 1900 y la tradicional entrada con un plano abierto y un moderno adición de dos plantas en el patio trasero. Una serie de espacios interiores, patios y cubiertas que se entrelazan entre sí crean un flujo sin fisuras entre el interior y el exterior. Un volumen de doble altura establece conexiones verticales formadas por claraboyas y ventanas, revelando vistas inesperadas a través de la residencia. El roble blanco teñido y el cedro crean una paleta suave en todas partes, conectando el suelo a los armarios, los armarios a la escalera principal, las paredes interiores a las paredes exteriores, y la fachada histórica a la parte posterior moderna. La Two-way House une la reconocible arquitectura de San Francisco con la forma en que los San Francisco de hoy en día, conocedores del diseño, disfrutan de vivir en sus hogares.

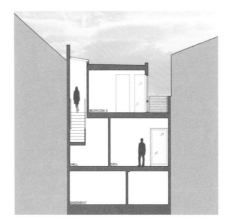

Section

South elevation

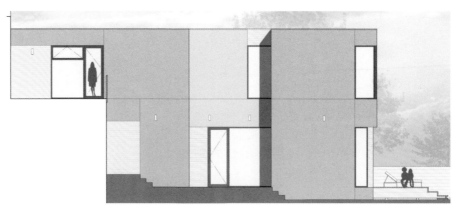

West elevation

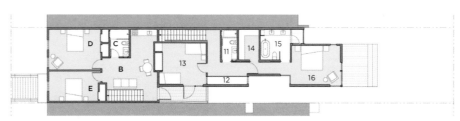

Second floor plan

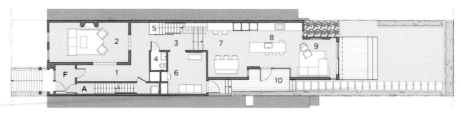

Ground floor plan

Common Area

F. Foyer

Main House

1. Entry hall
2. Parlor
3. Stair hall
4. Powder room
5. Main stair
6. Den/playroom
7. Office/dining
8. Kitchen
9. Family room
10. Courtyard
11. Bathroom 2
12. Open to below
13. Children's bedroom
14. Walk-in-closet
15. Bathroom 1
16. Parents' bedroom

Second Unit

A. Entry hall
B. Open Living
C. Bath
D. Bedroom 1
E. Bedroom 2

Located on a grassy hillside with a seasonal creek and shaded by oak trees, the site for this home is emblematic of Northern California's landscape. The clients requested a minimalist intervention as their escape from San Francisco to enjoy a secluded retreat. The natural landscape gives way to a plateau of decomposed granite and low retaining walls nestling the buildings into the earth. Two buildings, the main house and home office/garage, bend with the contours creating a courtyard that opens to a fruit orchard. Oversized windows frame views of the oak trees while the south deck extends under the oaks for summer shading. Zinc metal siding wraps the exterior while smooth cream stucco line the internal carved spaces at entries and decks.

An einem grasbewachsenen Hang mit saisonalem Bach und im Schatten von Eichen gelegen, ist der Standort dieses Hauses ein Symbol für die Landschaft Nordkaliforniens. Die Klienten forderten eine minimalistische Intervention als Flucht aus San Francisco, um einen abgeschiedenen Rückzugsort zu genießen. Die Naturlandschaft weicht einem Plateau aus zersetztem Granit und niedrigen Stützmauern, die die Gebäude an die Erde schmiegen. Zwei Gebäude, das Haupthaus und das Heimbüro/Garage, biegen sich mit den Konturen zu einem Innenhof, der sich zu einem Obstgarten öffnet. Übergroße Fensterrahmen bieten einen Blick auf die Eichen, während sich das Süddeck unter den Eichen erstreckt, um im Sommer Schatten zu erhalten. Zinkmetall-Siding umhüllt die Außenseite, während glatter, cremefarbener Stuck die Innenräume an Eingängen und Decks auskleidet.

Situé sur une colline herbeuse avec un ruisseau saisonnier et ombragé par des chênes, le site pour cette maison est emblématique du paysage du nord de la Californie. Les clients ont demandé une intervention minimaliste pour s'évader de San Francisco et profiter d'une retraite isolée. Le paysage naturel cède la place à un plateau de granit décomposé et à des murs de soutènement bas nichant les bâtiments dans le sol. Deux bâtiments, la maison principale et le bureau/garage de la maison, se courbent avec les contours créant une cour qui s'ouvre sur un verger. Des fenêtres surdimensionnées encadrent les vues sur les chênes tandis que le pont sud s'étend sous les chênes pour l'ombrage d'été. Un bardage en métal zingué enveloppe l'extérieur tandis qu'un stuc crème lisse tapisse les espaces intérieurs sculptés aux entrées et aux ponts.

Ubicada en una ladera de hierba con un arroyo estacional y a la sombra de los robles, el sitio de esta casa es representativo del paisaje del norte de California. Los clientes solicitaron una intervención minimalista para escapar de San Francisco y disfrutar de un retiro aislado. El paisaje natural da paso a una meseta de granito descompuesto y bajos muros de contención que enclavan los edificios en la tierra. Dos edificios, la casa principal y la oficina/garaje de la casa, se curvan creando un patio que se abre a un huerto de frutas. Las ventanas de gran tamaño enmarcan las vistas de los robles, mientras que la cubierta sur se extiende bajo los robles para dar sombra en verano. El revestimiento metálico de zinc envuelve el exterior mientras que el estuco crema liso recubre los espacios internos en las entradas y en las cubiertas.

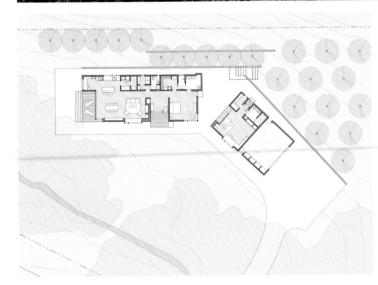

Floor plan

Front elevation

Side elevation

Atlassian is a tech company providing customized software business tools. With offices in Sydney, Amsterdam, and San Francisco, innovation, workplace transparency, and work-life balance are Atlassian's key values. Their first major office space in San Francisco—a casual elegant modernist interior—was a conscious alternative to the dot-com fun house mania found at other tech companies. The workplace, an unexpected oasis offset by its enigmatic warehouse exterior, offers a generous and open space designed to mimic its city analog. Focused around a "Town Square" with amphitheater seating for staff meetings and product launches, the space is egalitarian (no private offices) with transparent conference rooms and varied breakout areas and cafes promoting interaction and innovation.

Atlassian ist ein Technologieunternehmen, das kundenspezifische Software-Business-Werkzeuge anbietet. Mit Büros in Sydney, Amsterdam und San Francisco sind Innovation, Arbeitsplatztransparenz und Work-Life-Balance die wichtigsten Werte von Atlassian. Ihre erste große Bürofläche in San Francisco – ein lässiges, elegantes, modernistisches Interieur – war eine bewusste Alternative zu der Dot-Com-Spaßhaus-Manie anderer Technologieunternehmen. Der Arbeitsplatz, eine unerwartete Oase, die in das rätselhafte Äußere des Lagers eingebettet ist, bietet einen großzügigen und offenen Raum, der das analoge Stadtbild nachahmt. Der Raum, der sich um einen „Stadtplatz" mit Amphitheaterbestuhlung für Mitarbeiterversammlungen und Produkteinführungen dreht, ist egalitär (keine privaten Büros) mit transparenten Konferenzräumen und abwechslungsreichen Breakout-Bereichen sowie Cafés, die Interaktion und Innovation fördern.

Atlassian est une société de technologie qui fournit des outils d'affaires logiciels personnalisés. Avec des bureaux à Sydney, Amsterdam et San Francisco, l'innovation, la transparence sur le lieu de travail et la conciliation travail-vie privée sont les valeurs clés d'Atlassian. Leur premier grand espace de bureau à San Francisco - un intérieur moderniste élégant et décontracté - était une alternative consciente à la manie de la dot-com fun house que l'on trouve dans d'autres entreprises technologiques. Le lieu de travail, oasis inattendue contrebalancée par l'extérieur énigmatique de son entrepôt, offre un espace généreux et ouvert conçu pour imiter l'image de la ville. Centré autour d'une « place de la ville » avec des sièges d'amphithéâtre pour les réunions du personnel et les lancements de produits, l'espace est égalitaire (pas de bureaux privés) avec des salles de conférence transparentes et des espaces de détente et des cafés variés favorisant les interactions et l'innovation.

Atlassian es una empresa de tecnología que proporciona herramientas de negocio de *software* personalizadas. Con oficinas en Sídney, Ámsterdam y San Francisco, la innovación, la transparencia en el lugar de trabajo y el equilibrio entre la vida laboral y personal son los valores clave de Atlassian. Su primer espacio de oficinas importante en San Francisco —un interior modernista, elegante e industrial— fue una alternativa consciente al auge de las empresas ".com" (que recuperaban antiguos edificios industriales) que se encuentra en otras compañías de tecnología. El lugar de trabajo, un oasis inesperado compensado por su enigmático exterior estilo almacén, ofrece un espacio generoso y abierto diseñado para imitar a su análogo de la ciudad. Centrado en torno a una "plaza de la ciudad" con asientos de anfiteatro para reuniones de personal y lanzamiento de productos, el espacio es igualitario (sin oficinas privadas), con salas de conferencias transparentes y variadas áreas de descanso y cafeterías que promueven la interacción y la innovación.

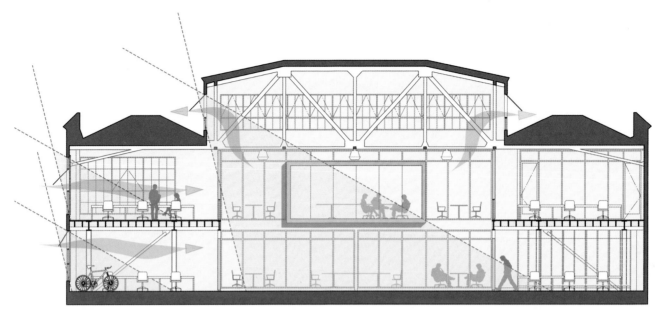

Sustainable strategies diagram

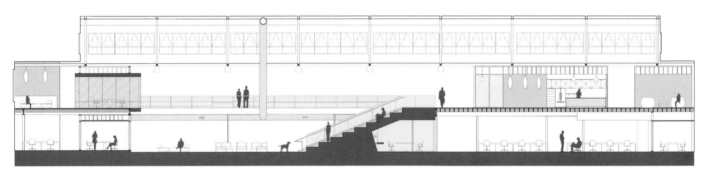

Longitudinal section

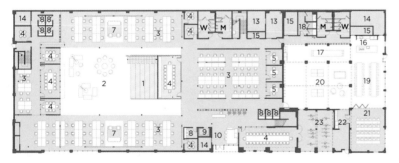

Ground floor plan

Second floor plan

1. Amphitheater
2. Event space/town square
3. Open work area
4. Conference room
5. Flexible office
6. Common lounge
7. Team lounge area/ future workstations
8. Skype booth
9. Elevator
10. Entry
11. Garden retreat
12. 2nd. floor café
13. Server/I.T. room
14. Mechanical room
15. Storage room
16. Main kitchen
17. Sandwich island
18. Coed. showers
19. Dining area
20. Game room
21. Training room
22. Coffee bar
23. Bike storage

STUDIO
VARA

PALO ALTO RESIDENCE

Photography: Matthew Millman Photography
Location: Palo Alto, California
Area: 4,500 Sq. Ft.
General Contractor: Von Clemm Construction
Landscape Contractor: Frank & Grossman
Civil Engineering: Hohbach-Lewin
Structural Engineering: FTF Engineering
Mechanical Engineering:
Monterey Energy Group
Lighting Consultant: Tucci Lighting Design
Audio Visual Consultant: Adaptive Systems
Geotechnical Engineering: Murray Engineers

SOMA LOFT

Photography: Bruce Damonte Photography
Location: San Francisco, California
Area: 1,700 Sq. Ft.
General Contractor: Upscale Construction
Furnishings: Toni Ambus/Design Details
Structural Engineering: Strandberg Engineering
Lighting Consultant: Tucci Lighting Design

MISSION BAY

Photography: Bruce Damonte Photography
Location: San Francisco, California
Area: 182,000 Sq. Ft.
Architect of record: Mithun Solomon
Associate Architect: Studio VARA
General Contractor: Nibbi Brothers
Developer: Tenderloin Neighborhood
Development Corporation
Landscape Architect: Surface Design
Structural Engineer: KPFF Consulting Engineers
MEP Engineering: Engineering 350
Civil Engineer: Urban Design Consulting Engineers
Geotechnical Engineer: Rockridge Geotechnical

Studio VARA is a San Francisco-based design practice driven by a deep commitment to architecture as a material craft and a discipline grounded in ideas. With the city as a reference point and inspiration for our work, we create holistic, well-considered design solutions and human-centered experiences at many scales. We believe that our practice is a design project. We have developed a process-oriented approach that allows design solutions to arise organically from the unique ecology of each project. Clients are engaged throughout the design and construction process in a working environment attuned to their aspirations and infused with ease and clarity. Together, we work side-by-side with our contractors and consultants to foster a truly team-oriented process. From the exterior form to the interior furnishings, this flexible, collaborative design approach builds trust and yields spaces that profoundly shape our clients' lives.

Studio VARA ist ein in San Francisco ansässiges Designbüro, das von einem starken Engagement für Architektur als Materialhandwerk und einer auf Ideen basierenden Disziplin geprägt ist. Mit der Stadt als Bezugspunkt und Inspiration für unsere Arbeit schaffen wir ganzheitliche, durchdachte Designlösungen und menschlich orientierte Erfahrungen auf vielen Ebenen. Wir glauben, dass unsere Praxis ein Designprojekt ist. Wir haben einen prozessorientierten Ansatz entwickelt, der es ermöglicht, Designlösungen organisch aus der einzigartigen Ökologie jedes Projekts entstehen zu lassen. Die Kunden werden während des gesamten Planungs- und Bauprozesses in einer Arbeitsumgebung einbezogen, die auf ihre Wünsche abgestimmt ist und mit Leichtigkeit und Klarheit erfüllt ist. Gemeinsam mit unseren Auftragnehmern und Beratern arbeiten wir daran, einen wirklich teamorientierten Prozess zu fördern. Von der Außenform bis zur Inneneinrichtung schafft dieser flexible, kollaborative Designansatz Vertrauen und Räume, die das Leben unserer Kunden nachhaltig prägen.

Le Studio VARA est un cabinet de design basé à San Francisco, animé par un profond engagement envers l'architecture en tant qu'art des matériaux et une discipline fondée sur les idées. Avec la ville comme point de référence et source d'inspiration pour notre travail, nous créons des solutions de conception holistiques et réfléchies et des expériences centrées sur l'être humain à plusieurs échelles. Nous croyons que notre pratique est un projet de design. Nous avons développé une approche orientée processus qui permet aux solutions de conception de découler organiquement de l'écologie unique de chaque projet. Les clients sont engagés tout au long du processus de conception et de construction dans un environnement de travail à l'écoute de leurs aspirations et infusé avec de la facilité et de la clarté. Ensemble, nous travaillons côte à côte avec nos entrepreneurs et nos consultants pour favoriser un processus véritablement axé sur le travail d'équipe. De la forme extérieure à l'ameublement intérieur, cette approche de conception flexible et collaborative crée la confiance et crée des espaces qui façonnent profondément la vie de nos clients.

Studio VARA es un estudio de diseño con sede en San Francisco impulsado por un profundo compromiso con la arquitectura como material artesanal y una disciplina basada en las ideas. Con la ciudad como punto de referencia e inspiración para nuestro trabajo, creamos soluciones de diseño holísticas y bien pensadas y experiencias centradas en el ser humano a muchas escalas. Creemos que nuestro estudio es un proyecto de diseño. Hemos desarrollado un enfoque orientado al proceso que permite que las soluciones de diseño surjan orgánicamente de la ecología única de cada proyecto. Los clientes están involucrados durante todo el proceso de diseño y construcción en un entorno de trabajo acorde con sus aspiraciones y dotado de facilidad y claridad. Juntos, trabajamos codo con codo con nuestros contratistas y consultores para fomentar un proceso verdaderamente orientado al equipo. Desde la forma exterior hasta el mobiliario interior, este enfoque de diseño flexible y colaborativo crea confianza y produce espacios que dan forma profundamente a las vidas de nuestros clientes.

A young Palo Alto couple with three children desired a modern home with ample room for their family and generous social spaces flowing seamlessly from the inside out. The landscape, architecture, and interiors were handled by Studio VARA to create a cohesive whole that highlights comfort, efficiency, spaciousness, and light. The house was positioned at the outermost corner to preserve the rear yard and the massing was optimized to achieve the maximum allowable interior volume. The various materials—board-formed concrete for the basement, cedar and larch siding for the main level, and dark panelized zinc for the top floor—harmonize to create a cohesive whole, lending a human scale and hand-crafted feel to this modern home.

Ein junges Palo Alto-Paar mit drei Kindern wünschte sich ein modernes Zuhause mit viel Platz und großzügigen Sozialräumen, die nahtlos ineinanderfließen. Die Landschaft, Architektur und Innenräume wurden von Studio VARA bearbeitet, um ein zusammenhängendes Ganzes zu schaffen, das Komfort, Effizienz, Geräumigkeit und Licht hervorhebt. Das Haus wurde an der äußersten Ecke positioniert, um den Hinterhof zu erhalten, und die Masse wurde optimiert, um das maximal zulässige Innenvolumen zu erreichen. Die verschiedenen Materialien – plattenförmiger Beton für das Untergeschoss, Zedern- und Lärchenverkleidung für das Hauptgeschoss und dunkles, paneliertes Zink für das Obergeschoss – harmonieren zu einem kohärenten Ganzen und verleihen diesem modernen Haus eine menschliche Dimension und ein gediegenes Gefühl.

Un jeune couple de Palo Alto avec trois enfants souhaitait une maison moderne avec suffisamment d'espace pour leur famille et des espaces sociaux généreux qui coulaient de l'intérieur vers l'extérieur. Le paysage, l'architecture et les intérieurs ont été traités par le Studio VARA pour créer un ensemble cohérent qui met en valeur le confort, l'efficacité, l'espace et la lumière. La maison a été positionnée au coin le plus à l'extérieur pour préserver la cour arrière et la volumétrie a été optimisée pour atteindre le volume intérieur maximum permis. Les différents matériaux - béton coffré pour le sous-sol, bardage en cèdre et mélèze pour le rez-de-chaussée et zinc lamellé-collé foncé pour le dernier étage - s'harmonisent pour créer un ensemble cohésif, donnant à cette maison moderne une dimension humaine et un aspect artisanal.

Una joven pareja de Palo Alto con tres hijos deseaba una casa moderna con amplio espacio para su familia y espacios sociales generosos que fluyeran sin problemas de adentro hacia afuera. El paisaje, la arquitectura y los interiores fueron tratados por Studio VARA para crear un conjunto cohesionado que resalta la comodidad, la eficiencia, la amplitud y la luz. La casa se ubicó en la esquina más exterior para preservar el patio trasero y se optimizó el volumen para lograr el máximo espacio interior permitido. Los diversos materiales —hormigón encofrado para el sótano, revestimiento de cedro y alerce para el nivel principal, y zinc oscuro panelizado para el piso superior— se armonizan para crear un conjunto cohesivo, dando una dimensión humana y una sensación de artesanía a esta casa moderna.

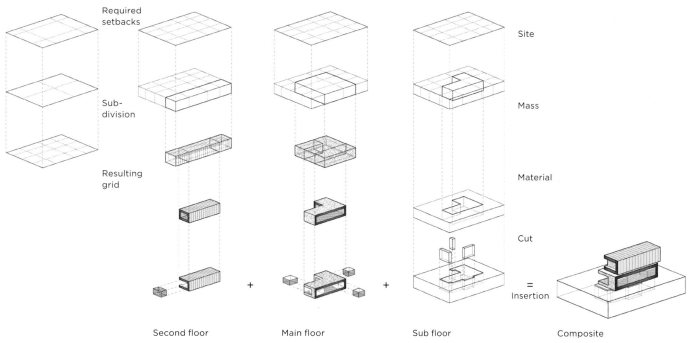

Required setbacks

Sub-division

Resulting grid

Site

Mass

Material

Cut

Insertion

Second floor + Main floor + Sub floor = Composite

Tectonic diagram

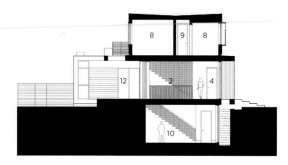

Sections

1. Dining room
2. Great room
3. Staircase
4. Entry
5. Half bathroom
6. Bathroom
7. Master bedroom
8. Bedroom
9. Hallway
10. Family room
11. Mechanical room
12. Deck

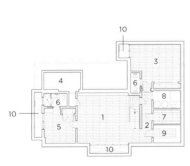

Basement plan

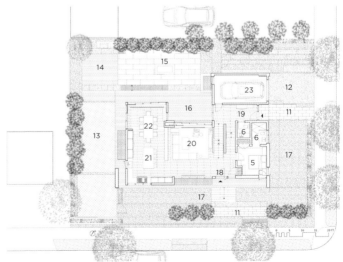

Ground floor plan

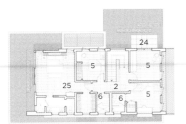

Second floor plan

Roof plan

1. Family room
2. Hallway
3. Exercise room
4. Crawl space
5. Bedroom
6. Bathroom
7. Wine room
8. Mechanical room
9. Storage
10. Lightwell
11. Entry path
12. Driveway
13. Play area
14. BBQ and dining patio
15. Fire pit patio
16. Porch
17. Entry garden
18. Entry
19. Foyer
20. Great room
21. Kitchen
22. Dining room
23. Garage
24. Deck
25. Master suite

0 5 10 15 20 ft

N

Offering spectacular Bay Bridge views, this two-level loft was an uninspired white box chopped up into many small rooms. Having worked with the owners on another home in the Carmel Valley, the designers wanted to bring a similar warm, modern and spacious character to this loft that celebrates the view while offering two-bedroom suites for overnight guests. To accomplish these goals, walls and soffits were first removed to expose concrete. Now pared down to the essentials, the space was reimagined and reconfigured as a composition of planes and volumes in warm materials: concrete, wire-brushed and waxed European white oak, gunmetal gray panels, and gallery white walls.

Dieses zweistöckige Loft mit spektakulärem Blick auf die Bay Bridge war eine uninspirierte, in viele kleine Räume geteilte weiße Box. Nachdem sie mit den Eigentümern an einem anderen Haus im Karmeltal gearbeitet hatten, wollten die Designer einen ähnlich warmen, modernen und geräumigen Charakter in dieses Loft bringen, der die Aussicht zelebriert, und gleichzeitig Suiten mit zwei Schlafzimmern für Übernachtungsgäste anbieten. Um diese Ziele zu erreichen, wurden zunächst Wände und Decken entfernt, um Beton freizulegen. Jetzt auf das Wesentliche reduziert, wurde der Raum neu konzipiert und als Komposition von Flächen und Volumen aus warmen Materialien neugestaltet: Beton, drahtgebürstete und gewachste europäische Weißeiche, rotmetallgraue Paneele und weiße Wände in der Galerie.

Offrant des vues spectaculaires sur le pont Bay Bridge, ce loft à deux niveaux était une boîte blanche sans inspiration, découpée en plusieurs petites pièces. Après avoir travaillé avec les propriétaires sur une autre maison dans la vallée du Carmel, les designers ont voulu apporter un caractère chaleureux, moderne et spacieux à ce loft qui célèbre la vue tout en offrant des suites de deux chambres à coucher pour les hôtes. Pour atteindre ces objectifs, les murs et les soffites ont d'abord été enlevés pour exposer le béton. Désormais réduit à l'essentiel, l'espace a été repensé et reconfiguré comme une composition de plans et de volumes dans des matériaux chauds : béton, chêne blanc européen brossé et ciré, panneaux gris gunmetal et murs blancs des galeries.

Ofreciendo espectaculares vistas del Bay Bridge, este *loft* de dos niveles era una caja blanca nada inspirada dividida en muchas estancias pequeñas. Después de haber trabajado con los propietarios en otra casa en el valle de Carmel, los diseñadores quisieron traer un carácter cálido, moderno y espacioso similar a este *loft* que celebra la vista al mismo tiempo que ofrece *suites* de dos dormitorios para los huéspedes que pernoctan. Para lograr estos objetivos, las paredes y los sofitos fueron eliminados primero para que quedar expuesto el hormigón. Ahora reducido a lo esencial, el espacio fue reimaginado y reconfigurado como una composición de planos y volúmenes en materiales cálidos: hormigón, roble blanco europeo cepillado y encerado, paneles color gris "gunmetal" y paredes blancas de las galerías.

PLASTER   WOOD   ZINC   STEEL   COMBINED

Axonometric diagram

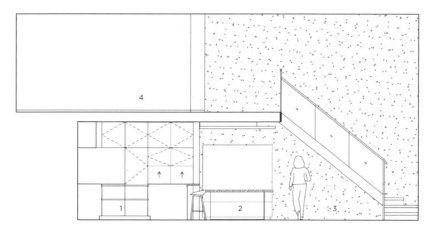

Proposed section

1. Kitchen
2. Dining nook
3. Living room
4. Loft

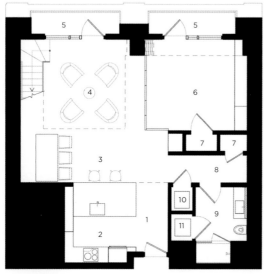

Lower floor plan

1. Entry
2. Kitchen
3. Dining nook
4. Living room
5. Balcony
6. Guest bedroom
7. Closet
8. Hall
9. Guest bathroom
10. Mechanical room
11. Laundry
12. Loft
13. Open to below
14. Master bedroom
15. Master bathroom
16. WC
17. Dressing room
18. Master closet

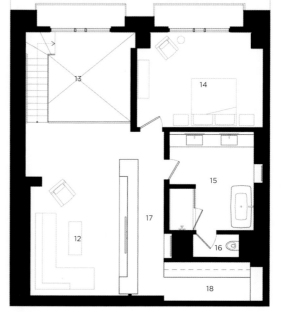

Upper floor plan

Studio VARA drew on its extensive experience with single-family residential townhouses to develop a row of 18 townhomes in a pair of three-story blocks that form part of this 143-unit development on one of the last residential sites in Mission Bay. The townhomes feature generous fenestration, a rhythm of projecting bay windows, and colorful accent panels to activate the facades and give scale to the landscaped pedestrian walkway. Individual ground-floor residential entry stoops activate the public realm, and double-aspect units provide access to daylight and eyes on the street. Studio VARA teamed with Mithun and TNDC to develop this housing project, making a meaningful contribution to the city by providing much-needed housing and articulating collective life.

Studio VARA nutzte seine umfangreiche Erfahrung mit Einfamilienhäusern, um eine Reihe von 18 Reihenhäusern in einem Paar dreistöckiger Blöcke zu entwickeln, die Teil dieser 143 Einheiten Entwicklung auf einem der letzten Wohngebiete in der Mission Bay sind. Die Stadthäuser verfügen über eine großzügige Fensterung, einen Rhythmus aus vorstehenden Erkern und farbenfrohe Akzentpaneele, um die Fassaden zu aktivieren und den landschaftlich gestalteten Fußgängerweg zu skalieren. Individuelle Einstiegsmöglichkeiten im Erdgeschoss aktivieren den öffentlichen Raum, und doppelseitige Einheiten ermöglichen den Zugang zu Tageslicht und Blick auf die Straße. Das Studio VARA entwickelte in Zusammenarbeit mit Mithun und TNDC dieses Wohnprojekt und leistete einen wichtigen Beitrag zur Stadt, indem es dringend benötigte Wohnungen bereitstellte und das kollektive Leben artikulierte.

Le Studio VARA s'est appuyé sur sa vaste expérience des maisons en rangée résidentielles unifamiliales pour développer une rangée de 18 maisons de ville dans une paire d'immeubles de trois étages qui font partie de ce projet de 143 appartements sur l'un des derniers sites résidentiels de Mission Bay. Les maisons en rangée sont dotées d'une fenestration généreuse, d'un rythme de baies vitrées en saillie et de panneaux d'accent colorés pour activer les façades et donner de l'ampleur à la voie piétonnière paysagée. Des perrons d'entrée individuels au rez-de-chaussée activent le domaine public et les logements avec fenêtres sur deux côtés apportent luminosité et visibilité vers la rue. Le Studio VARA s'est associé à Mithun et à TNDC pour développer ce projet de logement, apportant une contribution significative à la ville en fournissant des logements indispensables et en articulant la vie collective.

Studio VARA aprovechó su amplia experiencia con casas adosadas residenciales unifamiliares para desarrollar una hilera de 18 casas adosadas en un par de bloques de tres pisos con 143 viviendas en uno de los últimos núcleos residenciales de Mission Bay. Las casas adosadas tienen un ventanaje generoso, ventanas en voladizo que crean un ritmo de entrantes y salientes y paneles de colores que activan las fachadas y dan escala al paseo peatonal ajardinado. Las escaleras individuales de entrada a las viviendas de planta baja activan el dominio público. Por otro lado, las viviendas con ventanas a dos lados proporcionan luminosidad y visibilidad hacia la calle. El Estudio VARA se asoció con Mithun y TNDC para desarrollar este proyecto de viviendas, contribuyendo significativamente a la ciudad al proporcionar viviendas muy necesarias y articular la vida colectiva.

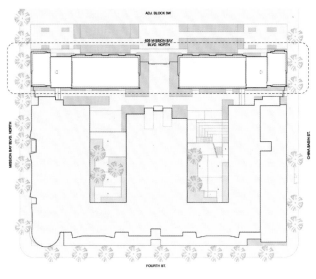

Proposed site plan

Third floor plan

Second floor plan

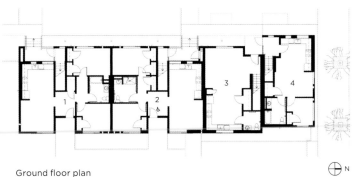

Ground floor plan

N

1. 2-bedroom, 1-level unit
2. 2-bedroom, 1-level unit (ADA)
3. 3-bedroom, 2-level unit
4. 1-bedroom, 1-level unit
5. 2-bedroom, 2-level unit

TIERNEY CONNER
ARCHITECTURE

BERKELEY HOUSE

Photography: **David Duncan Livingston**
Location: **Berkeley, California**
Area: **1,500 Sq. Ft. house + 450 Sq. Ft. studio**
Landscape Architecture: **Tierney Conner Architecture**
Structural Engineering: **PCTC Engineering**

OAKLAND HOUSE

Photography: **David Duncan Livingston**
Location: **Oakland, California**
Area: **3,000 Sq. Ft. house including 365 Sq. Ft. addition**
General Contractor: **Oliver Builders**
Landscape Architect: **Tierney Conner Architecture**
Structural Engineering: **Vaziri Structural Engineering**
Lighting Design: **Tierney Conner Architecture**

SONOMA HOUSE

Photography: **David Duncan Livingston**
Location: **Sonoma, California**
Area: **350 Sq. Ft. addition**
General Contractor: **Caldwell-Trouette General Contractors**
Landscape Architect: **Tierney Conner Architecture**
Structural Engineering: **Komendant Engineering**

Tierney Conner weaves together the fields of architecture, landscape, and interiors, creating inspired spaces that function and flow with ease. To us, this means dissolving the boundary between inside and out, indulging in a rich material expression, and leveraging small artistic details for big impact. Our designs provide a stage for the lives within, embracing the changing seasons and the patina of time. The following projects apply distinct strategies to introduce a modern aesthetic and to promote a connection to the landscape. They are reconceived spaces—interventions designed within the parameters of existing structures. Each result in unique spaces that developed out of the collaboration between the homeowners, the existing site and architecture, and our approach to integrating indoor and outdoor living.

Tierney Conner verbindet die Bereiche Architektur, Landschaft und Innenräume und schafft inspirierte Räume, die mit Leichtigkeit funktionieren und fließen. Für uns bedeutet das, die Grenze zwischen innen und außen aufzulösen, einem reichen materiellen Ausdruck zu frönen und kleine künstlerische Details für große Wirkung zu nutzen. Unsere Entwürfe bieten eine Bühne für das Leben im Inneren, die die wechselnden Jahreszeiten und die Patina der Zeit umfasst. Die folgenden Projekte wenden unterschiedliche Strategien an, um eine moderne Ästhetik einzuführen und eine Verbindung zur Landschaft zu fördern. Sie sind rekonzipierte Räume – Interventionen, die im Rahmen bestehender Strukturen konzipiert sind. Jedes Ergebnis führt zu einzigartigen Räumen, die sich aus der Zusammenarbeit zwischen den Hausbesitzern, dem bestehenden Standort und der Architektur sowie unserem Ansatz zur Integration von Innen- und Außenleben entwickeln.

Tierney Conner tisse ensemble les domaines de l'architecture, du paysage et des intérieurs, créant des espaces inspirés qui fonctionnent et coulent avec aisance. Pour nous, cela signifie abolir la frontière entre l'intérieur et l'extérieur, s'adonner à une expression matérielle riche et mettre à profit les petits détails artistiques pour obtenir un grand impact. Nos conceptions fournissent une scène pour la vie à l'intérieur, embrassant les saisons changeantes et la patine du temps. Les projets suivants appliquent des stratégies distinctes pour introduire une esthétique moderne et promouvoir un lien avec le paysage. Ce sont des espaces reconçus - des interventions conçues dans le cadre des paramètres des structures existantes. Chacun d'entre eux donne naissance à des espaces uniques qui sont le fruit d'une collaboration entre les propriétaires, le site et l'architecture existants, ainsi que de notre approche d'intégration de la vie intérieure et extérieure.

Tierney Conner entreteje los campos de la arquitectura, el paisaje y los interiores, creando espacios inspirados que funcionan y fluyen con facilidad. Para nosotros, esto significa disolver la frontera entre el interior y el exterior, permitirse una rica expresión material y aprovechar los pequeños detalles artísticos para lograr un gran impacto. Nuestros diseños proporcionan un escenario para la vida interior, abarcando las estaciones cambiantes y la pátina del tiempo. Los siguientes proyectos aplican estrategias distintas para introducir una estética moderna y promover una conexión con el paisaje. Son espacios reconcebidos, intervenciones diseñadas dentro de los parámetros de las estructuras existentes. Cada uno resulta en espacios únicos que se desarrollaron a partir de la colaboración entre los propietarios, el sitio y la arquitectura existentes, y nuestro enfoque para integrar la vida en el interior y en el exterior.

This home weaves public and private areas as well as interior and exterior spaces from the front yard to a backyard studio. The inherently public front yard leads to a semi-enclosed courtyard stepping up to the house entry. Inside, the entire floor plan is flipped, moving a bedroom to the front of the house and allowing formerly small spaces at the rear to be combined into an open living area. Skylights allow natural light to fill the living area, while the hallway to the bedrooms borrows daylight through openings in the wall and bookshelf without sacrificing privacy. At the rear of the lot, a garage is transformed into a studio apartment. A modern palette of weathered steel, stucco, and concrete connect the two structures. What was a dysfunctional space, is now an open and light-filled home for a young family.

Dieses Haus verwebt öffentliche und private Bereiche sowie Innen- und Außenräume vom Vorplatz bis zum Hinterhofstudio. Der von Natur aus öffentliche Vorplatz führt zu einem halbgeschlossenen Innenhof, der bis zum Hauseingang reicht. Im Inneren ist der gesamte Grundriss umgedreht worden, wodurch ein Schlafzimmer an die Vorderseite des Hauses verlagert wurde und ehemals kleine Räume im Heck zu einem offenen Wohnbereich kombiniert werden konnten. Dachfenster lassen natürliches Licht in den Wohnbereich eindringen, während der Flur Tageslicht zu den Schlafzimmern durch Öffnungen in Wand und Bücherregal leitet, ohne die Privatsphäre zu beeinträchtigen. Im hinteren Teil des Grundstücks wurde eine Garage in eine Studio-Wohnung umgewandelt. Eine moderne Palette aus verwittertem Stahl, Stuck und Beton verbindet die beiden Bauwerke. Was ein dysfunktionaler Raum war, ist heute ein offenes und lichtdurchflutetes Zuhause für eine junge Familie.

Cette maison tisse des espaces publics et privés ainsi que des espaces intérieurs et extérieurs de la cour avant à l'arrière-cour d'un studio. La cour avant, par nature publique, mène à une cour semi-fermée qui s'élève jusqu'à l'entrée de la maison. À l'intérieur, tout le plan de l'étage est renversé, déplaçant une chambre à coucher vers l'avant de la maison et permettant de combiner des espaces autrefois réduits à l'arrière pour en faire un espace de vie ouvert. Les lanterneaux permettent à la lumière naturelle de pénétrer dans l'espace de vie, tandis que le couloir menant aux chambres à coucher emprunte la lumière du jour par des ouvertures dans le mur et sur la bibliothèque sans sacrifier l'intimité. À l'arrière du terrain, un garage est transformé en studio. Une palette moderne d'acier vieilli, de stuc et de béton relie les deux structures. Ce qui était un espace dysfonctionnel, est maintenant une maison ouverte et lumineuse pour une jeune famille.

Esta casa teje áreas públicas y privadas, así como espacios interiores y exteriores desde el patio delantero hasta un estudio en el patio trasero. El patio delantero, público por naturaleza, conduce a un patio semicerrado que da paso a la entrada de la casa. En el interior, se da la vuelta a toda la planta, moviendo un dormitorio al frente de la casa y permitiendo que los espacios que antes eran pequeños en la parte trasera formen una sala de estar abierta. Las claraboyas permiten que la luz natural llene la sala de estar, mientras que el pasillo de las habitaciones recibe la luz del día a través de aberturas en la pared y en la estantería sin sacrificar la privacidad. En la parte trasera del terreno, el garaje se transforma en un estudio. Una moderna paleta de acero envejecido, estuco y hormigón conecta las dos estructuras. Lo que era un espacio disfuncional, es ahora un hogar abierto y lleno de luz para una familia joven.

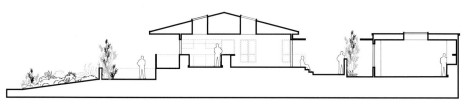

Section

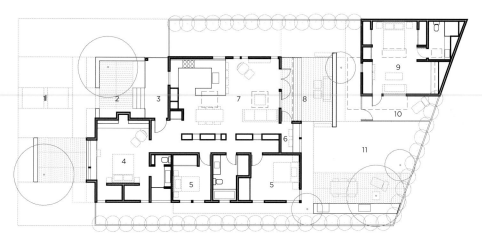

Floor plan

1. Front yard
2. Front courtyard
3. Entry porch
4. Ensuite bedroom
5. Bedroom
6. Office
7. Kitchen/living/dining
8. Deck
9. Studio apartment
10. Studio courtyard
11. Rear yard

Traditional features slowly turn into modern in this home, as one moves from the original front entry to the expansive double-story rear addition. The formal spatial organization around the staircase is maintained, but with the new rear spaces providing a modern interpretation of the original architecture. On the main floor, glass folding doors offer a seamless indoor-outdoor transition. The family gathering areas extend to the exterior, which is punctuated with bold strokes of planting and concrete walls. Upstairs the rear of the house continues the modern vocabulary with an open plan, rich materials, and floor-to-ceiling windows that take advantage of the sloping rear yard, and make the bedroom and bathroom feel like they are in a garden.

Traditionelle Merkmale werden in diesem Haus langsam zu modernen, wenn man vom ursprünglichen Vordereingang zum großzügigen doppelstöckigen Hinteranbau übergeht. Die formale räumliche Gliederung um das Treppenhaus herum ist erhalten geblieben, aber mit neuen Hinterräumen, die eine moderne Interpretation der ursprünglichen Architektur bieten. Im Erdgeschoss erstrecken sich die Bereiche des Familienlebens von innen nach außen. Starke Striche von Bepflanzungen, Betonwänden und Glasfalttüren lösen die Grenze zwischen den Räumen auf. Im Obergeschoss setzt die Rückseite des Hauses das moderne Vokabular mit einem offenen Grundriss, reichen Materialien und raumhohen Fenstern fort, die den schrägen Hinterhof nutzen und dem Schlafzimmer und dem Badezimmer ein Gefühl wie im Garten geben.

Les caractéristiques traditionnelles de cette maison se transforment lentement en modernité à mesure que l'on passe de l'entrée avant d'origine à l'agrandissement de l'arrière du double étage. L'organisation spatiale formelle autour de l'escalier est maintenue, mais les nouveaux espaces arrière offrent une interprétation moderne de l'architecture originale. Au rez-de-chaussée, les espaces de rassemblement familial s'étendent de l'intérieur à l'extérieur. Les coups de plantation audacieux, les murs de béton et les portes pliantes en verre dissolvent la limite entre les espaces. À l'étage, l'arrière de la maison continue le vocabulaire moderne avec un plan ouvert, des matériaux riches et des fenêtres du sol au plafond qui profitent de la cour arrière en pente pour donner l'impression que la chambre et la salle de bains sont dans un jardin.

Las características tradicionales se convierten lentamente en modernas en esta casa, a medida que se pasa de la entrada principal original a la amplia adición trasera de dos pisos. Se mantiene la organización espacial formal alrededor de la escalera, pero con los nuevos espacios traseros que proporcionan una interpretación moderna de la arquitectura original. En el piso principal, las puertas plegables de vidrio ofrecen una transición perfecta entre el interior y el exterior. Las áreas de reunión de la familia se extienden hacia el exterior, que está salpicado con trazos audaces de plantación y paredes de hormigón.. Arriba, la parte trasera de la casa continúa el vocabulario moderno con un plano abierto, materiales ricos y ventanas de suelo a techo que aprovechan el patio trasero inclinado para dar la impresión de que el dormitorio y el baño están en un jardín.

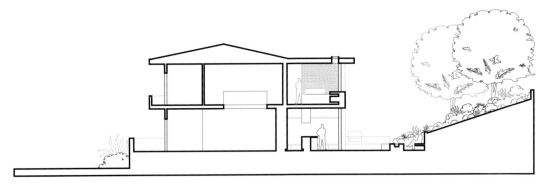

Section

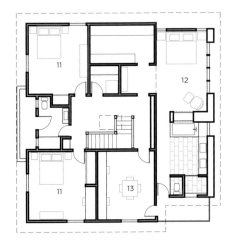

Second floor plan

1. Front yard
2. Entry porch
3. Foyer
4. Living room
5. Dining room
6. Family room
7. Kitchen
8. Fire pit area
9. Game room
10. Rear garden
11. Bedroom
12. Ensuite bedroom
13. Office

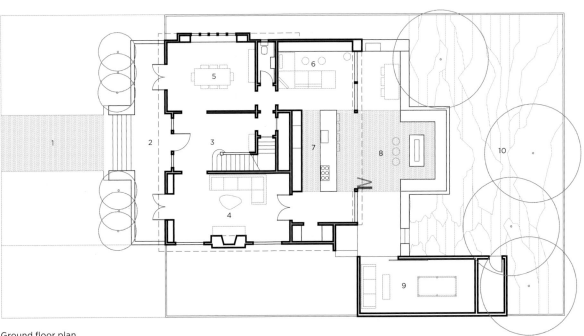

Ground floor plan

This addition to a wood-shingled Sonoma County farmhouse is a true juxtaposition of modern and traditional. Rather than replicate the aesthetics of the existing residence, the design takes its cues from the surrounding cascading decks. The farmhouse's connection to the landscape is phenomenal as much as physical, creating a space from which to take in the expansive views and enjoy the changing seasons. In winter, warmth and light from the low-lying sun flood the living spaces. In summer, the overhanging roofline provides much-needed shade, and walls of windows open for cool breezes from the valley below to flow through. The fireplace creates an inviting place combating the gray and wet winter days and the evening chill of summer and fall.

Diese Ergänzung zu einem holzverschindelten Sonoma-County-Bauernhaus ist eine echte Gegenüberstellung von Moderne und Tradition. Anstatt die Ästhetik der bestehenden Residenz nachzubilden, orientiert sich der Entwurf an den umliegenden Kaskadendecks. Die Verbindung des Bauernhauses mit der Landschaft ist sowohl phänomenal als auch physisch und schafft einen Raum, von dem aus man die weiten Aussichten genießen und die wechselnden Jahreszeiten erleben kann. Im Winter überfluten Wärme und Licht der tiefstehenden Sonne die Wohnräume. Im Sommer spendet die überhängende Dachlinie den dringend benötigten Schatten, und die Fensterwände öffnen sich, so dass kühle Brisen aus dem Tal hindurchströmen können. Der Kamin schafft einen einladenden Ort, der die grauen und nassen Wintertage und die abendliche Kälte von Frühling und Herbst bekämpft.

Cet ajout à une ferme du comté de Sonoma, en bardeaux de bois, est une véritable juxtaposition de moderne et de traditionnel. Plutôt que de reproduire l'esthétique de la résidence existante, le design s'inspire des terrasses en cascade environnantes. Le lien de la ferme avec le paysage est aussi phénoménal que physique, créant un espace d'où l'on peut admirer les vues imprenables et profiter des saisons changeantes. En hiver, la chaleur et la lumière du soleil des basses terres inondent les espaces de vie. En été, la ligne de toiture en surplomb offre de l'ombre et les murs des fenêtres s'ouvrent pour laisser passer les brises fraîches de la vallée en contrebas. La cheminée crée un lieu invitant pour lutter contre les journées grises et humides de l'hiver et le froid nocturne de l'été et de l'automne.

Esta adición a una granja del condado de Sonoma con tejas de madera es una verdadera yuxtaposición de lo moderno y lo tradicional. En lugar de replicar la estética de la residencia existente, el diseño se inspira en las cubiertas en cascada que la rodean. La conexión de la granja con el paisaje es fenomenal tanto como física, creando un espacio desde el que disfrutar de las amplias vistas y del cambio de estaciones. En invierno, el calor y la luz del sol de baja altitud inundan los espacios vitales. En verano, el alero del tejado proporciona una sombra muy necesaria, y las paredes de ventanas se abren para que las brisas frescas del valle fluyan a través de ellas. La chimenea crea un lugar acogedor que combate los días grises y húmedos del invierno y el frío vespertino del verano y el otoño.

Elevation

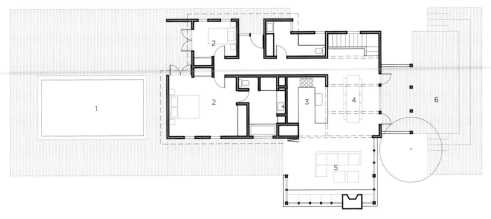

Floor plan

1. Pool
2. Bedroom
3. Kitchen
4. Dining area
5. Sunroom
6. Deck

TYREUS
DESIGN STUDIO

TOPSIDE WAY

Photography: Bart Edson
Location: Mill Valley, California
Area: 3,700 Sq. Ft.
General Contractor: Cogliandro Construction
Structural Engineering: Peoples Associates
Structural Engineers, Inc.

VIEWCREST

Photography: Bart Edson
Location: Sonoma, California
Area: 2,100 Sq. Ft.
General Contractor: Deveau Construction
Structural Engineering: MKM & Associates

ESPLANADE

Photography: Benny Chan
Location: Playa del Rey, California
Area: 1,894 Sq. Ft.
General Contractor: Glynn Design Build
Structural Engineering: Peter T. Erdelyi
& Associates, Inc.

Tyreus Design Studio maintains a fascination and dedication to reimagining existing structures. We work to transform buildings that lack connection to site or occupant into uniquely tailored spaces. In each project, we try to identify key features to retain or employ in a new way. Coupled with modern building practices, renovation can transform the ineffective, limiting, or uninspiring. The studio's focus is not just born out of a love for unrealized potential. We have an understanding of the larger context in which we work. Finding ways to reuse existing structures is important to preserve open space, rehabilitate aging infrastructure, and reduce construction waste. The studio's work spans a range of scales, from a small beach cottage to redeveloping 14 city blocks.

Das Tyreus Design Studio ist fasziniert von bestehenden Strukturen und widmet sich ihrer Neugestaltung. Wir arbeiten daran, Gebäude, die keine Verbindung zum Standort oder zur Person haben, in maßgeschneiderte Räume zu verwandeln. In jedem Projekt versuchen wir, die wichtigsten Merkmale zu identifizieren, die es zu erhalten oder auf neue Weise zu nutzen gilt. In Verbindung mit modernen Baupraktiken kann eine Renovierung das Ineffektive, Begrenzte oder Uninspirierende verändern. Der Fokus des Studios liegt nicht nur auf der Liebe zu unrealisiertem Potenzial: Wir haben ein Verständnis für den größeren Kontext, in dem wir arbeiten. Die Suche nach Möglichkeiten zur Wiederverwendung bestehender Strukturen ist wichtig, um Freiflächen zu erhalten, alternde Infrastrukturen zu sanieren und Bauschutt zu reduzieren. Die Arbeit des Studios umfasst eine Reihe von Maßstäben, vom kleinen Strandhaus bis hin zur Sanierung von 14 Wohnblöcken.

Tyreus Design Studio maintient une fascination et un dévouement à réimaginer les structures existantes. Nous travaillons à transformer les bâtiments qui n'ont pas de lien avec le site ou l'occupant en espaces sur mesure. Dans chaque pròjet, nous essayons d'identifier les caractéristiques clés à conserver ou à utiliser d'une nouvelle manière. Couplée aux pratiques modernes de construction, la rénovation peut transformer l'inefface, la limitation ou le manque d'inspiration. Le centre d'intérêt du studio n'est pas seulement né de l'amour pour le potentiel non réalisé. Nous comprenons le contexte plus large dans lequel nous travaillons. Il est important de trouver des moyens de réutiliser les structures existantes pour préserver les espaces ouverts, remettre en état les infrastructures vieillissantes et réduire les déchets de construction. Le travail de l'atelier s'étend sur une gamme d'échelles allant d'un petit chalet de plage au réaménagement de 14 îlots urbains.

Tyreus Design Studio mantiene una fascinación y dedicación para reimaginar las estructuras existentes. Trabajamos para transformar edificios que carecen de conexión con el lugar o el ocupante en espacios a medida. En cada proyecto, tratamos de identificar las características clave para mantenerlas o emplearlas de una manera nueva. Junto con las prácticas de construcción modernas, la renovación puede transformar lo ineficaz, lo limitante o lo poco inspirador. El enfoque del estudio no solo nace del amor por el potencial no realizado. Tenemos una comprensión del contexto más amplio en el que trabajamos. Encontrar formas de reutilizar las estructuras existentes es importante para preservar los espacios abiertos, rehabilitar la infraestructura obsoleta y reducir los desechos de la construcción. El trabajo del estudio abarca una amplia gama de escalas, desde una pequeña casa de campo en la playa hasta la reurbanización de 14 manzanas de la ciudad.

The Topside house was originally built to maximize square footage on a trapezoidal-shaped lot. This shape presented difficulties in plan due to acute angles, poor circulation, and limited views. We kept the original trapezoid foundation to reduce cost and permitting delays but shuffled the plan layout. Living and dining rooms now occupy space where the footprint expands towards a view of the San Francisco Bay. Large sliding doors face the naturally cooled bayside. Private bedrooms are placed in areas of the plan that narrow, creating a more intimate scale. The idea of a formal, front entry was discarded in favor of a planted courtyard serving as an outdoor foyer. This allowed for outdoor connections without giving up privacy to the adjacent street.

Das Maisonettehaus wurde ursprünglich gebaut, um die Quadratmeterzahl auf einem trapezförmigen Grundstück zu maximieren. Diese Form stellte uns aufgrund spitzer Winkel, schlechter Durchlüftung und eingeschränkter Sicht vor planerische Schwierigkeiten. Wir haben das ursprüngliche trapezförmige Fundament beibehalten, um Kosten zu senken und Verzögerungen zuzulassen, aber das Layout des Plans neu gestaltet. Wohn- und Esszimmer nehmen heute einen Raum ein, in dem sich die Grundfläche in Richtung der San Francisco Bay ausdehnt. Große Schiebetüren zeigen zum natürlich gekühlten Erker. Private Schlafzimmer sind in Bereichen des Grundrisses platziert, die sich verengen und eine intimere Dimension schaffen. Die Idee eines formalen, vorderen Eingangs wurde zugunsten eines begrünten Innenhofes als Außenfoyer aufgegeben. Dies ermöglichte Außenverbindungen, ohne den Schutz der Privatsphäre vor der angrenzenden Straße aufzugeben.

Site plan

La maison de surface a été construite à l'origine pour maximiser la superficie en mètres carrés sur un terrain de forme trapézoïdale. Cette forme présentait des difficultés dans le plan en raison des angles aigus, de la mauvaise circulation et des vues limitées. Nous avons conservé les fondations trapézoïdales d'origine pour réduire les coûts et permettre des délais, mais nous avons remanié la disposition du plan. Le salon et la salle à manger occupent maintenant de l'espace où l'empreinte de pas s'étend vers une vue sur la baie de San Francisco. De grandes portes coulissantes font face à la baie refroidie naturellement. Les chambres privées sont placées dans des zones du plan qui se rétrécissent, créant ainsi une échelle plus intime. L'idée d'une entrée principale formelle a été écartée au profit d'une cour plantée servant de foyer extérieur. Cela permettait des raccordements extérieurs sans renoncer à l'intimité de la rue adjacente.

La casa Topside fue construida originalmente para maximizar los metros cuadrados en un terreno de forma trapezoidal. Esta forma presentaba dificultades en planta debido a los ángulos agudos, la mala circulación y las vistas limitadas. Mantuvimos los cimientos trapezoidales originales para reducir los costes y permitir demoras, pero reestructuramos el diseño del plano. La sala de estar y el comedor ahora ocupan un espacio donde la huella se expande hacia una vista de la bahía de San Francisco. Las grandes puertas correderas dan al lado de la bahía que se refresca naturalmente. Las habitaciones privadas se ubican en zonas de la planta que se estrechan, creando una escala más íntima. La idea de una entrada delantera formal fue descartada en favor de un patio plantado que sirviera como vestíbulo al aire libre. Esto permitió conexiones al aire libre sin renunciar a la privacidad de la calle adyacente.

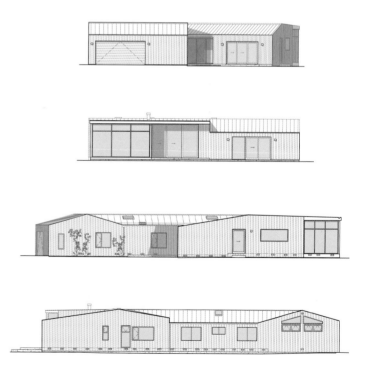

Elevations

Floor plan

1. Entry
2. Family room
3. Kitchen
4. Dining area
5. Living area
6. Laundry room
7. Master bedroom
8. Master bedroom
9. Office
10. Powder room
11. Bedroom
12. Bathroom
13. Den
14. Garage
15. Workshop
16. Courtyard

This single-story hilltop house sits on a southeast slope of Sonoma Mountain, west of downtown Sonoma. The site has privacy and views that extend above the fog line and across the valley floor. The design of the original house ignored the dramatic site, with small windows, low roofline, and limited access to outdoor space. The renovation raised ceiling heights throughout the main living areas with a deck cantilevering out towards the view. The existing bedroom wing anchors the house to the hillside, while entertaining spaces pinwheel above the slope. A boxlike volume added to the front of the house creates a connection between old and new forms while focusing circulation on the surrounding landscape.

Dieses einstöckige Hügelhaus liegt an einem Südosthang des Sonoma Mountain, westlich der Innenstadt von Sonoma. Der Standort bietet Privatsphäre und Ausblicke, die sich über die Nebelgrenze und über den Talboden erstrecken. Der Entwurf des ursprünglichen Hauses mit kleinen Fenstern, niedriger Dachlinie und begrenztem Zugang zum Außenbereich ignorierte den dramatischen Ort. Die Renovierung führte zu erhöhten Decken in den Hauptwohnbereichen mit einem zur Aussicht auskragenden Deck, der bestehende Schlafzimmerflügel verankert das Haus am Hang. Ein kastenförmiges Volumen an der Vorderseite des Hauses schafft eine Verbindung zwischen alten und neuen Formen und fokussiert die Zirkulation auf die umgebende Landschaft.

Cette maison de plain-pied est située sur le versant sud-est du mont Sonoma, à l'ouest du centre-ville de Sonoma. Le site offre une intimité et des vues qui s'étendent au-dessus de la ligne de brouillard et à travers le fond de la vallée. La conception de la maison d'origine ne tenait pas compte de l'emplacement spectaculaire, avec de petites fenêtres, d'un toit bas et d'un accès limité à l'espace extérieur. La rénovation a rehaussé les hauteurs sous plafond dans les principales pièces de vie avec une terrasse en porte-à-faux vers l'extérieur vers la vue. L'aile chambre à coucher existante ancre la maison au flanc de la colline, tout en divertissant les espaces de roues à aubes au-dessus de la pente. Un volume en forme de boîte ajouté à l'avant de la maison crée un lien entre les anciennes et les nouvelles formes tout en concentrant la circulation sur le paysage environnant.

Esta casa de un solo piso se encuentra en la ladera sureste de la Montaña de Sonoma, al oeste del centro de Sonoma. El sitio tiene privacidad y vistas que se extienden por encima de la línea de niebla y a través del valle. El diseño de la casa original no tenía en cuenta el espectacular emplazamiento, con ventanas pequeñas, techo bajo y acceso limitado al espacio exterior. La renovación elevó las alturas del techo a través de las áreas principales de la sala de estar con una cubierta en voladizo hacia la vista. El ala del dormitorio existente ancla la casa a la ladera, mientras que la zona de estar se sitúa por encima de la pendiente. Un volumen en forma de caja añadido a la fachada de la casa crea una conexión entre las formas antiguas y las nuevas, a la vez que centra la circulación en el paisaje circundante.

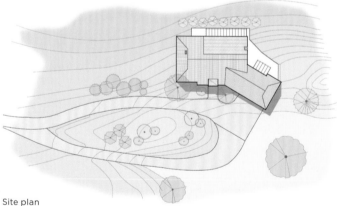

Site plan

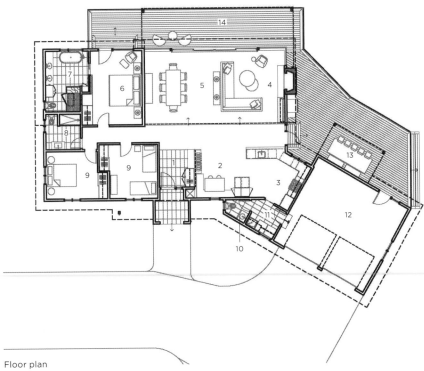

Floor plan

1. Entry
2. Breakfast nook
3. Kitchen
4. Living area
5. Dining area
6. Master bedroom
7. Master bathroom
8. Bathroom
9. Bedroom
10. Powder room
11. Laundry room
12. Garage
13. Outdoor dining
14. Deck

Located in a small California beach town, the original house was built over 80 years before our first discussions with the client. The house contained several small, distinct rooms rigidly divided between three stories. The interior needed more light, open space, and better views. The redesign focused on eliminating walls between living areas and maximizing water views. Vertical circulation spaces act as sunlit display areas between floors. Skylights in the south-facing roof direct diffused light into back corners of the floor plan. Exterior materials withstand the harsh demands of a beach climate. Engineered wood panels that resist fading cover the master bedroom wing next to a backdrop of smooth trowel stucco.

In einer kleinen kalifornischen Strandstadt gelegen, wurde das ursprüngliche Haus über 80 Jahre vor unseren ersten Gesprächen mit dem Kunden gebaut. Das Haus enthielt mehrere kleine, unterschiedliche Räume, die starr auf drei Stockwerke verteilt waren. Der Innenraum benötigte mehr Licht, mehr Freiraum und eine bessere Aussicht. Im Mittelpunkt des Neugestaltungsprozesses standen die Beseitigung von Wänden zwischen den Wohnräumen und die Maximierung der Ausblicke auf das Wasser. Vertikale Verkehrsflächen dienen als sonnenbeleuchtete Ausstellungsflächen zwischen den Etagen. Oberlichter im nach Süden ausgerichteten Dach leiten diffuses Licht in die hinteren Ecken des Grundrisses. Ausgesuchte Außenmaterialien widerstehen den harten Anforderungen des Strandklimas. Parkettplatten, die nicht verblassen, bedecken den Flügel des Hauptschlafzimmers vor der Kulisse aus glattem Spachtelstuck.

Située dans une petite ville de Californie, la maison originale a été construite plus de 80 ans avant nos premières discussions avec le client. La maison comprenait plusieurs petites pièces distinctes, divisées rigidement sur trois étages. L'intérieur avait besoin de plus de lumière, d'espace ouvert et de meilleures vues. La refonte visait à éliminer les murs entre les pièces à vivre et à maximiser les vues sur l'eau. Les espaces de circulation verticaux servent de zones d'affichage éclairées par le soleil entre les étages. Les lanterneaux du toit orienté vers le sud dirigent la lumière diffuse dans les coins arrière du plan de l'étage. Les matériaux extérieurs résistent aux rudes exigences d'un climat de plage. Des panneaux de bois d'ingénierie qui résistent à la décoloration recouvrent l'aile de la chambre à coucher principale à côté d'une toile de fond en stuc lisse à la truelle.

Ubicada en un pequeño pueblo de playa en California, la casa original fue construida más de 80 años antes de nuestras primeras conversaciones con el cliente. La casa contenía varias estancias pequeñas y bien diferenciadas, divididas rígidamente en tres plantas. El interior necesitaba más luz, espacio abierto y mejores vistas. El rediseño se centró en eliminar las paredes entre las áreas de la vivienda y maximizar las vistas al mar. Los espacios de circulación vertical actúan como expositores iluminados por el sol entre pisos. Los tragaluces en el techo orientado al sur dirigen la luz difusa hacia las esquinas traseras de la planta. Los materiales exteriores resisten las duras exigencias de un clima de playa. Los paneles de madera de ingeniería que resisten la decoloración cubren el ala del dormitorio principal junto a un fondo de estuco de paleta liso.

WDA | WILLIAM DUFF ARCHITECTS

BIG RANCH ROAD

Photography: **Matthew Millman**
Habitable area: **1,500 Sq. Ft.**
General Contractor: **Centric**
Landscape Architect: **Steve Arns**
Lighting Design: **Eric Johnson**
Structural Engineering: **GFDS Engineers**

BUTTERFLY HOUSE

Photography: **Matthew Millman**
Habitable area: **4,898 Sq. Ft.**
Landscape Designer: **The Garden Route**
Lighting Design: **Illuminosa**
Structural Engineering: **FTF Engineering**

We are a people-based, San Francisco, California practice. Founded in 1998 by William S. Duff, Jr.—who leads our management team, comprised of Jim Westover, Jonathan Tsurui, Phoebe Lam, and David K. Plotkin—we find inspiration in the talented people who live and work in our city and in the region's embrace of sustainability. From our location at the intersection of the city's historic manufacturing district, vibrant performing arts scene, and new technology zones, our firm delivers thoughtful, innovative architecture throughout the San Francisco Bay Area and beyond. Our commitment to a culture that fosters curiosity, collaboration, and innovation drives our success in projects across our residential, retail, and commercial studios.

Wir sind ein personenbasiertes Architekturbüro aus San Francisco, Kalifornien, gegründet 1998 von William S. Duff, Jr., der unser Management-Team leitet, bestehend aus Jim Westover, Jonathan Tsurui, Phoebe Lam und David K. Plotkin. Wir finden Inspiration in den talentierten Menschen, die in unserer Stadt leben und arbeiten und im Bewusstsein der Nachhaltigkeit der Region. Von unserem Standort an der Schnittstelle zwischen dem historischen Industriegebiet der Stadt, der pulsierenden Szene der darstellenden Künste und neuen Technologiezonen, liefert unser Unternehmen durchdachte, innovative Architektur in die gesamte San Francisco Bay Area und darüber hinaus. Unser Engagement für eine Kultur, die Neugier, Zusammenarbeit und Innovation fördert, befeuert unseren Erfolg bei Projekten in unseren Wohn-, Einzelhandels- und Geschäftsstudios.

Nous sommes un cabinet basé à San Francisco, Californie. Fondé en 1998 par William S. Duff, Jr. qui dirige notre équipe de direction composée de Jim Westover, Jonathan Tsurui, Phoebe Lam et David K. Plotkin, nous nous inspirons des gens talentueux qui vivent et travaillent dans notre ville et dans l'adoption de la durabilité par la région. De notre emplacement à l'intersection du quartier manufacturier historique de la ville, de la scène dynamique des arts de la scène et des nouvelles zones technologiques, notre cabinet offre une architecture réfléchie et innovatrice dans la région de la baie de San Francisco et au-delà. Notre engagement envers une culture qui favorise la curiosité, la collaboration et l'innovation est le moteur de notre succès dans nos projets résidentiels, commerciaux et de vente au détail.

Somos un estudio basada en la gente en San Francisco, California. Fundado en 1998 por William S. Duff, Jr. quien lidera nuestro equipo directivo, compuesto por Jim Westover, Jonathan Tsurui, Phoebe Lam y David K. Plotkin, encontramos inspiración en las personas talentosas que viven y trabajan en nuestra ciudad y en el abrazo de la sostenibilidad en la región. Desde nuestra ubicación en la intersección del histórico distrito manufacturero de la ciudad, la vibrante representación de las artes escénicas y las nuevas zonas de tecnología, nuestra firma ofrece una arquitectura pensada e innovadora en toda el área de la bahía de San Francisco y más allá. Nuestro compromiso con una cultura que fomenta la curiosidad, la colaboración y la innovación impulsa nuestro éxito en proyectos residenciales, comerciales y de venta al por menor.

Adventurous clients commissioned the unexpected transformation of this century-old former hay barn, an archetypal wine country form reflective of Northern California's history. Noted art patrons, philanthropists, and modern architecture connoisseurs, the couple loved the wood structure's utilitarian form and sought to preserve it, while adapting the interior in a provocative way for contemporary use. The barn—made from native California redwood—was relocated closer to the vineyard, surrounded by site-specific artwork. The region's crisp sunlight provided the catalyst for the concept, a contemplation on light. The wood-slatted shell screens cast ever-changing patterns on the stained concrete floors. Inside, two new opposing mirrored glass volumes reflect the barn and the surrounding environment. Internal illumination transforms the barn into a lantern at night.

Abenteuerlustige Kunden beauftragten die unerwartete Transformation dieser jahrhundertealten ehemaligen Heuschuppen in einem archetypischen Weinland, das die Geschichte Nordkaliforniens widerspiegelt. Das Paar, das von Kunstinteressierten, Philanthropen und Kennern der modernen Architektur geschätzt wird, liebte die nützliche Form der Holzstruktur und versuchte, sie zu erhalten, während es das Innere auf provokante Weise für den zeitgenössischen Gebrauch adaptierte. Die Scheune aus einheimischem kalifornischem Redwood wurde näher an den Weinberg verlegt, umgeben von ortsspezifischen Kunstwerken. Das frische Sonnenlicht der Region war der Auslöser für das Konzept, eine Betrachtung des Lichts: Die Holzlamellen-Siebe werfen immer wieder wechselnde Muster auf die gefärbten Betonböden. Im Inneren spiegeln zwei neue, gegenüberliegende Spiegelglas-Volumina den Stall und die Umgebung wider. Die Innenbeleuchtung verwandelt die Scheune nachts in eine Laterne.

Des clients aventureux ont commandé la transformation inattendue de cette ancienne grange à foin centenaire, une forme de pays viticole archétype qui reflète l'histoire de la Californie du Nord. Mécènes de renom, philanthropes et connaisseurs de l'architecture moderne, le couple aimait la forme utilitaire de la structure en bois et cherchait à la préserver, tout en adaptant l'intérieur de manière provocante pour un usage contemporain. La grange en séquoia californien d'origine a été déplacée plus près du vignoble, entourée d'œuvres d'art propres au site. L'ensoleillement vif de la région a été le catalyseur du concept, une contemplation de la lumière. Les moustiquaires en caillebotis de bois ont des motifs toujours changeants sur les planchers de béton teinté. À l'intérieur, deux nouveaux volumes de verre en miroir opposés reflètent la grange et l'environnement environnant. L'éclairage intérieur transforme la grange en lanterne la nuit.

Unos clientes aventurados encargaron la inesperada transformación de este antiguo granero de heno centenario, una forma arquetípica de un país vitivinícola reflejo de la historia del norte de California. Destacados mecenas, filántropos y conocedores de la arquitectura moderna, la pareja amaba la forma utilitaria de la estructura de madera y buscaba preservarla, a la vez que adaptaba el interior de una manera provocadora para el uso contemporáneo. El granero, hecho de madera de secuoya nativa de California, fue reubicado más cerca del viñedo, rodeado de obras de arte específicas del lugar. La nítida luz solar de la región fue el catalizador del concepto, una contemplación de la luz. Las rejillas de lama de madera proyectan patrones siempre cambiantes sobre los suelos de hormigón teñido. En el interior, dos nuevos volúmenes opuestos de vidrio espejado reflejan el granero y el entorno circundante. La iluminación interna transforma el granero en una linterna por la noche.

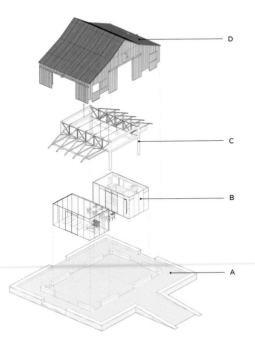

Exploded axonometric diagram: sustainability

A. New board-formed concrete path
B. New reflective glass interior volumes
   (conditioned space)
C. New structural support
D. Existing barn

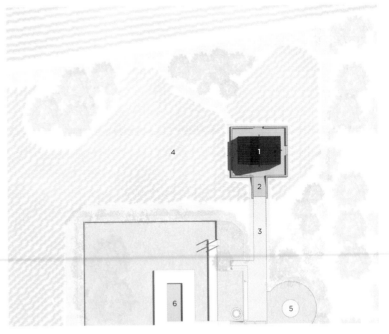

Site plan

1. Barn
2. Concrete plinth
3. Hardscape path
4. Vineyard
5. Sculpture
6. Pool

0 8 16   32 ft   N

This relaxing oasis for an intercontinental couple and their two young children fuses indoors and outdoors. Located in a neighborhood of similarly scaled homes, the house features an H-shaped plan that optimizes its lot size. With a focus on sustainability, materials include Western red cedar covering the walls of the two-story main volume, while smooth-troweled stucco coats the flanking one-story volumes. The house opens up in the rear through fully retractable floor-to-ceiling glass doors to an Ipe deck courtyard and surrounding garden. Internal spaces feature an equally layered palette of fumed-oak wood floors, stained vertical grain Douglas-fir paneling, stained Tay koto veneer cabinets, and a stained white oak staircase.

Diese Entspannungsoase für ein interkontinentales Paar und seine beiden Kleinkinder verschmilzt im Innen- und Außenbereich. Das Haus befindet sich in der Nähe ähnlich skalierter Häuser und verfügt über einen H-förmigen Plan, der die Grundstücksgröße optimal ausnutzt. Unter dem Gesichtspunkt der Nachhaltigkeit sind unter anderem westliches rotes Zedernholz für die Wände des zweistöckigen Hauptraumes gewählt sowie glatter Stuck an den flankierenden eingeschossigen Räumen. Das Haus öffnet sich im hinteren Teil durch vollständig versenkbare, raumhohe Glastüren zu einem mit Ipe-Holz gedeckten Hof und dem umgebenden Garten. Die Innenräume verfügen über eine ebenso mehrschichtige Palette von Holzböden aus geräucherter Eiche, gebeizten vertikalen Douglasie-Verkleidungen, gebeizten Koto-Furnierschränken und einer gebeizten Treppe aus Weißeiche.

Cette oasis de détente pour un couple intercontinental et leurs deux jeunes enfants fusionne à l'intérieur et à l'extérieur. Située dans un quartier de maisons de dimensions similaires, la maison présente un plan en forme de H qui optimise la taille de son terrain. En mettant l'accent sur la durabilité, les matériaux comprennent le Western Red Cedar qui recouvre les murs du volume principal de deux étages, tandis que le stuc lisse recouvre les volumes adjacents d'un étage. La maison s'ouvre à l'arrière par des portes vitrées entièrement escamotables, du sol au plafond, sur une cour intérieure en Ipé et sur le jardin environnant. Les espaces intérieurs comportent une palette de planchers de bois de chêne fumé, des lambris de Douglas taxifolié à grain vertical teinté, des armoires en placage Tay koto teinté et un escalier en chêne blanc teinté.

Este relajante oasis para una pareja intercontinental y sus dos hijos pequeños se fusiona en el interior y en el exterior. Ubicada en un barrio de casas de dimensiones similares, la casa tiene un plano en forma de H que optimiza el tamaño de su terreno. Con un enfoque en la sostenibilidad, los materiales incluyen el cedro rojo occidental que cubre las paredes del volumen principal de dos pisos, mientras que el estuco liso cubre los volúmenes laterales de un piso. La casa se abre en la parte trasera a través de puertas de cristal completamente retráctiles del suelo al techo a un patio con suelo de Ipe y al jardín circundante. Los espacios internos cuentan con una paleta de capas de madera de roble ahumado, paneles de abeto Douglas de grano vertical teñido, armarios de chapa Tay koto teñidos y una escalera de roble blanco teñido.

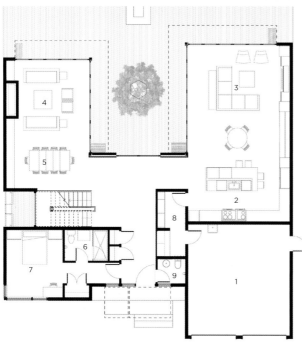

Ground floor plan

1. Garage
2. Kitchen
3. Casual living
4. Formal living
5. Dining area
6. Bathroom
7. Bedroom
8. Mudroom/pantry
9. Powder room

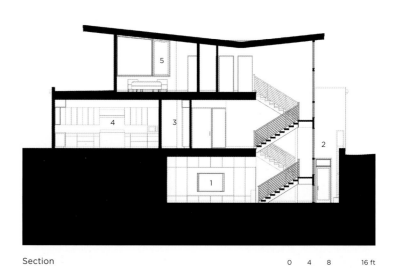

Section

1. Media room
2. Lightwell
3. Mudroom/pantry
4. Kitchen
5. Master bedroom

0   4   8   16 ft

ZACK | de VITO

LAIDLEY RESIDENCE

Photography: Bruce Damonte and Paul Dyer
Location: San Francisco, California
Area: 3,300 Sq. Ft.
Design team: Lise de Vito, Jim Zack, and Joe Lambert
General Contractor: Zack | de Vito
Structural Engineering: Double D Engineering
Prefabricated panel supplier: Forma (no longer in business)
Audio Consultant: JK Sound

RIDGEVIEW

Photography: Cesar Rubio Photography
Location: St. Helena, California
Lot area: 8.5 acres
Habitable area: 4,200 Sq. Ft
Design team: Lise de Vito, Jim Zack, Reggie Stump, Andrew Germann, Andy Drake, and Sarah Nicolas
Civil Engineering: Adobe Associates
Structural Engineering: Strandberg Engineering
Lighting design: Sherry Weller Architectural Lighting Design

STEELHOUSE 1 + 2

Photography: Bruce Damonte Photography
Location: San Francisco, California
Area: Front House/SteelHouse 1, two stories over garage, 1,400 Sq. Ft.;
Rear House/SteelHouse 2, two stories, 1,200 sq ft.; Shared garage
Design team: Lise de Vito, Jim Zack, Joe Benveniste, and Ryan Knock
General Contractor: Zack | de Vito
Landscape design: Lise de Vito
Lighting design: Lise de Vito
Structural Engineering: Double D Engineering
Project Development Partner and Lead Construction Manager: Bruce Wickstrom

Inspired by modernist principles and a deep value for craft, Zack | de Vito creates award-winning buildings and interiors that express a lifelong interest in how buildings are made and a dedication to design excellence. Principals Jim Zack and Lise de Vito approach architecture as a holistic practice—creating integrated, composed environments focused on detail, form, and materiality at all scales. In complement to the firm's architectural services, they provide comprehensive expertise for interior design and landscape architecture, as well as architect-led design-build construction and development projects. While the firm designs project-specific furniture, several custom furniture pieces by Jim Zack are in the permanent A+D collection of the San Francisco Museum of Modern Art.

Inspiriert von modernistischen Prinzipien und hoher Wertschätzung für das Handwerk, kreiert Zack | de Vito Architecture preisgekrönte Gebäude und Innenräume, die ein lebenslanges Interesse an der Herstellung von Gebäuden und ein Engagement für exzellentes Design zum Ausdruck bringen. Die Direktoren Jim Zack und Lise de Vito betrachten Architektur als eine ganzheitliche Praxis, die integrierte, komponierte Umgebungen schafft, die sich auf Details, Formen und Materialität auf allen Ebenen konzentrieren. Ergänzend zu den Architekturleistungen des Büros bieten sie umfassendes Know-how für Innen- und Landschaftsarchitektur sowie für architektonisch geführte Designbau- und Entwicklungsprojekte. Während das Unternehmen projektspezifische Möbel entwirft, befinden sich mehrere individuelle Möbelstücke von Jim Zack in der permanenten A+D-Kollektion des San Francisco Museum of Modern Art.

Inspiré par des principes modernistes et une valeur profonde pour l'artisanat, Zack | de Vito crée des bâtiments et des intérieurs primés qui expriment un intérêt de toute une vie dans la façon dont les bâtiments sont fabriqués et un dévouement à l'excellence en design. Les directeurs Jim Zack et Lise de Vito abordent l'architecture comme une pratique holistique, créant des environnements intégrés et composés, axés sur le détail, la forme et la matérialité à toutes les échelles. En complément des services d'architecture du cabinet, ils offrent une expertise globale en design d'intérieur et en architecture paysagère, ainsi qu'en conception-construction et en projets de développement dirigés par des architectes. Alors que l'entreprise conçoit des meubles spécifiques à un projet, plusieurs meubles personnalisés de Jim Zack font partie de la collection permanente A+D du San Francisco Museum of Modern Art.

Inspirado por principios modernistas y un profundo valor para la artesanía, Zack | de Vito crea edificios e interiores, que han sido galardonados, que expresan un interés de por vida en cómo se hacen los edificios y una dedicación a la excelencia del diseño. Los directores principales Jim Zack y Lise de Vito enfocan la arquitectura como una práctica holística — creando ambientes integrados y compuestos enfocados en el detalle, la forma y la materialidad a todas las escalas. Como complemento a los servicios arquitectónicos de la firma, proporcionan una amplia experiencia en diseño de interiores y paisajismo, así como en proyectos de diseño y construcción y desarrollo liderados por arquitectos. Mientras que la firma diseña muebles específicos para cada proyecto, varios muebles personalizados de Jim Zack forman parte de la colección permanente A+D del Museo de Arte Moderno de San Francisco.

Open plan, natural light and views, and environmental sensitivity were the central inspirations in designing this ground-up hillside home for a family of modernists. Composed of side-by-side three-story volumes, the north half of the building pushes out toward a panoramic view of San Francisco, while the south half recedes to invite light to penetrate the interior. Contemporary craft and purity of structure are expressed through a consistent palette of materials and graphic architectural detailing. Custom structural steel and wood cabinetry are used to define spaces throughout the home. The house was designed and built using sustainable principles, with energy efficiency, low consumption, and healthy materials as primary parameters.

Offener Grundriss, natürliches Licht und Ausblicke sowie Umweltsensibilität waren die zentralen Inspirationen bei der Gestaltung dieses Hanghauses für eine Familie von Modernisten. Die Nordhälfte des Gebäudes besteht aus drei Stockwerken und schiebt sich in Richtung eines Panoramablicks auf San Francisco, während die Südhälfte sich zurückzieht, um das Licht zur Durchdringung des Innenraums einzuladen. Zeitgenössisches Handwerk und Reinheit der Struktur werden durch eine einheitliche Palette von Materialien und grafische architektonische Details zum Ausdruck gebracht. Kundenspezifische Stahlkonstruktionen und Holzschränke werden verwendet, um Räume im gesamten Haus zu definieren. Das Haus wurde nach nachhaltigen Prinzipien entworfen und gebaut, wobei Energieeffizienz, geringer Verbrauch und gesunde Materialien die wichtigsten Parameter waren.

Le plan ouvert, la lumière naturelle, les vues et la sensibilité à l'environnement ont été les principales sources d'inspiration dans la conception de cette maison à flanc de colline pour une famille de modernistes. Composée de volumes de trois étages côte à côte, la moitié nord de l'édifice s'avance vers une vue panoramique de San Francisco, tandis que la moitié sud recule pour inviter la lumière à pénétrer à l'intérieur. L'artisanat contemporain et la pureté de la structure s'expriment à travers une palette cohérente de matériaux et de détails architecturaux graphiques. Des armoires en acier de charpente et en bois sont utilisées pour définir les espaces de la maison. La maison a été conçue et construite selon des principes de durabilité, avec comme paramètres principaux l'efficacité énergétique, une faible consommation et des matériaux sains.

Planos abiertos, luz natural y vistas, y sensibilidad ambiental fueron las inspiraciones centrales en el diseño de esta casa en la ladera de una colina para una familia de modernistas. Compuesto por volúmenes de tres pisos uno al lado del otro, la mitad norte del edificio sobresale hacia una vista panorámica de San Francisco, mientras que la mitad sur retrocede para invitar a la luz a penetrar en el interior. La artesanía contemporánea y la pureza de la estructura se expresan a través de una paleta consistente de materiales y detalles arquitectónicos gráficos. El acero estructural personalizado y los armarios de madera se utilizan para definir los espacios en toda la casa. La casa fue diseñada y construida con principios sostenibles, con eficiencia energética, bajo consumo y materiales saludables como parámetros primarios.

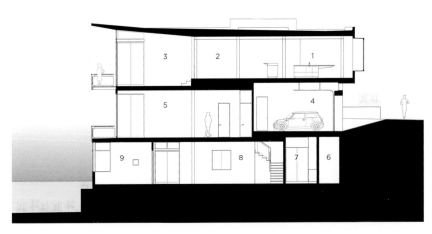

Section

1. Kitchen
2. Dining room
3. Living room
4. Garage
5. Master suite
6. Mechanical room
7. Bathroom
8. Family room
9. bedroom

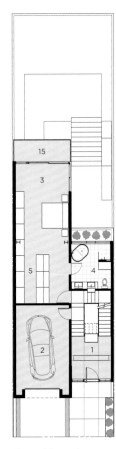

Basement floor plan

Ground floor plan

Second floor plan

1. Entry
2. Garage
3. Master suite
4. Bathroom
5. Walk-in closet
6. Guestroom
7. Kitchen
8. Dining room
9. Living room
10. Sitting room
11. Family room
12. Bedroom
13. Laundry room
14. Mechanical room
15. Patio/balcony

0 5 10 15 20 25 ft

Perched atop the western edge of Napa Valley's Vaca Range, over-
looking the heart of Northern California wine country, Zack | de Vito
designed this modern residence to nestle into the site's natural rock
outcroppings and native Oak and Manzanita trees, while maximizing
its exceptional views. The details at RidgeView are finely attuned—expressive of a deep regard for materials and craft, and the close relationship between designer and craftsman. Every aspect of the estate
was designed to visually, spatially, and functionally integrate inside
and outside spaces, and to promote indoor/outdoor living. Large windows bathe the living areas with ambient daylighting, and openings
on all sides give the option of channeling ridge-top breezes to mini-
mize air conditioning needs.

Auf dem westlichen Rand der Vaca Range des Napa Valley gelegen,
mit Blick auf das Herz des nordkalifornischen Weinlandes, sollte die-
se moderne Residenz nach dem Entwurf von Zack | de Vito sich in
die natürlichen Felsvorsprünge der Anlage und die einheimischen
Eichen- und Manzanita-Bäume einfügen und gleichzeitig ihre außergewöhnliche Aussicht maximieren. Die Details bei RidgeView sind
fein aufeinander abgestimmt – Ausdruck der tiefen Wertschätzung
für Materialien und Handwerk sowie der engen Beziehung zwischen
Designer und Handwerker. Jeder Aspekt des Anwesens wurde so gestaltet, dass er sich optisch, räumlich und funktional in Innen- und
Außenräume integriert und das Wohnen in beiden Bereichen fördert.
Große Fenster tauchen die Wohnbereiche in Tageslicht, und Öffnungen auf allen Seiten bieten die Möglichkeit, Windeinflüsse zu kanali-
sieren, um den Klimatisierungsbedarf zu minimieren.

Perché au sommet de l'extrémité ouest de la chaîne Vaca de la vallée
de Napa, surplombant le cœur de la région viticole du nord de la Cali-
fornie, Zack | de Vito a conçu cette résidence moderne pour se nicher
dans les affleurements rocheux naturels du site et dans les arbres
indigènes des chênes et manzanites, en maximisant ses vues excep-
tionnelles. Les détails de RidgeView sont en parfaite harmonie, té-
moignant d'un profond respect pour les matériaux et l'artisanat, ainsi
que de l'étroite relation entre le designer et l'artisan. Chaque aspect
du domaine a été conçu pour s'intégrer visuellement, spatialement et
fonctionnellement à l'intérieur et à l'extérieur, et pour promouvoir la
vie intérieure et extérieure. De grandes fenêtres baignent les pièces
à vivre de la lumière du jour ambiante et des ouvertures de tous les
côtés permettent de canaliser les brises de faîte pour minimiser les
besoins en climatisation.

Encaramada en el borde occidental de la cordillera Vaca del Valle de
Napa, con vistas al corazón de la región vinícola del norte de Califor-
nia, Zack | de Vito diseñó esta moderna residencia para enclavarse en
los afloramientos rocosos naturales del lugar y en los árboles nativos
de roble y manzanita, al mismo tiempo que aprovechaba al máximo
sus excepcionales vistas. Los detalles en RidgeView están finamente
sintonizados, expresando un profundo respeto por los materiales y
la artesanía, y la estrecha relación entre el diseñador y el artesano.
Cada aspecto de la finca fue diseñado para integrarse visual, espacial
y funcionalmente dentro y fuera de los espacios, y para promover la
vida en interiores y exteriores. Las grandes ventanas bañan las áreas
de la sala de estar con luz natural ambiental, y las aberturas en todos
los lados dan la opción de canalizar las brisas de la cima de la cresta
para minimizar las necesidades de aire acondicionado.

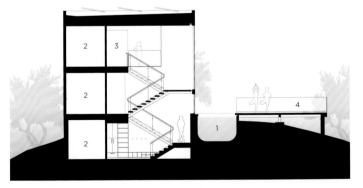

Section

0 5 8 10 13 15 ft

A. Pool
B. Storage
C. Office/study
D. Patio/balcony

Northwest elevation

Southeast elevation

Southwest elevation

0 5 10 15 20 ft

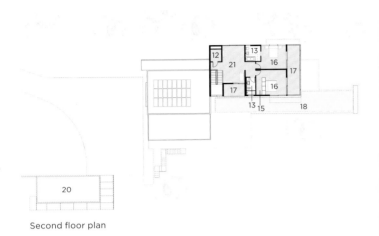

Second floor plan

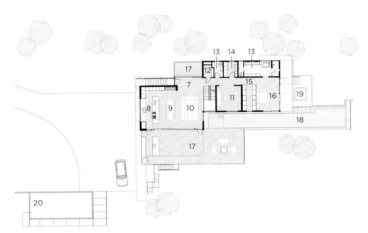

Ground floor plan

Basement plan

0   10   25 ft   N

1. Garage
2. Wine cellar
3. Storage
4. Guest bathroom
5. Guest bedroom
6. Guest living room
7. Entry
8. Kitchen
9. Dining room
10. Living room
11. Family room
12. Storage
13. Bathroom
14. Laundry room
15. Walk-in closet
16. Bedroom
17. Patio/balcony
18. Pool
19. Spa
20. Guest suite
21. Office/study

SteelHouse 1 + 2 is a resourceful response to modern urban infill housing—creating efficient multi-family homes and outdoor areas that offer beauty and comfort in the heart of a dense residential neighborhood. Zack | de Vito led the entire process of acquiring and transforming this property with a small, derelict cottage into an idyllic courtyard compound with two detached units. The existing structure, located at the back of the lot, was completely rebuilt and expanded into a modern two-level home, while a new, three-level home with shared garage was added at the front of the site. A common yard space is nestled between the two, balancing autonomy with maximal land use. Steel is the defining architectural feature throughout as exterior cladding and interior design gesture.

SteelHouse 1 + 2 ist eine einfallsreiche, moderne Antwort auf den städtischen Wohnungsbedarf – effiziente Mehrfamilienhäuser und Außenbereiche, die Schönheit und Komfort im Herzen einer dichten Wohngegend bieten. Zack | de Vito leitete den gesamten Prozess des Erwerbs und der Umwandlung dieser Liegenschaft mit einem kleinen, verfallenen Cottage in eine idyllische Hofanlage mit zwei freistehenden Einheiten. Die bestehende Struktur, die sich im hinteren Teil des Grundstücks befindet, wurde komplett um- und zu einem modernen zweistöckigen Haus ausgebaut, während ein neues, dreistöckiges Haus mit gemeinsamer Garage an der Vorderseite des Grundstücks hinzugefügt wurde. Zwischen den beiden befindet sich ein gemeinsamer Hofbereich, der die Autonomie mit maximaler Landnutzung in Einklang bringt. Stahl ist das bestimmende architektonische Merkmal als Außenverkleidung und Geste der Innenarchitektur.

SteelHouse 1 + 2 est une réponse ingénieuse aux habitations intercalaires urbaines modernes - créant des maisons multifamiliales et des espaces extérieurs efficaces qui offrent beauté et confort au cœur d'un quartier résidentiel dense. Zack | de Vito a dirigé tout le processus d'acquisition et de transformation de cette propriété avec un petit chalet abandonné en une cour idyllique avec deux unités indépendantes. La structure existante, située à l'arrière du terrain, a été complètement reconstruite et agrandie en une maison moderne à deux niveaux, tandis qu'une nouvelle maison à trois niveaux avec garage partagé a été ajoutée à l'avant du site. Une cour commune est nichée entre les deux, équilibrant l'autonomie et l'utilisation maximale du terrain. L'acier est la caractéristique architecturale qui définit l'ensemble du revêtement extérieur et de l'aménagement intérieur.

SteelHouse 1 + 2 es una respuesta ingeniosa a la vivienda moderna construidas en terrenos urbanos baldíos, creando hogares multifamiliares eficientes y áreas al aire libre que ofrecen belleza y comodidad en el corazón de un denso vecindario residencial. Zack | de Vito dirigió todo el proceso de adquisición y transformación de esta propiedad que contaba con una pequeña cabaña abandonada en un idílico complejo de patios con dos unidades independientes. La estructura existente, ubicada en la parte posterior del terreno, fue completamente reconstruida y expandida en una casa moderna de dos niveles, mientras que una nueva casa de tres niveles con garaje compartido fue añadida en la parte delantera del terreno. Entre las dos, un espacio común de patio, equilibra la autonomía con el uso máximo de la tierra. El acero es la característica arquitectónica que define todo, como revestimiento exterior y gesto de diseño interior.

East elevation

Section

1. Entry
2. Courtyard
3. Garage
4. Bedroom
5. Bathroom
6. Kitchen
7. Dining room
8. Patio/balcony

Ground floor plan

Second floor plan

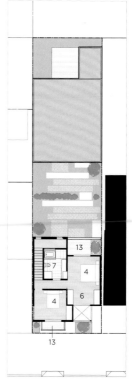

Third floor plan

1. Entry
2. Courtyard
3. Garage
4. Bedroom
5. Study/office
6. Walk-in closet
7. Bathroom
8. Laundry room
9. Mechanical room
10. Kitchen
11. Living room
12. Dining room
13. Patio/balcony

0   5   10   20 ft   N

ZUMAOOH

328
v

SONOMA COMPOUND

Photography: **David Wakely Photography**
Location: **Sonoma County, California**
Area: **13-acre lot, 3,000-Sq. Ft. residence and 2,000-Sq. Ft. pool house**
Architecture and Interior Design: **Zumaooh**
General Contractor: **Jungsten Construction**
Structural Engineering: **Spectrum Structural Engineering**
Civil Engineering: **Adobe Associates**
Mechanical Engineering: **Browne Heating & Metal Works**
Electrical Engineering: **Culley Electric**
Plumbing Engineering: **Borg Plumbing**
Lighting Consultant: **Loop Lighting**

332
v

INVESTMENT GROUP

Photography: **David Wakely Photography**
Location: **San francisco, California**
Area: **10,000 Sq. Ft.**
Architecture and Interior Design: **Zumaooh**
General Contractor: **BCCI Builders**
Mechanical Engineering:
Critchfield Mechanical
Electrical Engineering: **CBF Electrical**
Plumbing Engineering: **Pribuss Engineers**
Lighting Consultant: **Auerbach Glasow**
Audio Visual Consultant: **Creation Networks**

334
v

WINERY

Photography: **David Wakely Photography**
Location: **Hopland, California**
Area: **1,750 Sq. Ft.**
Architecture and Interior Design: **Zumaooh**
General Contractor: **FetzeRock**
MEP Engineering: **Design Build**

⊕ **www.zumaooh.com**

Zumaooh seamlessly combines architecture, interior design, and decoration to unleash the full potential of a client's vision. Seizing the dynamic between interior, exterior, light, space, views, landscape, materials, and color, zumaooh creates a greater whole. zumaooh is a longstanding partnership, with a shared vision and values. Michelle Wempe is the heart and soul of zumaooh, working closely with clients to shape and articulate their vision for a project. Mark Szumowski is the architectural conscience of zumaooh—a modernist committed to the honest use and expression of materials. Over the years, they have developed an exceptional synergy, language, and approach, enabling them to achieve a singular purpose: creating wonderful, client-responsive environments.

Zumaooh kombiniert nahtlos Architektur, Innenarchitektur und Dekoration, um das volle Potenzial der Vision eines Kunden auszuschöpfen. Zumaooh greift die Dynamik zwischen Innen- und Außenbereich, Licht, Raum, Ansichten, Landschaft, Materialien und Farbe auf und schafft ein größeres Ganzes. Zumaooh ist eine langjährige Partnerschaft mit einer gemeinsamen Vision und gemeinsamen Werten. Michelle Wempe ist das Herz und die Seele von zumaooh und arbeitet eng mit den Kunden zusammen, um deren Vision für ein Projekt zu formulieren. Mark Szumowski ist das architektonische Gewissen von zumaooh – ein Modernist, der sich dem ehrlichen Gebrauch und Ausdruck von Materialien verschrieben hat. Im Laufe der Jahre haben die beiden eine außergewöhnliche Synergie, Sprache und Herangehensweise entwickelt, die es ihnen ermöglicht, ein einzigartiges Ziel zu erreichen: die Schaffung wunderbarer, kundenorientierter Umgebungen.

Zumaooh combine harmonieusement l'architecture, le design intérieur et la décoration pour libérer tout le potentiel de la vision d'un client. Saisissant la dynamique entre l'intérieur, l'extérieur, la lumière, l'espace, les vues, le paysage, les matériaux et la couleur, zumaooh crée un ensemble plus grand. zumaooh est un partenariat de longue date, avec une vision et des valeurs communes. Michelle Wempe est le cœur et l'âme de zumaooh, travaillant en étroite collaboration avec les clients pour façonner et articuler leur vision pour un projet. Mark Szumowski est la conscience architecturale du zumaoooo, un moderniste engagé dans l'utilisation et l'expression honnête des matériaux. Au fil des ans, ils ont développé une synergie, un langage et une approche exceptionnels qui leur ont permis d'atteindre un objectif unique : créer des environnements merveilleux et à l'écoute du client.

Zumaooh combina a la perfección la arquitectura, el diseño interior y la decoración para liberar todo el potencial de la visión del cliente. Aprovechando la dinámica entre el interior, el exterior, la luz, el espacio, las vistas, el paisaje, los materiales y el color, zumaooh crea un todo mayor. zumaooh es una asociación de hace tiempo, con una visión y valores compartidos. Michelle Wempe es el corazón y el alma de zumaooh, trabajando estrechamente con los clientes para dar forma y articular su visión de un proyecto. Mark Szumowski es la conciencia arquitectónica de zumaooh, un modernista comprometido con el uso honesto y la expresión de los materiales. A lo largo de los años, han desarrollado una sinergia, un lenguaje y un enfoque excepcionales, lo que les ha permitido lograr un propósito singular: crear entornos maravillosos que respondan a las necesidades de los clientes.

Sited on 13 acres of meadowland running alongside a creek, the parents wanted to encourage the children to explore the landscape, play, and hang out. The family-centered environment exists on the meadow, comprised of a house, a pool house, and auxiliary buildings. The connection between the buildings is reinforced by the transparency of the living spaces, with extensive use of windows that create a seamless indoor-outdoor transition and also give the parents and children visual access throughout the day, creating boundaryless freedom and flexibility. The design throughout reflects the owners' style, with color, patterns, and texture enhancing their place on the meadow in which they live and play.

Auf einer Fläche von 5 Hektar Wiesenland, das entlang eines Baches verläuft, wollten die Eltern ihre Kinder ermutigen, die Landschaft zu erkunden, zu spielen und sich auszutoben. Auf der Wiese existiert die familienfreundliche Umgebung, bestehend aus einem Haus, einem Poolhaus und Nebengebäuden. Die Verbindung zwischen den Gebäuden wird durch die Transparenz der Lebensräume verstärkt, mit der weitgehenden Verwendung von Fenstern, die einen nahtlosen Übergang von innen nach außen schaffen und Eltern und Kindern den ganzen Tag über visuellen Zugang ermöglichen, was grenzenlose Freiheit und Flexibilität schafft. Das gesamte Design spiegelt den Stil der Besitzer wider, wobei Farbe, Muster und Textur ihren Platz auf der Wiese, auf der sie leben und spielen, unterstreichen.

Installés sur 5 hectares de prairie le long d'un ruisseau, les parents voulaient encourager les enfants à explorer le paysage, à jouer et à se promener. L'environnement centré sur la famille existe sur la prairie, composée d'une maison, d'un pool house et de bâtiments auxiliaires. Le lien entre les bâtiments est renforcé par la transparence des espaces de vie, avec l'utilisation extensive de fenêtres qui créent une transition transparente entre l'intérieur et l'extérieur et donnent également aux parents et aux enfants un accès visuel tout au long de la journée, créant une liberté et une flexibilité sans limites. Le design reflète le style des propriétaires, avec des couleurs, des motifs et des textures qui rehaussent leur place sur la prairie dans laquelle ils vivent et jouent.

Situados en 5 hectáreas de praderas que corren a lo largo de un arroyo, los padres querían animar a los niños a explorar el paisaje, jugar y pasar el rato. El ambiente centrado en la familia existe en el prado, compuesto de una casa, una casa para la piscina y edificios auxiliares. La conexión entre los edificios se ve reforzada por la transparencia de los espacios habitables, con el uso extensivo de ventanas que crean una transición perfecta entre el interior y el exterior y que también permiten a los padres y a los niños tener acceso visual durante todo el día, creando una libertad y flexibilidad sin límites. El diseño refleja el estilo de los propietarios, con colores, patrones y texturas que realzan su lugar en la pradera en la que viven y juegan.

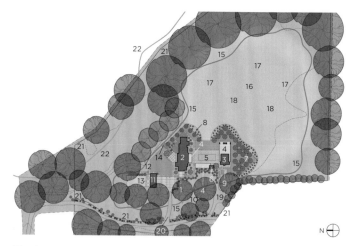

Site plan

1. Main entry
2. Residence
3. Pool house
4. Shaded patio
5. Pool
6. Pool equipment
7. Sculpture garden
8. Lavender fields
9. Vegetable garden
10. Meditation garden
11. Garage and autocourt
12. Water tanks
13. Sport court
14. Dock/overlook
15. Foot path
16. Meadow
17. Owl box
18. Raptor perch
19. Guest parking
20. Drive
21. Deer fence
22. Creek

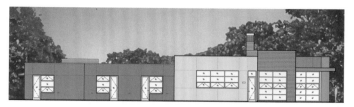

Residence North elevation

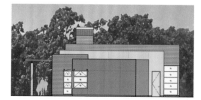

Residence East elevation

Residence South elevation

Residence West elevation

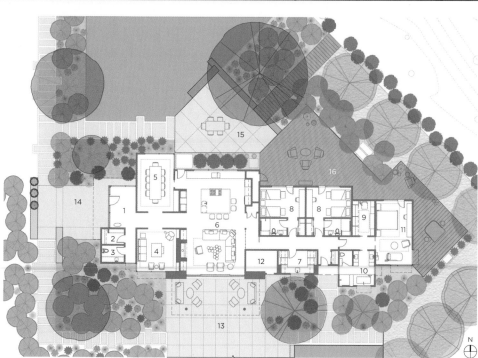

Residence floor plan and partial landscape plan

1. Entry	5. Dining area	9. Master closet	13. Pool patio
2. Coat closet	6. Great room	10. Master bathroom	14. Entry terrace
3. Powder room	7. Laundry room	11. Master bedroom	15. Kitchen terrace
4. Library	8. Guest suite	12. Mechanical room	16. Bedroom decks

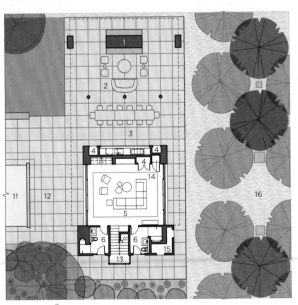

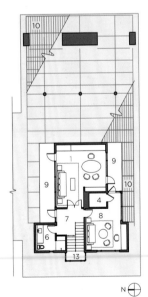

Pool house floor plan and partial landscape plan

1. Open fireplace	9.	Terrace
2. Shaded patio/lounge area	10.	Shade device
3. Outdoor kitchen/dining	11.	Pool
4. Storage	12.	Pool patio
5. Great room	13.	Staircase
6. Bathroom	14.	Laundry room
7. Foyer	15.	Mechanical room
8. Office	16.	Sculpture grove

The sophisticated, transparent offices of this fast-growing San Francisco hedge fund mirror its intellectually rigorous, forward-thinking, and entrepreneurial spirit: polished, without being intimidating; rich in detail, yet spare and clean; invigorating, but not chaotic. Creating an open and workable environment that feels all of a piece was no small feat in a narrow, rectangular space which was built for a single tenant and was never intended to be subdivided. The ceiling plane played an active role in delineating this challenging space. Contrasting frames and planes, varying ceiling heights, novel textures, and unexpected choices of fixtures served to separate the office's three domains while providing a seamless and cohesive experience.

Die anspruchsvollen, transparenten Büros dieses schnell Hedgefonds in San Francisco spiegeln seinen intellektuell rigorosen, zukunftsweisenden und unternehmerischen Geist wider: geschliffen, ohne einzuschüchtern; detailreich, aber maßvoll und sauber; belebend, aber nicht chaotisch. Die Schaffung einer offenen und arbeitsfähigen Umgebung, die sich wie ein Stück anfühlt, war keine leichte Aufgabe in einem engen, rechteckigen Raum, der für einen einzigen Mieter gebaut und nie zur Untergliederung vorgesehen war. Die Deckenebene spielte eine aktive Rolle bei der Abgrenzung dieses herausfordernden Raumes. Kontrastierende Rahmen und Flächen, unterschiedliche Deckenhöhen, neuartige Texturen und unerwartete Ausstattungsvarianten trennen die drei Bereiche des Büros und sorgen für ein nahtloses und zusammenhängendes Erlebnis.

Les bureaux sophistiqués et transparents de ce hedge fund de San Francisco en pleine expansion reflètent son esprit intellectuellement rigoureux, avant-gardiste et entrepreneurial : poli, sans être intimidant ; riche en détails, mais épuré et propre ; vivifiant, mais pas chaotique. Créer un environnement ouvert et fonctionnel qui donne l'impression d'être une pièce à part entière n'est pas une mince affaire dans un espace étroit et rectangulaire qui a été construit pour un seul locataire et n'a jamais été destiné à être subdivisé. Le plan du plafond a joué un rôle actif dans la délimitation de cet espace difficile. Des cadres et des plans contrastés, des hauteurs de plafond variables, des textures inédites et des choix inattendus de luminaires ont permis de séparer les trois domaines du bureau tout en offrant une expérience homogène et cohésive.

Las sofisticadas y transparentes oficinas de este fondo de inversión de San Francisco, de rápido crecimiento, reflejan su espíritu intelectual riguroso, progresista y emprendedor: pulido, sin ser intimidante; rico en detalles, pero sobrio y limpio; vigorizante, pero no caótico. La creación de un ambiente abierto y funcional que sienta toda una pieza no fue una hazaña pequeña en un espacio estrecho y rectangular que se construyó para un solo inquilino y que nunca fue concebido para ser subdividido. El plano del techo desempeñó un papel activo en la delimitación de este espacio desafiante. Marcos y planos contrastantes, alturas de techo variables, texturas novedosas y opciones inesperadas de accesorios sirvieron para separar los tres dominios de la oficina a la vez que proporcionaban una experiencia uniforme y cohesiva.

Floor plan

1. Elevator lobby
2. Reception
3. Lobby
4. Lounge
5. Library
6. Office
7. Conference room
8. Open offices
9. Copy room
10. Lunch room
11. Exit corridor

It is on a 600-acre ranch in the Northern California wine country that a winemaker couple chose to build its future. Taking the name from a setting in Tuscany, they founded Saracina Vineyards, a boutique winery, planting just 300 acres of organic vineyards on the banks of the Russian River. The owners, actively involved with the working vineyards, chose to live on the site. For their first project—a remodel of the original ranch-style house—they wanted to emphasize the connection between their home and the unique surrounding landscape. Next came a public tasting room and a winery production building, where visitors can sample Saracina's acclaimed wines and see where they are made. The overall design balances rustic simplicity with modern architecture, art, and landscaping.

Ein Winzerpaar beschloss, seine Zukunft auf einer 142 Hektar großen Ranch im nordkalifornischen Weinland aufzubauen. Es wählte einen typisch toskanischen Namen und gründete Saracina Vineyards, eine Boutique-Weinkellerei, die nur 121 Hektar biologische Weinberge am Ufer des Russischen Flusses bebaut. Die Eigentümer, die sich aktiv an der Bewirtschaftung der Weinberge beteiligen, entschieden sich für das Wohnen auf dem Gelände. Für ihr erstes Projekt – den Umbau des ursprünglichen Hauses im Ranchstil – wollten sie die Verbindung zwischen ihrem Zuhause und der einzigartigen Landschaft betonen. Es folgten ein öffentlicher Verkostungsraum und ein Produktionsgebäude, in denen die Besucher die renommierten Weine der Saracina nicht nur probieren, sondern auch einen Einblick in den Herstellungsprozess erhalten können. Das Gesamtdesign balanciert rustikale Einfachheit mit moderner Architektur, Kunst und Landschaftsbau.

C'est sur un ranch de 142 hectares dans le vignoble du nord de la Californie qu'un couple de vignerons a choisi de construire son avenir. Tirant son nom d'un lieu en Toscane, ils ont fondé Saracina Vineyards, un vignoble boutique, plantant seulement 121 hectares de vignes biologiques sur les rives de la rivière russe. Les propriétaires, activement impliqués dans le travail des vignes, ont choisi de s'installer sur le site. Pour leur premier projet - la rénovation de la maison d'origine de style ranch - ils voulaient mettre l'accent sur le lien entre leur maison et le paysage environnant unique. Viennent ensuite une salle de dégustation publique et un bâtiment de production viticole, où les visiteurs peuvent déguster les vins de Saracina et voir où ils sont produits. L'ensemble de la conception concilie la simplicité rustique avec l'architecture moderne, l'art et l'aménagement paysager.

Es en un rancho de 142 hectáreas en la región vinícola del norte de California donde una pareja de enólogos decidió construir su futuro. Tomando el nombre de un lugar de la Toscana, fundaron Viñedos Saracina, una bodega boutique, plantando solo 121 hectáreas de viñedos orgánicos a orillas del río ruso. Los propietarios, activamente involucrados con el trabajo de los viñedos, eligieron vivir en el lugar. Para su primer proyecto —una remodelación de la casa original de estilo rancho— querían enfatizar la conexión entre su casa y el paisaje único que la rodeaba. A continuación, una sala de catas pública y un edificio de producción de bodega, donde los visitantes pueden degustar los aclamados vinos de Saracina y ver dónde se elaboran. El diseño general equilibra la simplicidad rústica con la arquitectura moderna, el arte y el paisajismo.

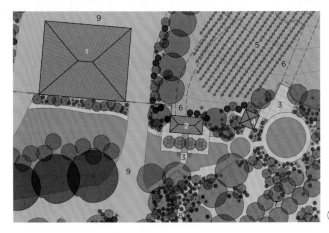

Site plan

1. Production facility
2. Tasting room
3. Plaza
4. Restrooms
5. Vineyard
6. Wine caves
7. Path to lake
8. Olive grove
9. Drive and parking